RAINBOWS

THE BOOK OF HOPE

Edited
BY
George W. Humphreys

Henry W. Sharadin

Foreword

In this volume are collected many old
favorites, old favorites of yours and of mine.
There was not space to enter all of them.
Selection has been made in the light of present
world conditions and in harmony with the universal quest for hope, comfort, and rededication.

G. W. H.

ACKNOWLEDGMENTS

The editor has endeavored to discover the authentic holders of copyrights covering the items quoted in this anthology. In some cases, painstaking and persevering search has not brought them to light. Great care has been taken in securing proper permission to use or quote.

If credit for any item has been incorrectly given or unknowingly withheld, apology is here offered for such mistake, whether of omission or commission.

To the following we wish to express our thanks for permissions granted:

HELEN COLDREN ANDERSON for contributing "The Ships."

W. RUSSELL BOWIE for quotations from his sermon in Best Sermons.

JOE MITCHELL CHAPPLE for poems by Josephine Dodge Daskam, Ellen H. Underwood and Elizabeth Akers Allen, in Heart Throbs, published by Chapple Publishing Company. Also for poems by Emily Dickinson and James Whitcomb Riley, from More Heart Throbs, published by Grossett and Dunlap, Incorporated.

JOSEPH B. DUNN for quotations from In the Service of the King, G. P. Putnam's Sons.

GEORGE ELLISTON (Mrs. Augustus T. Coleman) for use of her poems "How Beautiful" and "Friend Who Understands."

J. A. FRANCIS for "A Brief Description of a Life."

BESSIE CARROL HICKS (Mrs. Guy Hicks) for use of her poem "His Soul Has Wings."

SARA HENDERSON HAY HOLDEN for use of her poems "Mary" and "For a Little Bird."

HOWARD S. KISER for use of the poem "Unconquered," by his father, Samuel E. Kiser.

RICHARD LE GALLIENNE for quotations from Vanishing Roads, G. P. Putnam's Sons.

NELLIE BURGET MILLER for use of her poem "Prophecy."

MRS. M. S. RICE for quotations from "The Perfect Salvation," a sermon by M. S. Rice.

EDWARD HERSHEY RICHARDS for use of his poem "Today."

WILLIAM SCARLETT for quotations from his sermon "Does God Care?" in Best Sermons.

ISABEL CRAWFORD SCHOCH for use of her poem "Sentinels."

JOHN CALVIN SLEMP for use of his poems "God Is Law" and "Renascence."

L. BRADLEY SPAUN for use of his poems "A Song of the Hills" and "Do Not Ask."

WILLIAM L. STIDGER for "A Day," from I Saw God Wash the World Last Night, published by Rodeheaver-Hall Mack Company, and for "Lest Thou Forget," from Poems That Touch the Heart.

ERNEST FREMONT TITTLE for quotations from his sermon "Will Men Ever Follow Jesus?" in Best Sermons.

CLEMENT WOOD for use of his poems "De Glory Road," "Christmas Prayer," and "Sword Song."

WOMENS MISSIONARY SOCIETY U.L.C.A. for use of *"A Nurse's Prayer,"* by Ruth Winant Wheeler, and *"Ye Have Not Because . . .,"* author unknown.

THE ABINGDON-COKESBURY PRESS for quotations from *Cross Lots,* by George Clark Peck; and, from *The Light Shines Through,* passages by Clarence E. Flynn and Frederick Spense.

D. APPLETON-CENTURY COMPANY and Ruth Comfort Mitchell for use of her poem *"Voyagers."* Also, for quotations from *Moods and Truths* and *The Divine Romance,* by Fulton J. Sheen.

THE ASSOCIATED PRESS for quotations from *Twelve Tests of Character, The Meaning of Faith,* and *The Meaning of Prayer,* by Harry Emerson Fosdick.

THE CHRISTIAN CENTURY PRESS for use of *"You Who Have Dreams,"* by Mildred Cousens, and *"Gilead,"* by Mary Brennan Clapp.

THE CURTIS PUBLISHING COMPANY for use of *"Mothers with Little Sons,"* by Angela Morgan; *"Women Mending,"* by Nelle Graves McGill; and, *"Possessive Case,"* by May Richstone. All published in the *"Ladies Home Journal,"* the first in 1926 and the others in 1943.

E. P. DUTTON and COMPANY, INCORPORATED, for quotations from *Many Furrows,* by Alfred G. Gardiner.

THE EVANGELICAL PUBLISHERS for use of *"Jesus Christ—and We,"* by Annie Johnson Flint.

THE FLEMING & REVELL COMPANY for quotations from *A Pastor Speaks Out,* by George W. Humphreys; *The Open Door,* by Hugh Black; *The Empire of Love,* by W. J. Dawson; *Paths to Power,* by Frank W. Gunsaulus; *The Fatal Barter, The Blind Spot, The Bane and the Antidote,* and *The Evangelistic Note,* by W. L. Watkinson. Also for quotations from James Reid and F. B. Meyer in *British Preachers.*

HARPER & BROTHERS for quotations from *The Winds of God,* by John A. Hutton, and from *The Gift of God,* by W. A. Cameron.

THE LITERARY CLASSICS, INCORPORATED, for use of *"Lou Gehrig Was My Friend,"* by Stanley Frank; *"A Stroll with Anne,"* by Jenny Wrenn; and, *"Curley Head,"* by Howard Vincent O'Brien, all of which appear in *This Is Your America.*

LITTLE, BROWN & COMPANY for use of the poem *"Shall I Complain,"* by Louise Chandler Moulton.

THE MACMILLAN COMPANY for quotations from *"The World Within,"* by Rufus M. Jones.

THE CONDE NAST PUBLICATIONS, INCORPORATED, for use of *"Gardener's Prayer,"* published in 1934 in *"House and Garden."*

THE PENN PUBLISHING COMPANY for *"Losses,"* by Frances Browne, from 100 *Choice Selections.*

POETRY MAGAZINE (Chicago) for use of the poem *"Vigil,"* by Mabel Simpson.

THE PILGRIM PRESS for quotations from *The Godward Side of Life,* by Gaius Glenn Atkins.

"THE PULPIT" for quotations from Paul Sherer, Robert Freeman, M. H. Lichliter, Mrs. Calvin Coolidge, Thomas Curtis Clark, John G. Magee, Jr., Marguerite George, Charlotte Perkins Gilman, John R. Ewers, Sylvester Horne, and Harold C. Phillips.

THE REILLY & LEE COMPANY for use of the poems *"Only a Dad"* and *"My Creed,"* by Edgar A. Guest.

THE ROUND TABLE PRESS, INCORPORATED, for use of *"The Victor,"* by Charles Hanson Towne, and *"Wait On,"* by Dnyanodaya; both from *Poems for Daily Needs.*

SATURDAY REVIEW for use of Louis Golding's poem *"Second Seeing."*

CHARLES SCRIBNER'S SONS for use of quotations from Arthur Gossip's *From the Edge of the Crowd,* and from Edward Sanford Martin's *Windfalls of Observation.*

THE STRATFORD COMPANY for use of *"The Source,"* by Isla Paschal Richardson, from *Contemporary American Poetry.*

THE SUNSHINE PRESS for poems by Ray Burgess, Helen Welshimer, Ethel Rainey, John D. M. Brown, Marcella Hooe, Doris Couts, Thomas Curtis Clark, Paul Laurence Dunbar, William L. Stidger, Grace Haines, Edwin H. Stuart, Mary Davis Reed, Alice Whitson Norton, Nellie Good, J. S. Royer, Preston Bradley, Fanny Heaslip Lea, G. S. Harp, Elaine V. Emans, Ruth Smeltzer, Charles Cooke Woods, Charles S. Kinnison, Alice Cary, Katheryn C. Mertz, Phil Perkins, Christine Grant Curless, Beverley Nichols, Bovee, Marcella E. Minard, Elizabeth Thomas, Charlotte A. Perry, David Keppel, Willa Hoey, Frederic Lawrence Knowles, Sarah Doudney, Madeleine Sweeney Miller, and Roselyn C. Steere.

The editor also desires to render grateful thanks to Carrie Boudeman, Harriet Boudeman, Mary Coldren, Isabel Schoch and Donald Shoemaker for valuable assistance in tracing authentic authorships, copyrights, and other detail.

Contents

The Rainbow

It cannot be that the earth is man's only abiding place. It cannot be that our life is a mere bubble cast up by eternity, to float a moment on its waves, and then sink into nothingness. Else why is it that the glorious aspirations, which leap like angels from the temple of our hearts, are forever wandering unsatisfied? Why is it that all stars that hold their festival around the midnight throne are set above the grasp of our limited faculties, forever mocking us with their unapproachable glory? And why is it that bright forms of human beauty presented to our view are taken from us, leaving the thousand streams of our affections to flow back in Alpine torrents upon our hearts?

There is a realm where the rainbow never fades; where the stars will be spread out before us like islands that slumber in the ocean; and where the beautiful beings which now pass before us like shadows will stay in our presence forever.

What an achievement when one grows old!
Too many of us get old. When we grow old,
We never cease to be young.
                              W. Stuart Cramer

Growing Old Gracefully

Four-score! yet softly the years have
    swept by thee
Touching thee lightly with tenderest
    care;

Sorrow and death they have often brought
    nigh thee
Yet they have left thee but beauty to wear,
Growing old gracefully, graceful and fair.
                              Clara Heath.

❧

Titian at 98 painted his historic picture, "The Battle of Lepanto."

Chauncey M. Depew said: "Give me
five minutes' talk with a man about politics, or weather, or neighbors, or finances,
and I will tell you whether he is going
to reach 95 in good shape or not. If
he says he has the finest neighbors in
the world, and adds that times never
have been better, or politics cleaner, or
the weather finer, then you may be
pretty sure that he will be a winner at
95, or any other age. No matter how
long you live, there isn't time to worry."

Character gives splendor to youth and
awe to wrinkled skin and gray hairs.
                              Emerson.

1

The Well-Beloved

Whom the Gods love die young—

So down the ages sung
We shall grow old and die
And lay our beauty by;
And all our potent charms
Lie wasted . . . Vague alarms——
See now! The Gods decree
Eternal youth shall be;
And old age keep the thrill
Of its quick heart-beats still;
The mind alert, the soul
Impatient to its goal
Thrusts forward. So of me.
Dear Gods, in charity,
Of me let it be sung——
Who, being old, died young.

Enid Clay.

❧

But still when the mists of doubt prevail,
And we lie becalmed by the shores of age
We hear from the misty troubled shore
The voice of the children gone before
Drawing the soul to its anchorage.

Bret Harte.

❧

Age

I know the night is near at hand
The mists lie low on hill and bay,
The autumn sheaves are dewless, dry;
But I have had my day.

Yes I have had dear Lord the day;
When at Thy call I have the night,
Brief be the twilight as I pass
From light to dark from dark to light.

S. Weir Mitchell.

Nothing, so it seems to me, is more beautiful than the love that has weathered the storms of life . . .

The love of the young for the young, that is the beginning of life. But the love of the old for the old, that is the beginning——of things longer.

Jerome K. Jerome.

❧

Age

Age is a quality of mind.
If you've left your dreams behind,
If hope is cold;
If you no longer look ahead,
If your ambition fires are dead,
Then you are old.

Edward Tuck.

❧

Man is as old as his arteries it is said. He is not. He is as old as his soul. And some souls age so prematurely. By middle life they are grey-haired and dull and drowsy. But others remain young in sheer defiance of the years. Always they are eager, expectant, on tiptoe.

It is because they believe that wonderful news is likely to break through at any moment, from God.

A mind that is perpetually looking back and talking scornfully of today as a sad decadence, that is gloomy and pessimistic, that believes all things are hurtling hideously down to ruin, that keeps clutching the seat nervously ready to jump when the crash comes——well it's rather cowardly and surely not a little blasphemous.

Arthur Gossip.

2

Somehow, Somewhere, Sometime

Somehow, but God knows how we'll
    meet again
You'll see the firelight on the pane
Knock at the door, call "Come my dear"
You'll hear the bolt drawn——"You, love,
    here?"
And answer "Yes——no partings now
For all things have come right somehow."

Somewhere beyond the farthest western
    sea
My boat will reach a sun-washed quay,
White birds, brown sails, a topaz sky,
Your smile of welcome. You and I
Together with all time to spare
A brave new shining world——some-
    where!

Sometime . . . but now, how long have
    we to wait,
Gray hair, deaf ears, slow feeble gait,
The dull monotony of age
The book of life spelt page by page
Till sight fails, hope fails, then sublime
The great surprise of death——sometime.

               Winifred M. Letts.

✳✳

We can not control the evil tongues
of others; but a good life enables us to
despise them.   *Cato.*

✳✳

Nothing is really lost by a life of sacrifice; every thing is lost by failure to obey
God's call.

               H. P. Liddon.

Lower Road

The "Lower Road" over life's journey
is down grade all the way. It affords easy
means of transportation—there are tufted
seats in all conveyances—there are gay and
hysterical crowds to cheer you as you pass
—there are bands and orchestras to make
music—there are many mirages and opti-
cal illusions to lead you on and there is
much "leisure" among the happy-go-lucky
wayfarers.

Yes, this lower road offers enchant-
ments of a varied nature until you get by
the last connecting path to the great Highway of Progress—then you become thirsty
—you experience hunger for more prac-
tical and permanent things—you feel the
pang of wasted opportunities and suddenly you are jolted by the husky voice
of Failure crying out, "All off!—far as we
go."

✳✳

Cultivate the enduring qualities. Youth
must pass and beauty must fade. Covet
the abiding values. There can be glory
in the silver that the gold never held.

You cannot get up much real sentiment even by singing "Darling I Am
Growing Old" or "When You And I
Were Young, Maggie" if you are fifty
and trying to look like twenty-five.

Youth is wonderful, but trying to hold
on to it as it slips away or chasing it after
it has gone is pathetic.

A man once said to me, "My wife is
sixty years old and thank God she looks
it!" That couple probably will grow old
happily together.

               G. W. H.

Youth

Youth is not a time of life——it is a state of mind. It is not a matter of red cheeks, red lips and supple knees. It is a temper of the will; a quality of the imagination; a vigor of the emotions; it is a freshness of the deep springs of life.

Youth means a temperamental predominance of courage over timidity, of the appetite for adventure over a life of ease. This often exists in a man of fifty, more than in a boy of twenty.

Nobody grows old by merely living a number of years; people grow old by deserting their ideals. Years may wrinkle the skin, but to give up enthusiasm wrinkles the soul. Worry, doubt, self-distrust, fear and despair——these are the long, long years that bow the head and turn the growing spirit back to dust.

Whether seventy or sixteen, there is in every being's heart a love of wonder; the sweet amazement at the stars and starlike things and thoughts; the undaunted challenge of events, the unfailing childlike appetite for what comes next, and the joy in the game of life.

You are as young as your faith, as old as your doubts, as young as your self-confidence, as old as your fear, as young as your hope, as old as your despair.

In the central place of your heart there is a wireless station. So long as it receives messages of beauty, hope, cheer, grandeur, courage and power from the earth, from men and from the Infinite ——so long are you young. When the wires are all down and the central places of your heart are covered with the snows of pessimism and the ice of cynicism, then are you grown old indeed!

Samuel Ullman.

Old Age

"Old Age is the 'Front Line' of life moving into 'No Man's Land.' No Man's Land is covered with mist. Beyond that is eternity.

As we have moved forward the tumult that now lies behind us has died down. The sounds grow less and less. It is almost silence. There is an increasing feeling of isolation, of being alone. We seem so far apart.

Here and there one falls, silently, and lies a little bundle on the ground that the rolling mist is burying. Can we not keep nearer? It's hard to see one another. Can you hear me? Call to me. I am alone. This must be near the end.

Old age can only be reconciled insofar as it has something to pass on, children or grandchildren or some recollection of good deeds . . . something done that may give one the hope to say 'non omnis moriar'——I shall not all die.

Give me my stick. I'm going out to No Man's Land. I'll face it."

Thus *Stephen Leacock* begins and concludes his essay on "Three Score and Ten."

RAINBOWS — THE BOOK OF HOPE

Communion

God of the Heights! Give us to Share
Thy Kingdom in the Valleys Too.
Hubert L. Simpson

He Is God of the Valley Also

God of the heights where men walk free,
Above life's lure, beyond death's sting;
Lord of all souls that rise to Thee,
White with supreme self-offering;
Thou who hast crowned the hearts that
    dare,
Thou who hast nerved the hands to do,
God of the heights! give us to share
Thy kingdom in the valleys too.

Yet through the daily, dazing toil,
The crowding tasks of hand and brain,
Keep pure our lips, Lord Christ, from
    soil,

Keep pure our lives from sordid gain.
Come to the level of our days,
The lowly hours of dust and din,
And in the valley-lands upraise
Thy kingdom over self and sin.

Not ours the dawn-lit heights; and yet
Up to the hills where men walk free
We lift our eyes, lest faith forget
The Light which lighted them to Thee.
God of all heroes, ours and Thine!
God of all toilers! Keep us true,
Till Love's eternal glory shine
In sunrise on the valleys too.
Hubert L. Simpson.

5

The Empty Room

The empty room filled still with your
    sweet presence
The empty room where once you lived
    and loved and suffered.
Yet suffering, filled our lives with
    gladness.
Who basking in the sunlight of your
    smile,
Guessed not the depths of anguish
Whence your soul had garnered treasure
To lavish upon us.

How empty seems your room!
Tho' permeated with a subtle perfume
Distilled like rarest attar
From the crushed petals of a rose.
And in the silence of this empty chamber
I think I hear the rustle of an angel's
    wing.

             Rhoda Walker Edwards.

Well blest is he who has a dear one dead;
A friend he has whose face will never
    change——
A dear communion that will not grow
    strange;
The anchor of a love is death.
             John Boyle O'Reilly.

Along the Road

I walked a mile with Pleasure
She chattered all the way,
But left me none the wiser
For all she had to say.

I walked a mile with Sorrow
And ne'er a word said she
But, oh, the things I learned from her
When Sorrow walked with me!
             Robert B. Hamilton.

The Hidden Hand

I would go forward, stumbling through
    the dark,
    After my wayward will;
A hidden hand withholds me suddenly,
    Firm, strong and still.

I would go back to what I left behind——
    The laughter and the night;
The hidden hand quick grips me, turns
    me round
    Toward the light.

I feel the red wound in its beating palm;
    And, though I cannot see,
I guess that somewhere that deep bitter
    scar
    Was borne for me.

For me, or such another as myself!
    Wounding, and pain, and loss;
So I go forward, all the way of Love,
    Led by a Cross.
             Lauchlan Maclean Watt.

Go Apart

We can render no greater service to
our time or more worthily prepare ourselves for whatever the future holds for
us than to go apart with God.

Twice in each twenty-four hours the
tides of the ocean, soiled and discolored
through their contact with our shores,
withdraw themselves into the bosom of
the deep, there to be cleansed and rebaptized in the clean and salt immensity
of the sea, there to hear again the call
of the sun, the moon, and the stars, and
so cleansed to come back with a blessed
power upon the coasts which are unlovely
without them, and are kept sweet only
by their healing contact.

Life is like that. For we too are much stained through our contact with occupation or pleasure and all the coast of reality. The withdrawing tides of our souls need to be gathered again into the clean, the vast, and the unfailing; there to be rebaptized in goodness and vision; there to hear the voice of the eternal, to answer to the compulsion of the Unseen.

Out of such a communion as this we shall return again to our duties and our relationships, healed and recollected; to achieve——please God——in some vaster advance some new victory for the Kingdom of Christ and to release some deepened measure of love and power.

Gaius Glenn Atkins.

Conversion means transfiguration. We walk the same streets, see the same familiar folk but now a strange new transforming beauty shines upon all until the happy soul can sing with Masefield's plowman:

"O glory of the lighted mind,
How dead I'd been, how dumb, how
     blind.
The station brook, to my new eyes,
Was babbling out of Paradise;
The waters rushing from the rain
Were singing Christ has risen again!
I thought all earthly creatures knelt
From rapture of the joy I felt.
The narrow station-wall's brick ledge,
The wild hop withering in the hedge,
The lights in huntsman's upper storey
Were parts of an eternal glory,
Were God's eternal garden flowers.
I stood in bliss at this for hours."

Leslie D. Weatherhead.

Father's Voice

Years an' years ago, when I
Was jest a little lad,
An' after school hours used to work
Around the farm with Dad;
An' as the sun was settin' low
When eventide was come,
Then I'd get kinder anxious-like
About the journey home.
An' Dad, he used to lead the way,
An' once a while turn 'round an' say,
So cheerin'-like, so tender: "Come,
Come, my son, you're nearly home!"
That allers used to help me some,
And so I followed Father home.

I'm old an' gray an' feeble now,
An' tremble at the knee,
But life seems jest the same today
As then it seemed to me.
For I am still so wearied out,
When eventide is come,
An' still get kinder anxious-like
About the journey home.
An' still my Father leads the way,
An' once a while I hear him say,
So cheerin'-like, so tender: "Come,
Come, my son, you're nearly home!"
An' same as then, that helps me some.
And so I'm followin' Father home.

Unknown.

The Road to Bethlehem

It isn't far to Bethlehem town!
It's anywhere that God comes down
And finds in people's friendly face
A welcome and abiding place.
The road to Bethlehem runs right through
The homes of folks like me and you.

Madeleine Sweeney Miller.

Earth Angel

I walked the hills
   I talked with God.
I saw the place
   His feet had trod.

I felt His breath
   Upon me pass
Like wind that stirs
   The lowly grass.

I brushed His hand
   With one small wing
Now God and I
   Are everything.

Barbara Young.

❧❦

High Thoughts!
   They visit us,
In moments when the soul is dim and
   darken'd
   They come to bless,
After the vanities to which we harken'd:
When weariness hath come upon the
   spirit
(Those hours of darkness which we all
   inherit),
Bursts there not through a glint of warm
   sunshine,
A winged thought which bids us not
   repine!
In joy and gladness,
In mirth and sadness,
Come signs and tokens;
Life's angel brings
Upon its wings,
Those bright communings,
The soul doth keep——
Those thoughts of Heaven so pure and
   deep.

Robert Nicoll.

Just Ahead

Back in the tender days of long ago
   I used to wander with my father dear,
My hand in his; and oh, he loved me so!
   I was content; I had no harm to fear.
One day we wandered far and lost our
   way
   Well I remember what his dear lips
   said:
"Child I will find the path, and you
   must stay;
   I'll only be a little way ahead."

I waited for him very patiently;
   I knew no fear——I was so confident
He'd only gone to clear the way for me;
   He would return the very way he went.
When he came back he found a tired
   child;
   He carried me safe on his loving breast;
He spoke to me; his voice was sweet
   and mild:
   "Dear little one, we're going home to
   rest."

Father, the years have borne you in their
   flight
   To God's Own Land. They say that
   you are "dead".
I know you're searching for the Path
   of Light;
   You've only gone a little way ahead;
You'll come for me. Ah, very well I
   know!
   My feet are tired, heavy is my load.
You left me waiting, Dear, you loved
   me so,
   You'll come back for me when you've
   found the Road.

Florence Belle Anderson.

This is not he alone
Whom I have known,
This is all Christs since time began.
The blood of all the dead
His veins have shed
For he is God and Ghost and Everyman.

Louis Golding.

❧❧

Easter

I knew Thou wert coming, O Lord divine;
I felt in the sunlight a softened shine,
And a murmur of welcome I thought I
　　heard,
In the ripple of brook and the chirp
　　of bird;
And the bursting buds and the spring-
　　ing grass
Seemed to be waiting to see Thee pass;
And the sky, and the sea, and the
　　throbbing sod,
Pulsed and thrilled to the touch of God.

I knew Thou wert coming, O Love divine,
To gather the world's heart up to Thine;
I knew the bonds of the rock-hewn grave
Were riven, that living, Thy life might
　　save.
But blind and wayward, I could not see,
Thou wert coming to dwell with me.

Now let me come nearer, O Christ divine,
Make in my soul for Thyself a shrine;
Cleanse, till the desolate place shall be
Fit for a dwelling, dear Lord, for Thee.
Rear, if Thou wilt, a throne in my breast,
Reign, I will worship and serve my Guest.
While Thou art in me, and in Thee I
　　abide,
What end can there be to the Easter-tide?

Mary Lowe Dickinson.

"I cannot do it alone,
　　The waves run fast and high,
And the fogs close chill around,
　　And the light goes out in the sky.
But I know that we two
Shall win in the end——
　　Jesus and I.

"Coward and wayward and weak,
　　I change with the changing sky,
Today so eager and brave,
　　To-morrow, too feeble to try;
But He never gives in,
So we two shall win——
　　Jesus and I."

Dan Crawford.

All the Days

Yea I am with thee when there falls
　　no shadow
　　Across the golden glory of the day,
And I am with thee when the storm-
　　clouds gather,
　　Dimming the brightness of the on-
　　ward way;
In days of loss, and loneliness and sorrow,
　　Of care and weariness and fretting pain,
In days of weakness and deep depression,
　　Of futile effort when thy life seems
　　vain;
When courage fails thee for the un-
　　known future,
　　And the heart sinks beneath its weight
　　of fears;
Still I am with thee,——Strength and
　　Rest and Comfort,
　　Thy Counsellor through all Earth's
　　changing years.
　　Whatever goes, whatever stays,
　　　Lo, I am with thee all the days.

Annie Johnson Flint.

By Air

I visited with God to-day
And joined the angels in their play!
For just my joy the round earth rolled,
While I leaned down and swiftly told
Each tiny roof of gray or red,
And sent my love from overhead.

A hundred farms lay shining green,
With streams and shadowy trees between;
And widening strips of brown and black
Where small men crawled the plough-
    horse track.
Wee women stood in narrow plots;
The flocks of geese were clustered dots
White as the linen spread to dry——
I smiled upon them from the sky!
Toy cattle grazed, play windmills turned,
And threads of smoke, from hearth fires
    burned,
Showed where they spent their little days.
"Oh, look!" I called, "Look up and
    praise!
For life is more than work and food!
Oh, see how big it is and good!"

For I saw to-day what God can see.
And shared with Him eternity.

                    Eva Phillips Boyd.

❧

When *John Muir*, discoverer of the
Yosemite and explorer of glaciers and
peaks on the roof of the world, crossed
the great divide he wrote:

"John of the mountains, wonderful John,
Is past the summit and traveling on,
The turn of the trail on the mountain
    side,
A smile and a 'hail' where the glaciers
    slide,

A streak of red where the condors ride,
And John is over the Great Divide.

"John of the mountains camps to-day
On a level spot in the milky way,
And God is telling him how he rolled
The smoking earth from the iron mold,
And hammered the mountains till they
    were gold
And planted the redwood trees of old.

"And John of the mountains says: 'I knew
And I wanted to grapple the hand o' you,
And now we're sure to be friends and
    chums
And camp together till chaos comes.' "

To One Beloved

I cannot feel that you have journeyed far
    Beyond day's pulsing life, night's burn-
        ing star,
On to some dimness where pale shadows
    are.
    You loved Earth's beauty, saw it
        everywhere——
Spring's shy unfolding, Autumn's gallant
    flare
    Of crimson on the dark hills, treetops
        bare,
Wind - flung against a coldly lighted
    sky——
    Summer's long, vivid pageant sweep-
        ing by——
And praised all as God's glory. So I know
    That, seeking you, I have not far to go.
In dawn's brave promise, sunset's tender
    glow,
    In tapestry of blossoms woven on
        the sod,
Looking for beauty, I find you——and
    God.

                    Dora Aydelotte.

My Lord of Little Boats

Some find their Lord on Calvary,
And some in bleak Gethsemane;
My trysting place is less remote——
I find Him by a little boat.

I seem to see His Presence glow
In ev'ry little boat I know,
And, as in far-off Galilee,
His voice comes calling, "Follow Me!"

He sat within a boat and taught,
And so each little ship is fraught
With sanctity of sea and sky
That holds a whispered, "It is I."

In any tranquil, harbored sail
I hear that Galilean gale!
The roar of waves and tempest shrill——
And then His calming, "Peace . . . be
    still."

A fishing boat, a net, an oar——
And there He watches on the shore,
His Spirit brooding o'er the sea,
To breathe a wistful, "Lov'st thou Me?"

Some find their Lord on mountain top,
And some in Joseph's busy shop——
I find him where the shadows creep
By little boats that brave the deep.
Beatrice Plumb.

Solitude

There are people who cannot entertain themselves happily for one hour. And to be without human companionship for several consecutive hours would be sufficient torture to drive them almost frantic.

Man, of course, is a social creature. To be really good he must be good-for-something, he must be good to somebody. Yet R. H. Schauffler keenly observes that "if anyone hates to be alone with himself he probably has not much self to be alone with."

Sir Walter Scott (and no one could accuse him of ascetic tendencies) once said, "If I had to choose between being always in the companionship of my friends or forever banished from them I should have to say 'Jailer, lock the door.'"

So important did he deem it that there should be moments when uninterruptedly, his soul and his God should meet.

⚜

The door of Heaven is on the latch
Tonight, and many a one is fain
To go home for one night's watch
With his love again.

Oh where the father and mother sit
There's a drift of dead leaves at the door,
Like pitter-patter of little feet
That come no more.

Then thoughts are in the night and cold
Their tears are heavier than the clay;
But who is this at the threshold
So young and gay?

They are come from the land o' the young
They have forgotten how to weep;
Words of comfort on the tongue
And a kiss to keep.

They sit down and they stay awhile
Kisses and comfort none shall lack
At morn they steal forth with a smile
And a long look back.
Katharine Tynan.

"I have come from Thee——when I know
    not——like mist from the ocean's
    breast;
But the mist shall feed the river, and
    the river at last find rest.
I wander afar in exile, a wave-born flake
    of foam;
But the wheel must 'come full circle,'
    and the wanderer wander home.

I have come from Thee——why I know
    not; but Thou art, O God! what
    Thou art;
And the round of eternal being is the
    pulse of Thy beating heart.
Thou hast need of Thy meanest creature;
    Thou hast need of what once was
    Thine;
The thirst that consumes my spirit is
    the thirst of Thy heart for mine.

Draw me from shame and sorrow and
    pain and death and decay;
Draw me from hell to heaven, draw me
    from night to day;
Draw me from self's abysses to the self-
    less azure above;
Draw me to Thee, Life's Fountain, with
    patient passionate love."

Human things must be known to be
loved; but Divine things must be loved
to be known.

Pascal.

Hymn for a Household

Lord Christ, beneath Thy starry dome
We light this flickering lamp of home,
And where bewildering shadows throng
Uplift our prayer and evensong.
Dost Thou, with heaven in Thy ken
Seek still a dwelling-place with men,
Wandering the world in ceaseless quest?
O Man of Nazareth, be our guest!

Lord Christ, the bird his nest has found,
The fox is sheltered in his ground,
But dost Thou still this dark earth tread
And have no place to lay Thy head?
Shepherd of mortals, here behold
A little flock, a wayside fold
That wait Thy presence to be blest——
O Man of Nazareth, be our guest!

Daniel Henderson.

To give and to lose is nothing, but to
lose and to give still is the part of a great
mind.

Seneca.

There is a scene where spirits blend,
Where friend holds fellowship with
    friend;
Though sundered far, by faith they meet
Around one common mercy seat.

Hugh Stowell.

RAINBOWS   THE BOOK OF HOPE

COMRADESHIP

He walks with God upon the hills;
And sees, each morn, the world arise
New-bathed in light of Paradise.

Ina Donna Coolbrith

The New Patriot

Who is the patriot? He who lights
　The torch of war from hill to hill?
Or he who kindles on the heights
　The beacon of a world's good will?

Who is the patriot? It is he
　Who knows no boundary, race nor
　　creed;
Whose nation is humanity,
　His countrymen all souls that need.

Who is the patriot? Only he
　Whose business is the general good;
Whose keenest sword is sympathy,
　Whose dearest flag is brotherhood!

Frederic L. Knowles.

With God

To talk with God no breath is lost;
Talk on!
To walk with God no strength is lost;
Walk on!
To toil with God no time is lost;
Toil on!
Little is much, if God is in it;
Man's busiest day not worth God's
　minute.
Much is little everywhere
If God the business doth not share.
So, work with God,——then nothing's
　lost;
The highest gain at lowest cost.

Dnyanodaya.

13

Men exist for the sake of one another. Teach them or bear with them.

Marcus Aurelius.

❦

Perhaps we are apt to think of Calvary too utterly as just one isolated historic happening.

The fact is that the Lord Christ is being continually "crucified afresh" and that Calvary is an ever recurring sacrifice.

With fine insight *Haniel Long* puts it like this:

He bore the brunt of it so long
And carried it off with wine and song,
The neighbors paused and raised an eye
At hearing He had learned to die.

'Twas on a Friday that He died
But Easter Day His neighbors spied
His usual figure on the streets
And one and all were white as sheets.

"I died," said He, "On Good Friday,
But someone rolled the stone away;
And I came back to you alive
To die tonight at half past five.

"Monday at Babylon I fall
And Tuesday on the Chinese Wall;
Wednesday I die on the Thracian Plain
And Thursday evening at Campiegne.

"Saturday, Sunday, Monday too,
I die and come to life anew;
Neighbors like Thomas look and touch,
Amazed that I can live so much."

❦

Charity is the very livery of Christ.

Latimer.

Up to the hour of Christ's crucifixion there was no spot on earth *where* and there was no event in history *when* all men were shown to be equal.

Liberty, equality, fraternity, were lost words in a lost world . . . Suddenly there lifted against the sullen sky the victorious cross. For the first time in human history appeared a commanding fact before which all men stood in awe. Here at last all men were equal. Here at last democracy was born. . . .

From that day to this there has been a steady breaking down of the walls of separation between man and man. God's love has flowed over all. The begger has knelt at the same altar with the prince. The King has washed the feet of his slave. The valleys have been exhalted and the hills made low. And this is the perpetual programme of God.

Institutions of religion, systems of education which forget that all men are equal before God will have their brief day and cease to be.

Frank W. Gunsaulus.

❦

Possessive Case

I polish spoons until they shine,
Contentedly, because they're mine;

I wield a dust mop happily
Because the floors belong to me.

I iron, and my spirit sings
Because I own these lovely things.

There's joy in everything I do
Because my heart belongs to you.

May Richstone.

No poem could meet a more eager response from freemen everywhere, as 1945 moves in, than the stirring and, we hope, prophetic lines of *Edwin Markham:*

The crest and crowning of all good;
Life's final star, is Brotherhood;
For it will bring again to earth
Her long-lost Poesy and Mirth;
Will send new light on every face,
A kingly power upon the race.
And till it comes, we men are slaves
And travel downward to the dust of
        graves.

Come, clear the way, then, clear the way;
Blind creeds and kings have had their day.
Break the dead branches from the path;
Our hope is in the aftermath——
Our hope is in heroic men,
Star-led to build the world again.
To this event the ages ran;
Make way for Brotherhood——make way
        for Man.

Escape

I survey lives stained with folly, wrecked by weakness, or made detestable by sin and crime. Why am I not as these? There may be a hundred reasons, but scarce one which gives me cause for boasting. With their life to live, had I done better? Exposed to their temptations, deprived of all the helpful friendships that have interposed between my life and ruin, should I have done as well? In those wakeful hours of night when all my past life runs before me like a frieze of flame, how clearly do I see how frequently I grazed the snare, hung over gulfs of wild disaster, courted ruin, and escaped I know not how? Remembering this, can I be hard towards those who fell? Can I pride myself on an escape in which my will had little part, a deliverance which was a kind of miracle, wrought not by virtue or discretion, but by some outside force which thrust out a strong and willing hand to save me?

W. J. Dawson.

The Friendly Road

To travel on a weary road
To stumble 'neath a heavy load
To rise again and trudge along
And smile and sing a cheery song;
        That's living!

To rise at dawning brave and strong
To help a weaker one along
To heal a wound or right a wrong
To fill a heart with gladder song
        That's living!

To meet a stranger on the way
To shake his hand and pass the day
To speak a work of kindness too
And hide the sorrow deep in you
        That's living!

To stand for right with courage true
To show with pride the man in you
To fill your life with noble deeds,
A sacrifice to human needs;
        That's living!

To greet life's end with no disgrace
To meet your Maker face to face
To feel, along the path you've trod
That you have known both man and God
        That's living!
                Unknown.

Your Seeds Blow Into My Garden, Friend

Your seeds blow into my garden, friend,
Whenever the wind is right;
They blow on wings of the breeze by day,
And they ride on the gales by night.

Your seeds blow into my garden, friend,
And nestle among my flowers;
In the soft, sweet soil of my garden plot
They wait for the sun and the showers.

Whatever you grow in your garden,
    friend,
Of beauty, or ugly weed,
The Fall will come, and the wind will
    blow,
And over will come your seed.

Your words blow into my life, my friend,
Or, whether of good or ill,
Your thoughts fly over, like ships of love,
Or daggers that pierce and kill.

Your smiles blow into my heart, dear
    friend,
And neighbor across the way;
They blow and blossom in buds of
    love——
A blessing to life all day.

Your life is a garden to me, dear friend,
And planted with living deeds.
So ever and over the wall will blow
Into my garden, your seeds.

                    William L. Stidger.

❧

No one can be perfectly free till all
are free; no one can be perfectly moral
till all are moral; no one can be perfectly happy till all are happy.

                    Herbert Spencer.

"There's a little brae in Picardy,
    A weary brae to me.
Yet as often as I close my eyes
    Its grey-green slopes I see.
The trench, the wire, the sunken road,
    Are stabbed deep in my head;
For near a hundred of the lads
    I found there, lying dead.

"There's a little hill called Calvary,
    Where God's Son died for me.
What it is like I do not know,
    Its slopes I'll never see.
Yet now, whene'er I think of it,
    Whene'er the word is said,
How clear that brae in Picardy,
    And the laddies lying dead!"

                    Unknown.

Comrade

My own favorite word for Christ is
not "Compassion," as Victor Hugo has
it, but "Comrade." For it was not so
much the things He did as the com-
radely way in which He did them. That
He should heal the leper was quite natural
from my viewpoint. But the way in
which He healed him——that was the
thing. "He put forth his hand and
touched him." The miracle was the
touch of comradeship.

Marvelous that He could look into the
eyes of a wee child and catch the gleam
that brought the words, "Of such is the
kingdom of heaven." But perhaps the
larger fact was not what He said but
what He did——"He took them in his
arms."

Or take the incident of Christ curing the mother of Peter's wife——the woman flung into a fever brought on by worry, her daughter's man giving up his fisherman's trade and going off to follow one whom the religious men called an imposter. She was burning up with anxiety. Her one need was to meet Jesus. And He came, of course. But the wonderful way of it again. "He took her hand and the fever left her." The Comrade we have to preach is the Christ holding hands with a world.

And if Christ's best name is "Comrade" the minister should make comradeship the biggest thing in his life. A less selfish thing, perhaps, than usual, for comradeship so frequently is chumming up to the folks who can help us instead of those whom we can help. A comradeship that will never be shocked by coarse manners or speech, born of lack of cultural advantages.

The familiar incident of the two men seeing the Grand Canyon for the first time is in point. One was a minister, the other a cowboy. The minister said, "O Lord, how wonderful are Thy works;" the cowboy said, "Don't it beat hell!" They were equally reverent as they stood with hat or sombrero in hand.

A comradeship that will pass to the on the other side, but will pass to the other's side and stand by the other's side. For, unless one in the pastorate is entirely lacking the tenderness of sympathy, he will have learned that to stand with his hand in another's as that other stands in disgrace and shame is to discover that the other's hand is held by the hand once nailed to the tree.

G. W. H.

Never

There is never a day so dreary
But God can make it bright
And to the soul that trusts Him
He giveth songs in the night.

There is never a path so hidden
But God will lead the way
If we seek for His loving guidance
And patiently wait and pray.

There is never a cross so heavy
But the nail-scarred hands are there
Outstretched in tender compassion
The burden to help us bear.

There is never a heart so broken
But the loving Lord can heal
For the heart that was pierced on the
    hill top
Doth still for the sorrowing feel.

There is never a life so darkened
So hopeless and so unblest
But may be filled with the light of God
And enter His promised rest.

There is never a sin or sorrow
There is never a care or loss
But that we may bring it to Jesus
And leave at the foot of His cross.

Lilla M. Alexander.

To err is human; to forgive Divine.
Pope.

A man's nature runs either to herbs or weeds. Therefore, let him seasonably water the one and destroy the other.
Bacon.

17

Things Work Out

Because it rains when we wish it wouldn't, because men do what they often shouldn't, because crops fail and plans go wrong, some of us grumble the whole day long. But somehow in spite of the care and doubt, it seems at last that things work out.

Because we lose what we hoped to gain, because we suffer a little pain, because we must work when we'd like to play, some of us whimper along life's way. But, somehow, as day will follow night, most of our troubles work out all right.

Because we cannot forever smile, because we must trudge in the dust awhile, because we think that the way is long, some complain that life's all wrong. But yet we live, and our sky grows bright; and everything works out all right.

So bend to your trouble and meet your care, for the clouds must break, and the sky grow fair. Let the rain come down, as it must and will, but keep on working and hoping still, for in spite of the grumblers who stand about, somehow, it seems, all things work out.

❧

Art thou lonely O my brother?
Share thy little with another!
Stretch a hand to one unfriended,
And thy loneliness is ended.

John Oxenham.

Whenever we meet a character that does not indulge in resentment we recognize moral greatness. Stanton called Lincoln "a low cunning clown," nicknamed him "the original gorilla," said that Du Chaillu was a fool to wander all the way to Africa in search of what he could so easily have found at Springfield, Illinois. Then Lincoln, who knew well what Stanton had said, made Stanton Secretary of War because he was the best man for the place. Years afterward that same Stanton stood at the bedside of the martyred President in the little room across the street from Ford's theater and, looking at the silent face, said, "There lies the greatest ruler of men the world has ever seen." A large part of Lincoln's hold on our affection is due to his magnanimity. "You have more of that feeling of personal resentment than I have," he said on one occasion. "Perhaps I have too little of it, but I never thought it paid."

Harry Emerson Fosdick.

❧

"The night was dark, the shadows spread
  Far as the eye could see:
I stretched my hand to a human Christ,
  And He walked through the dark with me.
Out of the dimness we came at length,
  Our feet on the deep, warm, sod:
And I knew by the light of His wondrous face,
  That I walked with the Son of God."

Unknown.

RAINBOWS   THE BOOK OF HOPE

Courage is the standing army of the soul which keeps it from conquest, pillage and slavery.

Henry Van Dyke

Quo Vadis?

Fare not abroad, O Soul, to win
Man's friendly smile or favoring nod;
Be still, be strong, and seek within
    The Comradeship of God.

Beyond is not the journey's end,
The fool goes wayfaring apart,
And even as he goes His Friend
    Is knocking at His heart.

Myles E. Connolly.

❧

Courage is the standing army of the soul which keeps it from conquest, pillage and slavery.   *Henry Van Dyke.*

You and I have not the ordering of the world; and in the world as it is setbacks do occur. But let us remember that they are only setbacks, unless we want to make them failures. We are not to let go; we are to hold on, keep at it, and carry through; until the ground lost has been recovered, new advance has been made, and we lay hold upon victory, as companions of our victorious Saviour, who also wrestled with darkness and discouragement, and overcame, and who is with us through the fray:

"He that endureth to the end, the same shall be saved."

Russell Henry Stafford.

19

A Hero

He sang of joy; whate'er he knew of
    sadness
    He kept for his own heart's peculiar
      share;
So well he sang, the world imagined
    gladness
    To be sole tenant there.

For dreams were his, and in the dawn's
    fair shining,
    His spirit soared beyond the mount-
      ing lark;
But from his lips no accent of repining
    Fell when the days grew dark;

And though contending long dread Fate
    to master,
    He failed at last her enmity to cheat,
He turned with such a smile to face
    disaster
    That he sublimed defeat.

              Florence Earle Coates.

❧

There is a meaning in every blow that
falls upon your life. The glory consists
not in finding the meaning but in pledg-
ing to carry on bravely though the answer
to the mystery does not come.

❧

The world has no room for cowards.
We must all be ready somehow to toil,
to suffer, to die. And yours is not the
less noble because no drums beat before
you when you go out into your daily
battlefields, and no crowds shout about
your coming when you return from your
daily victory or defeat.

            Robert Louis Stevenson.

Life is a burden imposed upon you by
God. What you make of it, that it will
be to you. Either a millstone around
your neck, or a diadem on your brow.
Take it up bravely, bear it on joyfully,
lay it down triumphantly.

            Gail Hamilton.

❧

Straight from the Mighty Bow this truth
    is driven.
They fail, and they alone, who have
    not striven.

            Clarence Urmy.

On Down the Road

Hold to the course, though the storms
    are about you;
    Stick to the road where the banner
      still flies;
Fate and his legions are ready to rout
    you——
    Give 'em both barrels——and aim for
      their eyes.

Life's not a rose bed, a dream or a bubble,
    A living in clover beneath cloudless
      skies;
And Fate hates a fighter who's looking
    for trouble,
    So give 'em both barrels——and shoot
      for the eyes.

Fame never comes to the loafers and
    sitters,
    Life's full of knots in a shifting disguise;
Fate only picks on the cowards and
    quitters,
    So give 'em both barrels——and aim
      for the eyes.

            Grantland Rice.

There is a story told by Sir Francis Doyle which illustrates the value of enduring hardships.

Dr. Keate, the terrible head-master of Eton, encountered one winter morning a small boy crying miserably and asked him what was the matter.

The child replied that he was cold. "Cold!," roared Keate, "You must put up with cold, Sir! You are not at a girls' school!" . . .

It so chanced that in the little snivelling boy there lurked a spark of pride and a spark of humor and both ignited. He stopped crying and he never forgot the sharp appeal to manhood.

Fifteen years later he charged with the Third Dragoons at the strongly entrenched Sikhs on the banks of the Sutlej.

When the word was given, he turned to his superior officer, a fellow Etonian, and chuckled as he remarked: "As old Keate would say, this is no girls' school." And so saying rode to his death.

Contemplating this incident, we become aware that ease is not the only good in a world consecrated to the heroic business of living and of dying.

Agnes Repplier.

❧❧

Peace has its victories, but it takes brave men to win them.   *Emerson.*

❧❧

"With faces darkened in the battle flame,
Through wind, and sun, and showers of
     bleaching rain,
With many a wound upon us, many a
     stain,
We came with steps that faltered——yet
     we came."

Sentinels

My neighbor has a garden
Where hollyhocks stand guard
Over the other glories
Which grace her charming yard.

They flank the garden fences
Like soldiers, row on row;
Sturdy, straight and beautiful,
Victoriously they grow.

Some, peeping o'er the ramparts——
The tallest of the tall——
Like ever loyal sentries
Patrol the garden wall.

Watching, and ever faithful,
Through each long day and night,
Their blossomed banners waving,
Pink, crimson, cream and white.

Oh, guardians of the garden,
I fain like you would grow;
The secret of your sturdiness
My heart desires to know.

You offer me a challenge,
Inspiring me to try
To keep my purpose steady,
My faith and courage high.

Isabel Crawford Schoch.

❧❧

The one hopeful fact about humanity is that we have reservoirs of untapped heroism left in us. We can be hard, we can endure. Life never should be easy. Life for ages has been tough. It is hard to be a Christian. It is a religion for heroes only. If we are able to discern the essence of Christian living, we must perceive this rugged, enduring, sacrificial, heroic element. Without these qualities the diamond is only paste.   *Ewers.*

Our Knights

"It is long since knighthood was in flower,
There are no men to-day who tower
Above their kind——the knights are dust,
Their names forgot, their good swords
    rust,"
We idly say. And yet, in truth——
The brave soul has eternal youth,
Like the great lighthouse rising free,
Whose far-flung beams guide ships at sea.
God lifts above his fellow man
A steadfast soul to dare and plan,
A king of men, by right divine,
Who in his forehead bears the sign——
He walks along the city street;
Unknowing, in the fields we meet
A modern knight in whose hand lies
A mighty Nation's destinies.

Then say no more the knights are gone,
Honor and truth and Right live on.
And men to-day would keep the bridge
Horatius kept——from rocky ridge
Heroic youth would still fling down
His horse, himself, to save the town.
    Columbia calls!
Off with your hats and lift them high,
Our own, our sons are passing by.
          Susan Hooker Whitman.

❧

    For all our complaints against life's misery and for all our inability to understand it in detail, who would not hesitate, foreseeing the consequence, to take adversity away from men?

    He who banishes hardship banishes hardihood; and out of the same door with Calamity walk Courage, Fortitude, Triumphant Faith, and Sacrificial Love. If we abolish the cross in the world, we make impossible the Christ in man. It becomes more clear the more one ponders it, that while this is often a hard world in which to be happy, to men of insight and faith it may be a great world in which to build character.

          Harry Emerson Fosdick.

❧

    Man is not the creature of circumstances. Circumstances are the creatures of men.   *Disraeli.*

My Resolve

Though all the roads be gray through
    long tomorrows, let us follow
To the mountaintops and seek the chalice
    that is the dawn.
To cherish dreams of loveliness, of silver
    and of blue,
To find the trail of fairyland, where all
    the paths are new;
To make a garden blossom with old for-
    gotten flowers;
To find a gleam of beauty as I watch the
    passing hours;
To find a better pattern for the warp
    that I must weave;
To know that life is always good, though
    sometimes I must grieve;
To read a shining splendor in the tales
    the far stars tell;
To laugh through weeping raindrops and
    to feel that all is well;
To look for golden rainbows, to love the
    simple things,
The dream-blue of the summer sky, the
    song the robin sings;
To dare to send my ships to sea, but
    find a gallant crew;
To keep their crimson sails afloat . . .
    this I resolve to do!

          Helen Welshimer.

The Spires of Oxford

I saw the spires of Oxford
  As I was passing by,
The grey spires of Oxford
  Against a pearl grey sky;
My heart was with the Oxford men
  Who went abroad to die.

The years go fast in Oxford,
  The golden years and gay,
The hoary colleges look down
  On careless boys at play.
But when the bugles sounded war
  They put their games away.

They left the peaceful river,
  The cricket- field, the Quad,
The shaven lawns of Oxford
  To seek a bloody sod——
They gave their merry youth away
  For country and for God.

God rest you merry gentlemen,
  Who laid your good lives down,
Who took the Khaki and the gun,
  Instead of cap and gown.
God bring you to a fairer place
  Than even Oxford town.

Winifred M. Letts.

Given then Christ and His Cross, and the assurance of God's Fatherhood which lives in them and shines through them, given the possibilities and prophesies of each time born self, given life with its tasks, its battles, its unfoldings, its transforming experiences, given this world of ours, as the stage of our pilgrimage, given ministrant days and loving comradeship and truth and beauty, music by which to march, and the Dayspring from on high across the hills of time, and in our steadfastness we shall win our souls. This is what life and time are for. If this world of ours were meant for joy alone, its conditions are hard to justify; if it were meant for petty success it is not worth the cost; if it were meant for smug well-being it would better never have been created; but if it be meant for a place in which to win a soul——then whatever worlds, tethered to other suns, are lost in far-flung constellations, ours is the peer of them all.

Gaius Glenn Atkins.

The Rose and the Knife

Gardener of God, if wild and weak desires
Choke the true growth, and rod the soul
    of power,
Use thy sharp knife on wandering shoots
    and briars,
Cut the weak stem hard back and let it
    flower.

Alfred Noyes.

No man can hope to accomplish anything great in this world until he throws his whole soul, flings the force of his whole life, into it.

In Phillips Brooks's talks to young people he used to urge them to be something with all their might.

It is not enough simply to have a general desire to accomplish something. There is but one way to do that; and that is, to try to be somebody with all the concentrated energy we can muster.

Any kind of a human being can wish for a thing, can desire it; but only strong, vigorous minds with great purposes can do things.

Orison Swett Marden.

23

The Fighter

I fight a battle every day
  Against discouragement and fear;
Some foe stands always in my way
  The path ahead is never clear!
I must forever be on guard
  Against the doubts that skulk along;
I get ahead by fighting hard,
  But fighting keeps my spirit strong.

I hear the groanings of Despair,
  The dark predictions of the weak;
I find myself pursued by Care,
  No matter what the end I seek;
My victories are small and few,
  It matters not how hard I strive;
Each day the fight begins anew,
  But fighting keeps my hopes alive.

My dreams are spoiled by circumstance,
  My plans are wrecked by Fate or Luck;
Some hour, perhaps, will bring my chance,
  But that great hour has never struck;
My progress has been slow and hard,
  I've had to climb and crawl and swim,
Fighting for every stubborn yard,
  But I have kept in fighting trim.

I have to fight my doubts away,
  And be on guard against my fears;
The feeble croaking of Dismay
  Has been familiar through the years;
My dearest plans keep going wrong,
  Events combine to thwart my will,
But fighting keeps my spirit strong,
  And I am undefeated still!
                    Samuel E. Kiser.

❧

Self - reverence, self - knowledge, self-control——these three lead life to sovereign power.   *Tennyson.*

When in biography or among our friends we see folk face crushing trouble, not embittered by it, made cynical, or thrust into despair, but hallowed, sweetened, illumined, and empowered, we are aware that noble characters do not alone bear trouble, they use it.
                    Harry Emerson Fosdick.

❧

I'm wounded sore but not yet slain
I'll just lie down and bleed awhile
And then I'll rise and fight again.

Volunteers

[Written forty-five years ago but supremely significant now.]

The war is over: but the country is not saved. The hardest battles are yet to fight. In these days, when the republic is encompassed with new difficulties and menaced with old dangers, there is need for an abiding and increasing patriotism.

When the call came for volunteers, what a response it had! Men who had been living quiet lives, doing homely tasks, making no clamor in the world, accounted commonplace enough by their next neighbors, showed themselves akin to all the gallant knights and captains of the past, and manifested anew the mighty forces which are hidden beneath the surface of society.

Now we want that strength and sacrifice, blessed with a new and unfailing consecration, applied to the new deeds. We want the soldiers of the war, who have shown that they love the country enough to die for it if need be, to prove that love again by living for it. We want their courage in the battles of peace.
                    George Hodges.

Carry On

Carry on! Carry on!
Fight the good fight and true;
Believe in your mission, greet dawn with
a cheer;
There's big work to do, and that's why
you are here,
Carry on! Carry on!
Let the world be the better for you;
And at last, when you die, let this be
your cry:
'Carry on, my soul! Carry on!'

Anon.

❧

It is a great story, the passion of that epic of the Scottish quest for education. It is a great story that of the roads, never grass grown, they have run all these centuries from the loneliest glens and the most unlikely places to our schools and universities; of the pinching and the scraping together and the long cheerful self-denial in many a cottage home, till at last it had come, and yet another boy lay unable to sleep, with eyes wide open, staring out into the wonderful to-morrow when he too would start out, his meager bundle of possessions bobbing on his back, would wave farewell from the top of the brae, be really over it and in the great world; of the lads, aye and the girls too these days, starving in many a bare garret in the cities, doggedly fighting their way through to that on which their hearts are fixed. Of those who started at the university with me four were dead, as the result of sheer privation, before the seven years slipped past. Or take Whyte of St. George's, lodging with another in a little room with a bed that could hold only one of them, so that they took it turn about to sit and work, six hours a shift, all through the night, paying less than a dollar per week for their garret and their food— evidently meager fare enough——and yet spending on occasion for a book fifteen dollars, gathered from who knows where; and by what desperate self-denials. Or, listen to Barrie on his youth: "The greatest glory that has ever come to me was to be swallowed up in London, not knowing a soul, with no means of subsistence, and the fun of working till the stars went out." What can you do with men like that? You cannot deny them, you cannot hold them back. If they want it, want it as much as that, and are prepared to lay down the full price, then they must have it that's all.

Arthur Gossip.

❧

Rules for the Road

Stand straight:
Step firmly, throw your weight:
The heaven is high above your head,
The good gray road is faithful to your
tread.

Be strong:
Sing to your heart a battle song:
Though hidden foemen lie in wait,
Something is in you that can smile at Fate.

Press through:
Nothing can harm if you are true.
And when the night comes, rest:
The earth is friendly as a mother's breast.

Edwin Markham.

A Man

I want to walk by the side of a man
Who has suffered and seen and knows,
Who has measured his pace on the battle
    line
And given and taken the blows.
Who has never whined when the scheme
    went wrong,
Nor scoffed at the failing plan——
But taken his dose with a heart of trust
And the faith of a gentleman;
Who has parried and struck and sought
    and given,
And, scarred with a thousand spears——
Can lift his head to the stars of Heaven
And isn't ashamed of his tears.

I want to grasp the hand of a man
Who has been through it all and seen,
Who has walked in the dark of an un-
    seen dread
And refused to sag or lean;
Who has bared his breast to the wind
    of dawn
And thirsted and starved and felt
The sting and the bite of the bitter blasts
That the mouths of the foul have dealt;
Who was tempted and fell and rose again,
And has gone on trusty and true,
With God supreme in his manly heart
And his courage burning anew.

I'd give my all——be it little or great——
To walk by his side today
To stand up there with the man who
    has known
The bite of the burning fray
Who has gritted his teeth and clenched
    his fist
And gone on doing his best
Because of the love for his fellowman
And the faith in his manly breast.

I would love to walk with him, hand in
    hand,
Together journey along
For the man who has fought and struggled
    and won
Is the man who can make men strong.
              Scottish Rite Magazine.

Heroism

The incident of the sailor on the sinking ship "Formidable" in the first World War should never be allowed to die.

He had won by ballot the last place in the last life boat. His ship was going down but he was to be saved. He had but to step into the life boat to be taken to the shore and safety.

He looked around at his old comrades who lost in the ballot to bid them goodbye. There they stand on the sinking vessel doomed to death. The passion for life surges in the young sailor, even as he looks at the cold cruel sea awaiting its victims. Then there comes his great moment. He beckons to one of his comrades, "You've got parents," he said, "I haven't." And with that heroic word he makes the other take his place in the life boat and a few moments later himself goes down beneath the waves.

All Army Engineers School graduates leave with understanding and belief in the motto that has a prominent place on Major Pellish's crowded desk:

"The Difficult We Do at Once;
The Impossible Takes a Little Longer."

They either believe in that motto or they don't graduate.
              Brad Wilson.

Life

Let me but live my life from year to year,
With forward face and unreluctant soul;
Not hurrying to, nor turning from the
goal;
Not mourning for the things that dis-
appear
In the dim past, nor holding back in fear
From what the future veils: but with
a whole
And happy heart that pays its toll
To Youth and Age, and travels on with
cheer.

So let the way wind up the hill or down,
O'er rough or smooth, the journey will
be joy;
Still seeking what I sought when but a
boy,
New friendship, high adventure, and a
crown,
My heart will keep the courage of the
quest,
And hope the road's last turn will be
the best.

Henry Van Dyke.

People's faces kindle at thought of
Stevenson's big heart——and little wonder!
You remember how at Hyeres, while
pinned to his bed by sciatica, and all but
killed by a desperate hemorrhage, he was
afflicted by a horrible ophthalmia, and
lay there for days with bandaged eyes,
threatened with permanent loss of sight;
and how, when his wife said bitterly, "I
suppose you will say, as usual, that things
have fallen out all for the best, if only
we look at them in the right way?"
"Why, now," he answered, "it's odd you
should say that, for that's exactly what
I have been thinking. What I needed
was a rest, and this has forced me into it."

Or that other day, when cramp in both
arms would not let him write, and, taking to dictating, his voice flickered and
went out.

And it was in such desperate case that,
refusing, as he said, to let the medicine
bottles on his mantelpiece be the limit
of his horizon, or the blood on his hand-
kerchief the chief fact in his life, he kept
writing articles so gallant, so full, not of
valor only, but of golden sunshine and
the joy of life, so certain that any one——
yes, even in the most desperate circumstances——can come through with his
heart unbeaten and with a lilt in his soul.

Slogan

Don't prate about what is your right,
But bare your fists and show your might;
Life is another man to fight
Catch as catch can.

Don't talk of Life as scurvy Fate,
Who gave you favors just too late,
Or Luck who threw you smiles for bait
Before he ran.

Don't whine and wish that you were dead,
But wrestle for your daily bread,
And afterward let it be said
"He was a man."

Jane M'Lean.

Even if the doctor does not give you
a year, even if he hesitates about a month,
make one brave push and see what can
be accomplished in a week.

Robert Louis Stevenson.

Voyagers

A tired old doctor died today and a baby
    was born——
A little new soul that was pink and frail
    and a soul that was gray and worn,
And——halfway here and halfway there——
On a white high hill of shining air
They met and passed and paused to
    speak in the flushed and hearty dawn.

The man looked down at the soft, small
    thing with wise and weary eyes,
And the little chap stared back at him
    with startled, scared surmise;
And then he shook his downy head——
"I think I won't be born," he said
"You are too gray and sad." He shrank
    from the pathway down the skies.

But the tired old doctor roused once
    more at the battle cry of birth,
And there was memory in his look of
    grief and toil and mirth.
"Go on!" he said, "It's good——and bad:
It's hard! Go on! It's ours, my lad!"
He stood and urged him out of sight,
    down to the waiting earth.
Ruth Comfort Mitchell Young.

❧

O friend never strike sail to a fear.
Come into port greatly, or sail with God
the seas.
Emerson.

If ever any one had a difficult conclusion to face, it was Jesus. Yet if He had given up in Gethsemane, unable to finish, all His teachings would have been forgotten, His works of mercy would have dropped into oblivion, and the life divine would have been wasted. His victory lay in His power to say on Calvary, "It is finished." If ever a man might have been tempted to give up it was Paul. Yet if in Nero's prison he had collapsed, unable to finish, all his fine start on the Damascus Road would have gone for nothing and his long arduous labor would have lost its fruit. The significance of his life hung on his ability at last to say, "I have finished the course, I have kept the faith."

Harry Emerson Fosdick.

❧

Resolve

To keep my health!
To do my work!
  To live!
To see to it I grow and gain and give!
Never to look behind me for an hour!
To wait in weakness and walk in power.
But always fronting onward toward the
    right,
Robbed, starved, defeated, fallen, wide
    astray——
On with what strength I have
Back to the way!
Charlotte Perkins Gilman.

RAINBOWS   THE BOOK OF HOPE

Though civilization is said to be measured by its care for human life, the greatness of a man is measured by his indifference to death.

G. W. H.

Calling

"The trumpets are calling, I've come to
the sea,
But far out in the moon-lighted glow,
I still hear the trumpets they're calling
to me,
The trumpets are calling——I go.
And lo, a strange boatman is here with
his bark,
And he takes me, all silent and dumb;
But my trumpets! my trumpets! they peal
through the dark
The trumpets are calling——I come."
Unknown.

Afterglow

The day died in a flood of crimson flame
That bathed the hills in beauty richly rare,
And all the world bowed down and I too
came
To stand in wonder and to worship there.

And then a small voice seemed to ques-
tion me;
"When death shall come and I must
gladly go,
Will there be one to love my memory?
O Lord, shall I, too, leave an afterglow?"
Edgar Daniel Kramer.

Called Death

"They called him Death, who sat beside
    me here,
    His tender smile alight with com-
      fortings——
They cried in agony of fear,
    Hearing his wings.
He came with silver fingers, cool and kind,
    To ease the pain of tortured, struggling
      breath.
With him were all the dreams I tried to
    find;
    They called him Death.
He bore me up in great strong arms of
    light,
    Upon his lips a song that did not cease,
As like a shaft of flame we cleft the
    night——
    I called him Peace."

                            V. J. Foley.

A God who said "Let there be light and life" and a world that says "Let there be darkness—and death" brilliantly portrayed by *Clement Wood.*

From the dark scabbard of the night
God drew his virgin blade of light,
Scimitar-curved, slim for bending,
Firm in his grip, and its tip unending.

He pinked a ball of drying mud.
Life leaped, when light lanced the flood.
It followed the beam from beach to
    height,
Fish, trees and insects, beasts, birds,
    sight . . .

The cold moon is hidden away,
And there is a black death to-day . . .
A tired God sheathes his blade of light
In the dark scabbard of the night.

The conviction growing with the gathering years, that we are not native here, we are native there, is deepened by such a poem as *William Watson's:*

Strange the world about me lies,
Never yet familiar grown——
Still disturbs me with surprise,
Haunts me like a face half-known.

In this house with starry dome,
Floored with gemlike plains and seas,
Shall I never feel at home
Never wholly be at ease?

On from room to room I stray,
Yet my host can ne'er espy,
And I know not to this day
Whether guest or captive I.

So, between the starry dome
And the floor of plains and seas
I have never felt at home,
Never wholly been at ease."

Proofs

We linger here a little while,
And then are gone
Like ghostly dews that disappear,
When comes the dawn,
And like the flaming dawn that dies
Before the day,
Which fades, when darkness falls, we too
Soon pass away.

But since the dew returns to kiss
The trembling grass,
Since darkness comes and dawning makes
The shadows pass,
I laugh at Death, for when I go
From hill and glen,
I know that I shall leave this clay
To live again.

                        Edgar Daniel Kramer.

Let Me Die Working

Let me die working,
Still tackling plans unfinished, tasks
  undone,
Clean to its end, swift may my race be
  run;
No lagging steps, no faltering, no shirking,
  Let me die working.

Let me die thinking,
Let me fare forth still with an open mind
Fresh secrets to unfold, new truths to
  find.
My soul undimmed, alert, no question
  blinking,
  Let me die thinking.

Let me die laughing,
No sighing o'er past sins, they are for-
  given.
Spilled on this earth are all the joys of
  heaven.
The wine of life, the cup of mirth still
  quaffing,
  Let me die laughing.

Let me die giving.
Not gloating o'er my gains though dearly
  won,
But finding joy in sharing, like God's Son,
Yielding my all, ungrudged, in selfless
  living.
  Let me die giving.

Let me die aspiring.
Still pressing onward to obtain the prize;
Viewing the future with expectant eyes;
In labor for the kingdom never tiring,
  Let me die aspiring.

                              S. Hall Young.

"If you should go before me, dear, walk
    slowly
  Down the ways of death, well-worn
    and wide,
For I would want to overtake you quickly
  And seek the journey's ending by your
    side.
I would be so forlorn not to descry you
  Down some shining highroad when I
    came.
Walk slowly, dear, and often look behind
    you
  And pause to hear if someone calls
    your name."

                              Adelaide Love.

❧

The Ship

I am standing upon the seashore. A
ship at my side spreads her white sails
to the morning breeze and starts for the
blue ocean.

She is an object of beauty and strength
and I stand and watch her until at length
she is only a ribbon of white cloud just
where the sea and sky come to mingle
with each other. Then some one at my
side says:

"There! She's gone!"

Gone——where? Gone from my sight
——that is all. She is just as large in mast
and hull and spar as she was when she
left my side and just as able to bear her
load of living freight——to the place of
destination.

Her diminished size is in me, not in
her and just at the moment when some
one at my side says: "There! She's gone!"
other voices are ready to take up the
glad shout "Here, she comes!"

And that is dying.

                    Helen Coldren Anderson.

I Have a Rendezvous With Death

I have a rendezvous with death
At some disputed barricade,
When Spring comes round with rustling
     shade
And apple blossoms fill the air.
I have a rendezvous with Death
When Spring brings back blue days and
     fair.

It may be he shall take my hand
And lead me into his dark land
And close my eyes and quench my breath;
It may be I shall pass him still.
I have a rendezvous with Death
On some scarred slope of battered hill,
When Spring comes round again this year
And the first meadow flowers appear.

God knows 'twere better to be deep
Pillowed in silk and scented down,
Where love throbs out in blissful sleep,
Pulse nigh to pulse, and breath to breath,
Where hushed awakenings are dear.
But I've a rendezvous with Death
At midnight in some flaming town,
When Spring trips north again this year,
And I to my pledged word am true,
I shall not fail that rendezvous.
                    Alan Seeger.

❧

We should be panic-stricken at the
idea of this life never coming to an end,
with no possibility of escape from it.
The pleasure of life would vanish into
pathos.

We should yearn for death as the condemned prisoner yearns for life. We do
not want to die now but to be comfort-
able we want to know that we shall die
some day. Being under sentence of death
we cling to life but if we were sentenced
to life, we should shriek for death.

We should hate the sunset that we
were doomed to see for ever and ever
and loathe the autumn that mocked us
with its falling leaves.

We like to know that the curtain will
fall and that a little weary and sleepy
we shall be permitted to go home. We
are in no hurry but we like to know
that the curtain is there.
                    Alfred G. Gardiner.

"The Funeral"

Now He didn't give you that baby, by a
     hundred thousand mile,
He just think you need some sunshine,
     and He lent him for a while.
                    Will Carleton.

❧

We are reminded in the following
lines that we have a covenant to fulfill,
a tryst to keep, a sacred pledge to redeem
with some, who having gone on before,
now watch and wait:

O the way sometimes is low
And the waters dark and deep
And I stumble as I go.
But I have a tryst to keep;
It was plighted long ago
With some who lie asleep.

And though days go dragging slow
And the sad hours graveward creep,
And the world is hushed in woe,
I neither wail nor weep,
For He would not have it so,
And I have a tryst to keep.

"The Tryst," by
                    Lauchlan MacLean Watt.

God was the gentlest man that ever lived and was crucified for it; the kindest friend anyone ever had, and was betrayed for it, with thirty pieces of silver clinking coldly in a leather bag. God has been in the midst of all human tears. He lost his Son there. A friend of mine once said, speaking of his own son that was killed, "If I had lost my son and God had not lost his, I should have had a depth of experience denied even to God Himself."

There is One who came over on our side of the gulf, and picked up somewhere worse scars than mine. Our tragedies are light against the darkness of His cross. I think He has a right now to take all weary folk in His arms, and say to them great, tender, knowing words, and not let them go. Calvary is the last comfort God has to give when life throws all its weight against a man! And isn't it enough? Isn't it enough?

Paul Sherer.

❧

Charles Frohman, as the Lusitania was sinking, "Why fear death? It is life's most beautiful adventure."

❧

Death in Life

He always said he would retire
　When he had made a million clear,
And so he toiled into the dusk
　From day to day, from year to year.

At last he put his ledgers up
　And laid his stock reports aside——
But when he started out to live
　He found he had already died.

Anderson M. Scruggs.

The Journey

When Death, the angel of our higher
　dreams,
Shall come far-ranging from the hills of
　light
He will not catch me unaware; for I
Shall be as now communing with the
　dawn.
For I shall make all haste to follow him
Along the valley, up the misty slope,
Where life lets go and Life at last is born.
There I shall find the dreams that I have
　lost
On toilsome earth, and they will guide
　me on
Beyond the mists unto the farthest height.
I shall not grieve except to pity those
Who cannot hear the songs that I shall
　hear.

Thomas Curtis Clark.

❧

Earth with its dark and dreadful ills
Recedes and fades away
Lift up your heads ye Heavenly Hills
Ye gates of death give way.
My soul is full of whispered song
My blindness is my sight
The shadows that I feared so long
Are all alive with light.
The while my pulses faintly beat
My faith doth so abound
I feel grow firm beneath my feet
The green immortal ground.
That faith to me a courage gives
Low as the grave I go
I know that my Redeemer lives
That I shall live I know.
The palace walls I almost see
Where dwells my Lord and King;
O grave, where is thy victory,
O death, where is thy sting?

Alice Cary.

It seemeth such a little way to me,
Across to that strange country, the
Beyond;
And yet, not strange, for it has grown
to be
The home of those of whom I am so fond.
They make it seem familiar and most
dear,
As journeying friends bring distant
regions near.

So close it lies that when my sight is clear
I think I almost see the gleaming strand,
I know I feel those who have gone from
here
Come close enough sometimes to touch
my hand
I cannot make it seem a day to dread,
When from this earth so dear I journey
out
To that still dearer country of the dead,
And join the lost ones so long dreamed
about.
I love this world, yet shall I love to go
And meet the friends who wait for me,
I know.

I never stand by casket side and see
The seal of death set on some well loved
face

But what I think, "One more to welcome
me,
When I shall cross the intervening space
Between this land and that one over
there;
One more to make the strange beyond
seem fair."

And so to me there is no sting of death,
And so the grave has lost its victory.
It is but crossing with abated breath,
And white, set face——a little strip of sea,
To find the loved ones waiting on the
shore,
More beautiful, more precious than
before.

Ella Wheeler Wilcox.

So live that when thy summons comes
to join
The innumerable caravan which moves
To that mysterious realm, where each
shall take
His chamber in the silent halls of death.
Thou go not, like the quarry-slave at night
Scourged to his dungeon, but sustained
and soothed
By an unfaltering trust approach thy grave
Like one who wraps the drapery of his
couch
About him, and lies down to pleasant
dreams.

William Cullen Bryant.

I was ever a fighter, so——one fight more,
The best and the last!
I would hate that death bandaged my
eyes, and forbore
And bade me creep past
No! let me taste the whole of it . . .

Robert Browning.

RAINBOWS   THE BOOK OF HOPE

Dreams

Keep thou Thy dreams! The tissue of all
wings is woven first of them. Dreams are
such precious and imperishable things.

Anon.

When we die we shall lose our sleep
but we shall not lose our dreams.

❧

A Mystery

But from the vision ere it passed
　A tender hope I drew,
And, pleasant as a dawn of spring,
　The thought within me grew,

That love would temper every change,
　And soften all surprise,
And, misty with the dreams of earth,
　The hills of Heaven arise.

John Greenleaf Whittier.

To Dreamers Everywhere

And if your own and time betray you

If all you hoped and wrought for does
　　not come,

Why should that dismay you?

Why should creeping doubt benumb

The leaping pulses of your will?

Have patience and be strong.

Seems your waiting long?

One has waited longer, who is waiting
　still.

Amelia Josephine Burr.

Ode

We are the music makers,
And we are the dreamers of dreams,
Wandering by lone sea-breakers,
And sitting by desolate streams;
World losers and world-forsakers,
On whom the pale moon gleams:
Yet we are the movers and shakers
Of the world for ever, it seems.

With wonderful deathless ditties
We build up the world's great cities,
And out of a fabulous story
We fashion an empire's glory;
One man with a dream, at pleasure,
Shall go forth and conquer a crown;
And three with a new song's measure
Can trample an empire down.

We, in the ages lying,
In the buried past of the earth,
Built Ninevah with our sighing
And Babel itself with our mirth.
And o'erthrew them with prophesying
To the old of the new world's worth;
For each age is a dream that is dying,
Or one that is coming to birth.

Arthur O'Shaughnessy.

✦✦

Light

O Lord of Light, steep Thou our souls
in Thee,
Then when the daylight trembles into
shade,
And falls the silence of mortality,
And all is done, we shall not be afraid,
But pass from light to light; from earth's
dull gleam
Into the very heart and heaven of our
dream.

Richard Watson Gilder.

I pray that never may my dreams contract
To such dimensions that I reach with
ease
The shelves whereon their sundry wares
are stacked
And fill as many pockets as I please.

Adelaide Love.

You Who Have Dreams

The ocean's width is but a wing's bright
span,
Islands are stepping stones to continents;
Desert and jungle cannot hinder man,
While mountains hardly constitute a
fence.

Only the mind disdains to leave its cell,
To ride the wind, to telescope the miles;
The snail-like soul clings to its narrow
shell
And keeps on crawling in familiar aisles.

You who have dreams of human brother-
hood,
The time has come for you to teach us
how
To have the faith so little understood——
For all the living world is neighbor now.

Mildred Cousens.

✦✦

Only the anointed eye
Sees in common things—
Gleam of wave and tint of sky—
Heavenly blossomings.

To the hearts where light was birth
Nothing can be drear;
Budding through the gloom of earth,
Heaven is always near.

Lucy Larcom.

There Was a Man

There was a man, a plain and lowly
    man——
And yet a man who held a godly dream.
Above his sordid age he saw a gleam
From Heaven's own light. His prophet
    eyes could scan
A world of greed and hate, yet hold to
    hope.
He saw the hapless poor entrapped by
    fate,
A friendless people doomed by laws of
    state.
He saw a warring nation blindly grope.

But he had faith, believed in God and
    good,
Holding that freedom is man's heritage.
He wrote a creed of love on life's dark
    page,
And preached a gospel of world brother-
    hood.
There was a man——so long ago he
    died!——
And his high dream our age has crucified.
            Thomas Curtis Clark.

※

There was once a man who had an
idea that India rubber could be made
useful. People laughed at him, but for
eleven years he struggled with hardships
to make his dream come true. He pawned
his clothing and the family jewels to buy
food for his children. His neighbors
called him insane. But he still insisted
that India rubber could be made of prac-
tical use. The man was Charles Good-
year. Dreams do come true——if you
make them.

            Katheryn C. Mertz.

Let me sit and hold high converse with
    the mighty dead.
My days among the dead are passed;
Around me I behold,
Where'er these casual eyes are cast,
The mighty minds of old;
The never failing friends are they
With whom I converse day by day.
            Robert Southey.

※

One of the really interesting things
of life is the magic of a once familiar
fragrance to bring back memories of the
long ago.

This faculty of familiar fragrances is
sometimes one of God's subtle agencies
of redemption.

In the following fine lines *Dana Burnet*
shows how in the most unlikely place
the scent of roses brings an angel
memory:

A wan-cheeked girl with faded eyes
Came stumbling down the crowded car
Clutching her burden to her heart
As though she held a star.

Roses I swear it! Red and sweet
And struggling from her pinched white
    hands
Roses——like captured hostages
From far and fairy lands.

The thunder of the rushing train
Was like a hush . . . the flower scent
Breathed faintly on the stale whirled air
Like some dim sacrament.

I saw a garden stretching out
And morning on it like a crown——
And o'er a bed of crimson bloom
My Mother——stooping down.

You cannot prevent the birds of sorrow from flying over your head, but you can prevent them from building nests in your heart.

❧

Kindness

If any little word of ours, can make one
    life the brighter;
If any little song of ours, can make one
    heart the lighter;
God help us speak that little word, and
    take our bit of singing
And drop it in some lonely vale, to set
    the echoes ringing.

If any little love of ours, can make one
    life the sweeter;
If any little care of ours, can make one
    step the fleeter;
If any little help may ease, the burden of
    another;
God give us love and care and strength,
    to help along each other.

If any little thought of ours, can make
    one life the stronger;
If any cheery smile of ours, can make its
    brightness longer;
Then let us speak that thought today,
    with tender eyes aglowing
So God may grant some weary one, shall
    reap from our glad sowing.

Author Unknown.

What can I do? I can talk out when others are silent. I can say man when others say money. I can stay up when others are asleep. I can keep on working when others have stopped to play.

I can give life big meanings when others give life little meanings. I can say love when others say hate. I can say every man when others say one man. I can try events by a hard test when others try it by an easy test.

What can I do? I can give myself to life when others may refuse themselves to life.

Horace Traubel.

❧

Happiness is not perfected until it is shared.

Jane Porter.

❧

And will there sometime be another world? We have our dream. The idea of immortality, that like a sea has ebbed and flowed in the human heart, beating with its countless waves against the sands and rocks of time and fate, was not born of any creed, nor of any book, nor of any religion.

It was born of human affection, and it will continue to ebb and flow beneath the mists and clouds of doubt and darkness, so long as love kisses the lips of death.

Robert G. Ingersoll.

RAINBOWS   THE BOOK OF HOPE

FAITH

Into the breast that gives the rose
Shall I with shuddering fall?
George Meredith

I Haste No More

I haste no more
At dawn or when the day is done
  The sun comes calmly to his place:
I've learned the lesson of the sun.

    I haste no more
For Spring and Autumn earth decrees
  The leaves shall bud, the leaves shall
    fall:
I've learned the lesson of the trees.

    I haste no more
At flood or ebb as it may be,
  The ocean answers to the moon:
I've learned the lesson of the sea.

    I haste no more
Whate'er, whoe'er is mine—these must
  On God's ways meet me in God's time
I've learned the lesson and I trust.
           Minot J. Savage.

Build a Little Fence

Build a little fence of trust
  Around today;
Fill the place with loving deeds
  And therein stay;
Look not through the sheltering bars
  Upon tomorrow;
God will help thee bear what comes
  Of joy or sorrow.
         Mary Frances Butts.

I Must Have God

I must have God; This life's too dull
    without,
Too dull for aught but suicide. What's
    man
To live for else? I'd drink myself blind
    drunk
And see blue snakes if I could not look up,
To see blue skies, and hear God speak-
    ing through
The silence of the stars. How is it proved?
How can you prove a victory before
It's won? How can you prove a man
    who leads
To be a leader worth following,
Unless you follow to the death, and out
Beyond mere death, which is not anything
But Satan's lie upon eternal life.
God is my leader, and I hold that He
Is good and strong enough to work
    His plan
And purpose out to its appointed end.
I am no fool, I have my reason for this
Faith, but they are not the reasonings,
The coldly calculated formulae
Of thought divorced from feeling. They
    are true,
Too true for that. There's no such thing
    as thought
Which does not feel, if it be real thought
And not thought's ghost——all pale and
    sicklied o'er
With dead conventions——abstract truth
    ——man's lie
Upon this living, loving, suffering Truth
That pleads and pulses in my very veins,
The blue blood of all beauty, and the
    breath
Of Life itself.
I must have God!

G. A. *Studdert-Kennedy.*

Everything we cherish, our order of life, our institutions, all that we call our civilization, have come to us as a heritage from the past.

They are the labors of countless generations of men who have lived and died in that faith, and we have entered into their labours. Craven must we be, if we lay down the load and put an end to the dream.

Even if we thought it only a forlorn hope, there is that in us that would still call us to join the goodly company of the seekers——saints, and seers and sages ——who through the ages have sought. What seek they? They seek the city that hath foundations, whose builder and maker is God.

It is a long way we have come, a long and toilsome climb, and there are blood marks on every stage of the flinty track. The story catches the breath with its pathos and beauty as well as its tragedy and squalor.

The checkered human career has in it deeds of high emprise, acts of sacrifice, tales of heroism that glorify the race. Lives have been lived with patience and courage and selfless love that create in us reverence for man.

They are not confined to the great ones or saints of old of whom we have heard with the hearing of the ears. There are the humble saints whom we ourselves have known, maybe have loved and lost, whose memory clings like a fragrance.

They make it easy for us to believe great things of the race to which they and we belong. We are unworthy of our past heritage and our present privilege if we forget the great society of the noble living and the noble dead.

Faith in the people rests on the belief that in spite of ignorance and folly and mob passion, and all the rest of the indictment which we know so well, yet the average man is honest and fair and wants to do right. I do not see how you can be a real democrat on any other basis.

We make an appeal too often to the baser side of man, to prejudice and self interest. The better side of man is the stronger side, if we would believe it seriously and apply the faith unflinchingly.

I have asked more than once. What is America? I ask it again with a new note of interrogation. If it is merely a place where we can achieve ever more material prosperity, a place where human maggots can grow ever fatter, it will mean nothing for the world in the end of the day.

America is a great political adventure, dedicated to the incredible proposition that men are born equal. I know all the criticism of that in fact and logic, but if America fails here she fails entirely. Christianity is a great spiritual adventure, dedicated to the incredible proposition that men are born sons of God. Has it our vote to be so if it can?

Hugh Black.

❧

Tolerance

Call no faith false which e'er hath brought
Relief to any laden life,
Cessation from the pain of thought
Refreshment 'mid the dust of strife.

Sir Lewis Morris.

Sonnet

In the "cosmic ray" Dr. Robert A. Millikan thinks he sees the workings of a Force continually renewing the universe; in other words, "a Creator continually on the job." To Millikan I dedicate this sonnet.——M. B.

In the cold depths of interstellar spaces
Science has found the "finger-prints of
   God,"
I, too, have found them, but in nearer
   places——
In little hidden ways my feet have trod——

In my own heart cold depths of grief re-
   revealed Him
And warmer depths of love have shown
   Him near;
False reasoning, alone, at times concealed
   Him
Obscuring faith, oppressing me with fear.

To one He gives the electroscope of
   Reason——
Or microscope——to find the "cosmic
   ray,"
To me, a hungry heart and Winter season
To find Him by life's truer simpler
   way——

By tears of grief that water darkling root,
By sun of love that ripens faith to fruit.
Mary Ballard.

❧

Evil is unnatural——goodness the natural state of man. Earth has no hopeless islands or continents. We live in a redemptive world.

Poverty will end; sin will die; love will triumph, and hope will plant flowers on every grave.

David Swing.

Miracle

We muse on miracles who look
  But lightly on a rose!
Who gives it fragrance or the glint
  Of glory that it shows?

Who holds it here between the sky
  And earth's rain-softened sod?
The miracle of one pale rose
  Is proof enough of God!

Edith Daley.

❧❧

"I Will Draw All Men Unto Myself"

The secret of that optimism was an abiding confidence in God. Our faith is clouded and intermittent. It floods and ebbs like the tide. Jesus never doubted. His vision was unclouded. His trust was absolute. He saw God. He realized God. He hid Himself in God. In God he lived and moved and had His being. He was no cheerful optimist who had shut His eyes to the sorrow and heart-break of the world. Never were eyes wider open than His. He saw suffering in its every form. He faces facts as they are and He predicts grander facts which are to be. He sees both sides—the bright side and the dark side—and having seen both sides. His face has light on it. He felt the fury of the storm and was certain of the calm which was to follow. He could measure the dimensions of the night and also see the dawning of glorious morning. His optimism was the optimism of God because He knew the secret of perfect trust.

W. A. Cameron.

I've comforted here and I've succored there.
I've faced my foes, and I've backed my friends;
I've blundered, and sometimes made amends.
I have prayed for light, and I've known despair.
Now I look before, as I look behind,
Come storm, come shine, whatever befall,
With a grateful heart and a constant mind,
For the end I know is the best of all.

William Ernest Henley.

❧❧

After the Crucifixion

"Except ye become as little children . . ."

We were the children Jesus loved.
Jonathan sat upon His knee
That morning in the marketplace
Of Galilee.

Benjamin was the little boy
Who had the lunch of fish and bread
Which Jesus blessed——and Benjamin saw
Five thousand fed.

And Miriam was sick, and slept
And would not wake——and she can tell
How Jesus came and took her hand,
And she was well!

We were all children, everywhere,
Who looked upon His face. We knew,
That day they told us He had died,
It was not true.

We wondered why our parents wept
And doubted Him and were deceived,
For we remembered what He said,
And we believed!

Sara Henderson Hay.

42

Authority

Ours is a religion with history behind it. A faith with a background. We offer no untested theories. Across the years rise generations of witnesses——ages of testimony——centuries of Saints who declare that God was their refuge and strength, their very present help in trouble. It is the holiest and mightiest tradition of the yesterdays.

Gilbert Chesterton has written "Tradition means giving votes to the most obscure of all classes: our ancestors. It is the democracy of the dead. Tradition refuses to submit to the small and arrogant oligarchy of those who merely happen to be walking about.

All democrats object to men being disqualified by the accident of birth, tradition objects to their being disqualified by the accident of death."

Who is your authority for that? On what precedent do you base your claim? is the frequent question of judge to attorney. And the claim is vindicated by reference to some ruling by one in his grave these hundred years or more. The authority of the wisest and best over nineteen centuries of time, attests the validity of Christianity.

G. W. H.

Ye Have Not Because . . .

If you had been living when Christ was
   on earth,
  And had met the Saviour kind,
What would you have asked Him to do
   for you,
  Supposing you were blind?

The child considered, and then replied,
  I expect that without a doubt,
I'd have asked for a dog, and a collar
   and chain,
  To lead me safely about.

And how oft thus in our faithless prayers
  We acknowledge with shamed surprise,
We have only asked for a dog and chain,
  When we might have had Opened
   Eyes.

Anon.

The world is wide
In time and tide,
And——God is guide——
  Then do not hurry!

That man is blest
Who does his best,
And——leaves the rest,
  Then do not worry!

Charles F. Deems.

Whether one's house be built on rock or sand, on both, as Jesus said, the rains descend and the floods come and the winds blow. In this experience of crushing trouble nothing but religious faith has been able to save men from despair or from stoical endurance of their fate.

To face the loom of life and hopefully to lay oneself upon it, as though the dark threads were as necessary in the pattern as the light ones are, we must believe that there is a purpose running through the stern forbidding process. What men have needed most of all in suffering, is not to know the explanation, but to know that there is an explanation.

Harry Emerson Fosdick.

43

Had We

Had we been on the mountainside of Capharnaum some twenty centuries ago, mingled with the shepherd and fisherman audience of Galilee; had we felt the upland breath of that autumn evening on whose wings the great Teacher's accents rose and died away; had we marked the eyes of Jesus, invited by the note of a bird whirling overhead or caught by the beauty of a distant lily floating in the Lake of Galilee or as He pointed to the pastures brilliant with gold amaryllis and heard His praise of the flowers that toil not; had we seen Him point to the green grass which carpets the mountainside and heard Him draw from all other beauties of nature lessons that Heaven tells . . . we should have been ashamed of our want of trust in Him who made us. *Fulton J. Sheen.*

❦❦

I recall how some time ago, when Mr. Blatchford was contributing papers to the Clarion newspaper subversive of men's Christian faith, various writers replied on the Christian side. The replies were all of them excellent, careful, learned. But only Chesterton seemed to me to deal properly with his opponent. Mr. Blatchford had said something to the effect that in these days——in days which had witnessed such additions to our knowledge——in these days, no really educated man could honestly still believe. How did Mr. Chesterton reply? He said, in effect, "Well, I may not be a really educated man; but one thing is certain, I am simply prancing with belief." *John A. Hutton.*

This crust of selfishness and sin
That shuts my better self within,——
If Thou canst make it soft and fine,
So bloom and fruitage there may shine
In answer to Thy dew and sun,
I can but say: Thy will be done!
For where the deepest cuts Thy plough,
And all is bare and broken now,
Faith sees the tender grain-rows spring,
The teeming valleys laugh and sing!

Riches in Christ

"In the summer of 1929, I go to Europe. I have sold nearly all my securities. My money is deposited in four banks, I am expecting a crash. It comes. In 1931 England chooses the lesser of two evils and goes off the gold basis, arresting deflation. I think we shall follow. The decline has been unprecedented and I buy heavy. I buy public utilities. At one time I had been President of the holding company of the Westinghouse public utility interests. I think I know about utilities. My expectations are not fulfilled.

We do not go off the gold basis until 1932. At this point I have lost 97% of my capital. I spend part of my time disposing of the things I have accumulated all my life. I get an allowance of a hundred dollars on my seventeen thousand dollar car in trade for a Ford. No one wants cars that are expensive to run. I am glad I have been very rich. I know money does not in itself bring happiness . . . I spend five long evenings with God asking Him to search my heart . . . Now I know Jesus is the Son of God . . . Now I know Him in whom I have believed." *Albert L. Kramer.*

God Is Law

Believe in God in such a time as this——
When tyrants rule the earth with brutal
    sway,
When death and hell hold gruesome
    holiday,
When wrong prevails and justice is
    remiss?
Believe in Christ who walked in Galilee
And talked of light, of hope, of life,
    of love,
Of sparrows in the care of God above,
Of certainty of truth that sets men free?
I do! Ten thousand times, I do! I know
That God is law, as well as love; that
    man,
In full accord with God's eternal plan,
Will reap at last in kind as he did sow.
'Tis but the spring time now, and from
    the sod
Leap up ten thousand arguments for God.

John Calvin Slemp.

The Believing Heart

Upon the white sea sand
There sat a pilgrim band
Telling the losses that their lives had
    known,
While evening waned away
From breezy cliff and bay,
And the strong tides went out with
    weary moan.

There were some who mourned their
    youth
With a most tender ruth,
For the brave hopes and memories ever
    green;
As one upon the West
Turned an eye that would not rest

For the fair hills whereon its joys had
    been.
Some talked of vanished gold,
Some of proud honors told,
Some spoke of friends who were their
    friends no more;
And one of a green grave
Far away beyond the wave,
While he sits here so lonely on the shore.

But when their tales were done,
There spoke among them one,
A stranger, seeming from all sorrow free:
"Sad losses ye have met,
But mine are sadder yet,
For the believing heart has gone from
    me."
"Then, alas!," those pilgrims said,
"For the living and the dead,
For life's deep shadows and the heavy
    cross,
For the wrecks of land and sea;
But howe'er it came to thee,
Thine, brother, is life's last and sorest loss,
For the believing heart has gone from
    thee——
Ah, the believing heart has gone from
    thee."

Frances Browne.

Symbol

My faith is all a doubtful thing,
  Wove on a doubtful loom,——
Until there comes, each showery spring,
  A cherry-tree in bloom;

And Christ who died upon a tree
  That death had stricken bare,
Comes beautifully back to me,
  In blossoms, everywhere.

David Morton.

It was a wise resolve of the Psalmist when he said "What time I am afraid I will trust in the Lord." It was a still wiser resolve when he said "I will trust in the Lord and not be afraid." For while it is a good thing to be brought out of the pit and miry clay, it is a better thing not to fall into it.

The faith that keeps us from fear is far preferable to the faith that rescues us from it.

A Creed

God sends no messages by me. I am
    mute
When Wisdom crouches in her farthest
    cave;
I love the organ but must touch the
    lute . . .

No controversies thrust me to the ledge
Of dangerous schools and doctrines hard
    to learn
Give me the white throat whistling in
    the hedge.

Why should I fret myself to find out
    ought?
Dispute can blight the soul's eternal corn
And choke its richness with the tares
    of thought.

I am content to know that God is great,
And Lord of fish and fowl, of air and
    sea——
Some little points are misty. Let them
    wait . . .   *Norman Gale.*

Not what, but Whom, I do believe!
That, in my darkest hour of need,
Hath comfort that no mortal creed
To mortal man may give.
  Not what but Whom!
For Christ is more than all the creeds,
And His full life of gentle deeds
Shall the creeds outlive.
Not what do I believe, but Whom!
Who walks beside me in the gloom?
Who shares the burden wearisome?
Who all the dim way doth illume
And bids me look beyond the tomb
The larger life to live?
Not what do I believe, but Whom!
  Not what, but Whom!
               John Oxenham.

And when I face the dark, and must
    resign
Love's tender human touch; must disen-
    twine
Its dear detaining clasp; when fears
    depress,
Those mortal fears I cannot quite repress,
For all my faith and trust——O Love
    divine
Hold Thou my hands.
              James T. White.

Trust says, "I may not know what the future holds but I know Who holds the future."

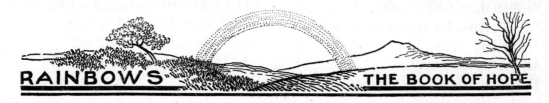

FRIENDSHIP

*My friends are little lamps to me; their ra-
diance warms and cheers my ways.*

Minutes of Gold

Two or three minutes——two or three
    hours;
What do they mean in this life of ours?
Not very much if but counted as time——
But minutes of gold and hours sublime
If only we'll use them once in a while
To make someone happy, to make some-
    one smile!
A minute may dry a little lad's tears:
An hour sweep aside the troubles of years.
Minutes of my time may bring to an end
Hopelessness somewhere——and give me
    a friend!

                Unknown.

A Little Town

I like to live in a little town, where
the trees meet over the street. You wave
your hand and say "Hello!" to every man
that you meet.

I like to stop for a minute outside of
a grocery store, and hear the kindly gossip of the folks moving in next door. For
life is interwoven with friends you learn
to know, and you feel their joys and sorrows as they daily come and go.

So I'm glad to live in a little town, and
care no more to roam, for every house
in a little town is more than a house——
it's a home!——

                Anon.

Values

What I have rested in His hands
Remains to me through all my days;
What I have hoarded secretly
Is lost in many shallow ways.

Some kindly acts that love dreamed out,
Dim smiles that shone in lowly faces;
I find all these again come back
To make a light in pallid places.

What I have shared is bright on high
Now as the road turns to its end;
I mark it down——life has been nothing
Save where I used it for a friend.

George Elliston.

❧

To Be Desired

Give me the love of friends, and I
Shall not complain of cloudy sky,
Or little dreams that fade and die.
Give me the clasp of one firm hand,
The lips that say, "I understand,"
And I shall walk on holy land.
For fame and fortune burdens bring,
And winter takes the rose of spring;
But friendship is a Godlike thing!

Anon.

❧

Little Song

These are the good things: work we love
  And rest that follows after,
Books near us, silver stars above,
  Gay courage, music, laughter——
Love that endures, though Life must end,
  And, O! the luxury of a friend!

Elaine V. Emans.

I Lost a Friend

For twenty years his friendship was one of my most cherished possessions. It was not that we saw eye to eye——we had arguments that sometimes lasted into the wee hours of the morning. Our trust in each other was manifested in the way we bared the innermost secrets of our lives, and shared our highest aspirations and fondest dreams.

Then he began to rise. The public took him to its heart. His name was always in the papers; at many public functions he was at the speaker's table. A much sought after position was only a little way ahead. Though we no longer moved in the same circles, we were friends. But my friend had one great weakness. I refused to believe the things whispered about him. Then he crashed. Everything he had built tumbled like a house of cards upon him.

Since that my friend has avoided me. I lost him because he was ashamed, and feared my disapproval. I am not sure of his place of abode, but some day I must seek him. I want to shake his hand, and say: "Listen pal, someone has said, 'A true friend is one who knows all about you, but is a friend for all that.' Come let us make up for lost time."

Adapted from J. S. Royer.

❧

Great merit or great failings will make you respected or despised; but trifles, little attentions, mere nothings, either done or neglected, will make you either liked or disliked. It is the general run of the world.

Michael Angelo.

48

A Friend

The lovely woman whose pen name is John Oliver Hobbs——who as a little girl used to play with Joseph Parker, of the City Temple in London——in her story entitled Life for a Life, wrote these golden words: "Oh, the comfort, the inexpressible comfort of feeling safe with a person: having neither to weigh thoughts nor to measure words, but pour them all right out just as they are, chaff and grain together, knowing that a faithful hand will take and sift them, keep what is worth keeping, and with the breath of kindness blow the rest away."

That is a perfect description of a friend: one to whom we can bare our hearts without restraint and without regret, finding sympathy, forgiveness, understanding, encouragement, and the strength of fellowship. There is only one such Friend, stronger than man, more merciful than woman, Whom life cannot tire nor death take away.

Joseph Fort Newton.

A Friend in Need

"A friend in need," my neighbor said
    to me;
"A friend in need, is what I mean to be.
In time of trouble I will come to you,
And in the hour of need you'll find me
    true."
I thought a bit, then took him by the
    hand;
"My friend," I said, "you do not under-
    stand
The inner meaning of that simple rhyme;
A friend is what the heart needs all the
    time."   *Anon.*

Prayer

Anything, God, but hate . . .
I have known it in my day,
And the best it does is to scar your soul
And eat your heart away.
We must know more than hate
As the years go reeling on,
For the stars survive
And the spring survives . . .
Only man denies the dawn.
God——if one prayer be mine——
Before the cloud-wrapped end . . .
I am sick of hate and the waste it
    makes——
Let me be my brother's friend.
Fanny Heaslip Lea.

A friend is most a friend of whom the best remains to learn.
Lucy Larcom.

All Inside

Last eve I walked a certain street
And met such gloomy folk;
I made great haste to pass them by,
And neither smiled nor spoke.
The giant elms drooped sullenly,
The very sun was dim——
I met a friend, and said, "I hope
I've seen the last of him."

Today I walked the selfsame street,
And loved the folks I met;
If business had not made me leave
I would have been there yet.
Of course, I've solved the mystery,
'Tis very plain to see;
The day I met the gloomy folks,
The gloom was inside me.
Anon.

Thousands of appeals for pardon came to Lincoln from soldiers involved in military discipline. Each appeal was as a rule supported by letters from influential people. One day a single sheet came before him, an appeal from a soldier without any supporting documents.

"What!" exclaimed the President. "Has this man no friends?"

"He is so worthless he has no friend," said an adjutant.

"Then," said Lincoln, "I will be his friend."

A Prayer

It is my joy in life to find
  At every turning of the road,
The strong arm of a comrade kind
  To help me onward with my load.
And, since I have no gold to give
  And love alone must make amends;
My only prayer is, while I live,
  God, make me worthy of my friends!
Frank Dempster Sherman.

"Who is my friend?" *Elbert Hubbard* once remarked. "The man who tells me the unpleasant 'truth' about myself? I can get as much of that as I need from my enemies. My friend is the man who sees the best in me, and reminds me of it occasionally."

Friend Who Understands

For people mean so much to me,
The things they do and what they say;
I can be happy any day
With clouds or stars or sunny sea,
But not for long for I must find
About me always, ever this:
Companionship, a lover's kiss
And thoughts and dreams and human
    kind.

The world is such a lovely place,
I love the grass and night and day,
I love my work and dreams and play,
But most of all a human face.
And more than that, the touch of hands
And words and songs that people sing;
Oh nothing life can offer, bring,
Is like a friend who understands.

George Elliston.

Lamps

My friends are little lamps to me;
Their radiance warms and cheers my ways,
And all my pathway, dark and lone,
Is brightened by their rays.

I try to keep them bright by faith,
And never let them dim with doubt,
For every time I lose a friend,
A little lamp goes out.

Anon.

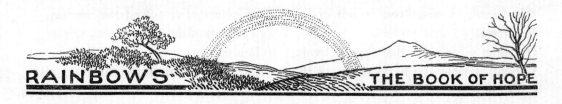

RAINBOWS — THE BOOK OF HOPE

In the day of prosperity we have many refuges to resort to; in the day of adversity, only one.
                                    Horatius Bonar

"I feel the winds of God to-day,
To-day my sail I lift,
Though heavy oft with drenching spray
And torn with many a rift;
If hope but lights the water's crest,
And Christ my barque will use,
I'll seek the seas at His behest,
And brave another cruise.

"If ever I forget Thy love
And how that love was shown,
Lift high the blood-red flag above,
It bears Thy name alone.
Great Pilot of my onward way,
Thou wilt not let me drift.
I feel the winds of God to-day
To-day my sail I lift."   Unknown.

Enough for me to feel and know
That He in whom the cause and end,
The past and future, meet and blend,——
Guards not archangels feet alone
But deigns to guide and keep my own;
Speaks not alone the words of fate
Which worlds destroy, and worlds create,
But whispers in my spirit's ear,
In tones of love, or warning fear,
A language none beside may hear.
To Him, from wanderings long and wild,
I come, an over-wearied child,
In cool and shade His peace to find,
Like dew-fall settling on my mind.
Assured that all I know is best,
And humbly trusting for the rest.
                    John Greenleaf Whittier.

For a Little Bird That Blundered Into Church

God, that harnesseth the winds
And the lordly striding sun,
Turn from Heaven a little space
Pity this, Thy frightened one!
Thou who knowest the sparrow's way
Set these beating pinions free.
God, if Thou art in Thy house
Show him where the windows be.

> *Sara Henderson Hay.*

❧

Today

O Father, guide these faltering steps
today,
  Lest I fall!
Tomorrow? Ah, tomorrow's far away;
  Today is all.
If I but keep my feet till evening time,
  Night will bring rest;
Then, stronger grown, tomorrow I shall
  climb
  With newer zest.

Oh, may I stoop to no unworthiness
  In pain or sorrow,
Nor bear from yesterday one bitterness
  Into tomorrow!
Then, Father, help these searching eyes
  today
  The path to see.
Be patient with my feebleness. The way
  Is steep to Thee.

> *Unknown.*

❧

The vision of the Divine presence ever takes the form which our circumstances most require.

> *Alexander Maclaren.*

Leaving Home in the Old Days

Private interviews and sacred family scenes took place, solemn vows and pledges were given and taken the night before he left. That night, or the last Sabbath evening at home (if the good old custom of family worship was kept) it was, I warrant, at the 28th chapter of Genesis that the Big Bible was opened, where they all heard again how Jacob went out from his father's house, how he fared the first night he spent away from home, how a convoy of angels bore him company, how God pledged Himself to be the traveller's guardian, and how he in turn pledged himself to the God of his fathers at the break of day. And if they sang together, it was the old hymn they struggled through:

'O God of Bethel, by whose hand
  Thy people still are fed;
Who through this weary pilgrimage
  Hast all our fathers led:
Our vows, our prayers, we now present
  Before Thy throne of grace:
God of our fathers: be the God
  Of their succeeding race. . . .
O spread Thy coverings wings around,
  Till all our wanderings cease
And at our Father's loved abode
  Our souls arrive in peace.'

What the prayer was — halting, broken, yet confidently committing body and soul to Heaven's care—not one of them can remember; but none can ever forget the baptising, consecrating, sacramental impression it left.

> *R. E. Welsh.*

God is at the fag end of the church. There are some poor creatures there. Many of us are weak and faltering enough, ready to drop away, to slip back to Egypt. But God regards the frailest and most spiritless amongst us with compassion and sympathy. He is not only in the front with the positive, the militant, the illustrious saints, but He is in the rear with the doubtful, the faint, the dull, the heavy-hearted, the "almost gone."

Dear brethren, let us arise to-day to pursue our march with fresh courage and hope. God is before us and anticipates all our needs and perils. God closes our procession, gathering us, keeping us from the perils in our rear. "Ye shall not go out with haste, nor go by flight." March on with dignity, assurance, peace. We are winning; we shall win. We are marching; we shall arrive.

W. L. Watkinson.

"Across the Waiting Hills a Flame Will Pass"

Harvests have been once more.
There was no sound
Of straining bolt, no crash of steel on steel,
No mutinous r o a r at power's swift release,
No plaint of captive wheel,
Yet from the ground
Surged quiet strength and from the bending sky
Streamed challenging light and cool clean showers of peace,
As in the way of turning years untold
Green became gold.

There was no sound,
And there shall be no sound
But presently
Across the waiting hills a flame will pass,
A crimson certainty. Garden paths will blaze
With scarlet sage; the humblest field be found
Adorned with purple splendor.
Mist-wrapped roads will wind
Between proud plumes of goldenrod.

Earth in her autumn ecstacy of praise
Puts sound to shame:
There are no words for days
That burn and burn and yet are not consumed.
There is no sound,
There is no need for sound,
Earth throbs with truth, age-old and infinite;
The Heart that knows thy heart is unforgetting,
The Love that draws thy love is allenfolding,
"Be still——, Be still and know that I am God!"

Molly Anderson Haley.

All's Well

The clouds, which rise with thunder, slake
  Our thirsty souls with rain;
The blow most dreaded falls to break
  From off our limbs a chain;
And wrongs of man to man but make
  The love of God more plain.
As through the shadowy lens of even
  The eye looks farthest into heaven
On gleams of star and depths of blue
  The glaring sunshine never knew!

John Greenleaf Whittier.

Divine Compassion

Long since, a dream of heaven I had,
  And still the vision haunts me oft;
I see the saints in white robes clad,
  The martyrs with their palms aloft;
But hearing still, in middle song,
  The ceaseless dissonance of wrong;
And shrinking, with hid faces, from the
    strain
    Of sad, beseeching eyes, full of remorse
      and pain.

The glad song falters to a wail,
  The harping sinks to low lament;
Before the still uplifted veil
  I see the crowned foreheads bent,
Making more sweet the heavenly air,
  With breathings of unselfish prayer;
And a Voice saith: "O Pity which is pain,
    O Love that weeps, fill up my suffer-
      ings which remain!

"Shall souls redeemed by me refuse
  To share my sorrow in their turn?
Or, sin-forgiven, my gift abuse
  Of peace with selfish unconcern?
Has saintly ease no pitying care!
  Has faith no work, and love no prayer!
While sin remains, and souls in darkness
    dwell,
    Can heaven itself be heaven, and look
      unmoved on hell?"

Then through the Gates of Pain, I dream,
  A wind of heaven blows cooly in;
Fainter the awful discords seem,
  The smoke of torment grows more
    thin,
Tears quench the burning soil, and
    thence
    Spring sweet, pale flowers of penitence;

And through the dreary realm of man's
    despair,
    Star-crowned an angel walks, and lo!
      God's hope is there!

Is it a dream? Is heaven so high
  That pity cannot breathe its air?
Its happy eyes forever dry,
  Its holy lips without a prayer!
My God! my God! if thither led
  By thy free grace unmerited,
No crown nor palm be mine, but let
    me keep
    A heart that still can feel, and eyes
      that still can weep.
                    John Greenleaf Whittier.

❧

Was Christ right, then, when He said the key to the riddle of the Universe was to be found in the words "our Father," with all of the implications of that high conception——Some One Who cares, Some One Who values, Some One Who never forgets!

Let me borrow this illustration: The first child of James Martineau and his wife died in infancy, and was laid away in a little French cemetery near the city of Dublin. And years passed, many years, until there were only two people in the world who remembered that little child, its father and its mother. More years passed and the mother died, and there was then but one person who recollected that once a life, like a lovely flower, had blessed their home. More years passed, and at length at the age of eighty-seven James Martineau returned to Dublin to attend the Tercentenary of the University. And one day the famous old man left a brilliant function and slipped out to a little French cemetery on the outskirts of Dublin, and baring his head he knelt beside the grave of the little child buried there over sixty years before.

Surely Fatherhood means this: that back of all the flux of circumstance there is Some One Who loves, Who values, Who cares, Who can never forget.

William Scarlett.

Does God Care?

Does God care? I am willing to take the word of Jesus about that. I am willing to take His word, Who, to say the least, knew a great deal more of God and of man than any of us do.

If Jesus Christ, looking out from a life more troubled than any of our lives, with the shadow of the cross darkening the end of it, looking into a world whose pain and sin He saw far more clearly than any of us see, could confront this great unsolved problem of human sorrow with God's power on one side of the equation and man's pain on the other side, and could somehow work it out so as to get "Love" for an answer, if He could say "God cares," I am content with that. I believe that God does care. I am willing to stop just there and to rest simply upon that.

It is not likely that God cares greatly when we miss some of our ambitions. Some of our social and commercial worries do not distress Him. Sometimes we are tempted to say that God does not care whether we are good or bad, because He seems to treat us all alike. If there is any difference, it is the rascals who get the triumphs, and the righteous who get the tribulations.

And a man will say: "I have served God all my life and here I am poor, and sick, and miserable; while my neighbor across the way, who has not said his prayers for a dozen years is living in his own house and has a good name at the bank. Surely God does not care."

Yes, friend, God cares, but He does not show His care in quite that way. He cares so much that He rewards those who serve Him with the very best. But you are making a mistake about the best. Is it houses and lands? Is it fame and position? Is it a dearth of doctor's bills? Evidently something is wrong if God's best is any of these.

Shall God bless virtue with successful investments? Shall He reward piety with horses and carriages? Shall He compensate purity with silver money? Blessed are the pure in heart, for every one of them shall have a hundred thousand dollars——is that what Jesus said?

Is it after this fashion that God will reward the good? Will He balance thus the earthly against the spiritual, and pay for one in terms of the other?

Never, in any world. The work itself is the wages for those who work for God. The life itself is the blessing which God gives to those who live it. To be good is the reward of goodness. To be honest is the reward of honesty. The pure in heart shall see God.

And religion, looking out into the world, adds to the declaration of the wisdom and the righteousness of God, the assertion of His love. For every one of us God cares. Every soul of us the eternal Father loves.

George Hodges.

Herod

And so the Magic-worker comes at last!
Three years he's shown his wondrous
    might to men.
They say his touch has power, that fever
    flees
Before his fingers, even blind eyes see;
To-day perhaps he'll show that power
    to me.

Youth slips from me, my body's growing
    old,
Older than my years warrant. I have lived
With wine and song and merry Roman
    girls
And merry Roman boys in Caesar's house,
And now I pay the price. Perhaps this
    man
Will touch me and will bring my youth
    again.
I'll try him, seek a sign, and then I'll draw
Him close beside me, offer him his
    freedom,
All he desires as well, if he will work
The miracle that brings me youth again.
He has his price, I'm sure, like any man.
Then Rome once more, while Caesar
    stares agape
At my new strength——and nights of wine
    and song!

He stood and looked and answered not
    a word.
But, oh! how deep he looked within
    my soul
Past places where I had not looked for
    years
Such men as he and John would drive
    me mad
And so he goes to Pilate——and his end!

              William E. Brooks.

A Brief Description of a Life

Here is a man who was born in an obscure village, the child of a peasant woman. He grew up in another obscure village. He worked in a carpenter shop until he was thirty, and then for three years he was an itinerant preacher. He never owned a home. He never had a family. He never went to college. He never put his foot inside a big city. He never traveled two hundred miles from the place where he was born. He never did any of the things which usually accompany greatness. He had no credentials but himself.

He had nothing to do with in this world but the naked power of his divine manhood. While still a young man the tide of popular opinion turned against him. His friends ran away. One denied him. Another betrayed. He was turned over to his enemies. He went through the mockery of a trial. He was nailed upon a cross between two thieves. While he was dying his executioners gambled for his robe——the only piece of property he had on earth. When he was dead he was taken down and laid in a borrowed grave through the pity of a friend.

Nineteen wide centuries have come and gone and today he is the world's only hope.

I am far within the mark when I say that all the armies that ever marched, and all the navies that were ever built, and all the parliaments that ever sat, and all the kings that ever reigned, put together, have not affected the life of man upon this earth as powerfully as has that one solitary life.

              J. A. Francis.

He led us on
By paths we did not know.
Upward He led us, though our steps
    were slow,
Though oft we'd faint and falter on the
    way,
Though storm and darkness oft obscured
    the day:
Yet when the clouds were gone
We saw He led us on.

Through all the unquiet years,
Past all our dreamland hopes and doubts
    and fears
He guides our steps; through all the
    tangled maze
Of sin and sorrow and o'er-clouded days,
We know His will is done
As still He leads us on.

After the weary strife
And the restless fever we call life,
After the dreariness, the aching pain,
The wayward struggles which have proved
    in vain,
The joys, the satisfactions, the sunlight
    and the rain,
Oh, still He'll lead us on
And on and on!

William Scarlett.

A Son at Sea

O God, through tomorrow and the next
    day and the next,
  Watch o'er the sea!
  Let starlit nights prevail,
    I ask of Thee!
Be Master of the waves that toss the
    ship upon the deep,
And safely guard a little boy I used to
    rock to sleep!

Margery Ruebush Shank.

De Massa Ob De Sheepfol

De Massa ob de sheepfol
Dat guards de sheepfol bin
Look out in de gloomerin meadows
Wha'r de long night rain begin——
So he call to de hirelin' shepha'd
"Is my sheep——is dey all come in?
My sheep, is dey all come in?"

Oh den says de hirelin' shepha'd
"Dey's some, dey's black and thin,
And some, dey's po' ol' wedda's——
Dat can't come home again.
Dey's some black sheep an' ol' wedda's
But de res' dey's all brung in——
De res' dey's all brung in."

Den de massa ob de sheepfol'
Dat guards de sheepfol' bin,
Goes down in de gloomerin meadows
Wha'r de long night rain begin——
So he let down de ba's ob de sheepfol'
Callin' sof', "Come in! Come in,"
Callin' sof', "Come in! Come in."

Den up t'ro de gloomerin meadows,
T'ro de col' night rain an' win'
And up t'ro de gloomerin' rain-paf'
Whar de sleet fa piercin thin,
De po' los' sheep ob de sheepfol'
Dey all comes gadderin' in
De po' los' sheep ob de sheepfol'
Dey all comes gadderin' in.

Sarah Greene.

❧

   Had the prophets of Baal been as
earnest in seeking God as they were in
pouring water upon His altar, they would
have been saved.

E. P. Brown.

Be near me when my light is low
When the blood creeps and the nerves
    prick
And tingle and the heart is sick
And all the wheels of being slow.
Be near me when the sensuous frame
Is racked with pangs that conquer trust
And Time a Maniac scattering dust
And Life a Fury slinging flame.
Be near me when my faith is dry
And when the flies of latter spring
That lay their eggs and sting and sting
And weave their petty cells and die.
Be near me when I fade away
To point the terms of human strife
And on the low dark verge of life
The twilight of eternal day.

Alfred Tennyson.

❧

Through love to light! Oh, wonderful
    the way
That leads from darkness to the perfect
    day!
From darkness and from sorrow of the
    night
To morning that comes singing o'er the
    sea!
Through love to light! Through light, O
    God, to Thee
Who art the love of love, the eternal
    light of light!

Richard Watson Gilder.

Out of the strain of the Doing
Into the peace of the Done
Out of the thirst of Pursuing
Into the rapture of Won
Out of the grey mist into brightness
Out of pale dusk into Dawn——
Out of all wrong into rightness,
We from these fields shall be gone.
"Nay" say the saints "Not gone but come,
Into Eternity's Harvest Home."

W. M. L. Fay.

❧

For who that leans on His right arm
  Was ever yet forsaken?
What righteous cause can suffer harm
  If He its part has taken?
    Though wild and loud
    And dark the cloud,
    Behind its folds
    His hand upholds
  The calm sky of to-morrow.

Martin Luther.

❧

For the world knows not of the peace
    that comes
To a soul at one with God.
It is only those who are travelling on
In the faith the Master trod
Who can feel through the dark that
    loving hand
And, holding it fast, can understand.

❧

Instead of going to heaven at last
I'm going all along.

Emily Dickinson.

RAINBOWS   THE BOOK OF HOPE

GRATITUDE

A man of a grumbling spirit may eat a very
poor dinner from silver plate, while one
with a grateful heart may feast upon a crust.

E. P. Brown

We Give Thanks

"For sunlit hours and visions clear,
For all remembered faces dear,
For comrades of a single day,
Who sent us stronger on our way,
For friends who shared the year's long
    road,
And bore with us the common load,
For hours that levied heavy tolls,
But brought us nearer to our goals,
For insight won through toil and tears,
We thank the Keeper of our years."

Clyde McGee.

Today

This little rift of light,
'Twixt night and night,
Let me keep bright
    Today!
And let no trace of sorrow
Nor shadow of tomorrow
From its brightness borrow
    Today!
I take the gift of heaven,
In love and mercy given,
And if tomorrow shall be sad,
Or never come at all, I've had
    Today! *Edward Hershey Richards.*

Humility

There was a time when faith began to
    slip,
When I had lost all that I had to lose——
Or so it seemed to me——I lost home,
My job——
I had no house, no food, no shoes.
Then, suddenly, I felt myself ashamed,
For I, who talked of shoes,
Then chanced to meet
Upon the busy highway of my life,
A man
Who had no feet!

Marcella Hooe.

Shall I Complain

Shall I complain because the feast is o'er,
And all the banquet lights have ceased
    to shine?
For Joy that was, and is no longer mine;
For Love that came and went and comes
    no more;
For Hopes and Dreams that left my
    open door;
Shall I, who hold the Past in fee, repine?
Nay! there are those who never quaffed
    Life's wine——
That were the unblest fate one might
    deplore.
To sit alone and dream, at set of sun
When all the world is vague with com-
    ing night——
To hear old voices whisper, sweet and
    low,
And see dear faces steal back, one by one,
And thrill anew to each long-past
    delight——
Shall I complain, who still this bliss
    may know?

Louise Chandler Moulton.

Thank God

Thank God for life!
E'en though it bring much bitterness
    and strife,
And all our fairest hopes be wrecked
    and lost,
E'en though there be more ill than good
    in life
We cling to life and reckon not the cost
    Thank God for life!

Thank God for love!
For though sometimes grief follows in
    its wake,
Still we forget love's sorrow in love's joy,
And cherish tears with smiles for love's
    dear sake;
Only in heaven is bliss without alloy
    Thank God for love!

Thank God for pain!
No tear hath ever yet been shed in vain,
And in the end each sorrowing heart
    shall find
No curse, but blessings in the hand of
    pain
Even when he smiteth then is God most
    kind.
    Thank God for pain!

Thank God for death!
Who touches anguished lips and stills
    their breath
And giveth peace unto each troubled
    breast;
Grief flies before thy touch, O blessed
    death;
God's sweetest gift; thy name in heaven
    is Rest.
    Thank God for Death!

Author Unknown.

Gratitude

For starry night and dawn of day,
For winds that in the willows play,
For every gift that comes my way,
  I'm grateful.
For sunshine bright and silvery rain,
For harvest time and ripening grain,
For joy that ever follows pain,
  I'm grateful.
For steeple bells that gaily ring,
For homing birds upon the wing,
And love that only worth can bring,
  I'm grateful.
For furrowed field and upturned sod,
For paths that I alone have trod,
For faith that lifts my soul to God,
  I'm grateful.

Alice Whitson-Norton.

A young man in his early twenties was to graduate from college within three weeks. He had striven hard, too hard, for his comparatively frail body to endure. Before graduation day arrived he was rushed to a sanitarium in a very critical condition. Within a short time, due to a complication of diseases, he lost his sight completely. The doctors told him that he could never see again, but that his other ailments might respond to treatment and rest, and that one day he might be well enough to be released.

For two years now this young man has been confined to his bed. He has not grown bitter, petulant, or rebellious. While he may not actually glory in his tribulation, he rejoices in the power that is his to endure patiently.

Already he is turning his tribulation into a testimony. In his blindness he has learned to typewrite, and is cultivating a latent talent for writing poetry—verses like the following, which reveals a fine philosophy, born of deep affliction:

I'm thankful, Lord, for loving care;
I'm thankful, too, for something more;
I'm thankful, Lord, that I can bear
The things that I'm not thankful for.

Claire Sanford.

A Little Thankful Song

For what are we thankful? For this;
For the breath and the sunlight of life.
For the love of the child, and the kiss
On the lips of the mother and wife.
  For roses entwining,
  For bud and for bloom,
  And hopes that are shining
  Like stars in the gloom.

For what are we thankful? For this:
The strength and the patience of toil;
For ever the dreams that are bliss——
The hope of the seed in the soil.
  For souls that are whiter
  From day unto day:
  And lives that are brighter
  From going God's way.

For what are we thankful? For all:
The sunlight——the shadow——the song;
The blossoms may wither and fall,
But the world moves in music along!
  For simple sweet living,
  'Tis love that doth teach it
  A heaven forgiving
  And faith that can reach it!

Frank L. Stanton.

Challenge

The words written by *Alfred G. Gardiner* on the day of the interment of the "Unknown Soldier" in Westminster Abbey ought to be preserved:-

"None of us will look on that moving scene without emotion. But something more will be required of us than a spasm of easy, tearful emotion that exhausts itself in being felt.

What have we the living to say to the dead who pass by in shadowy hosts? They died for no mean thing. They died that the world might be a better and a cleaner place for those who lived and for those who come after.

As that unknown soldier is borne down Whitehall he will issue a silent challenge to the living world to say whether it was worthy of his sacrifice.

And if we are honest with ourselves we shall not find the answer easy."

❧

A judicious silence is always better than truth spoken without charity.
> *Francis De Sales.*

❧

The World

This world that we're a-livin' in
Is mighty hard to beat;
You get a thorn with every rose,
But ain't the roses sweet!
> *Frank L. Stanton.*

We Are Thankful for These

These to be thankful for: a friend,
A work to do, a way to wend,
And these in which to take delight;
The wind that turns the poplars white,

Wonder and gleam of common things,
Sunlight upon a sea-gull's wings,
Odors of earth and dew-drenched lawns,
The pageantry of darks and dawns;

Blue vistas of a city street
At twilight, music, passing feet,
The thrill of Spring, half joy, half pain,
The deep voice of the Autumn rain.

Shall we not be content with these
Imperishable mysteries?
And jocund-hearted take our share
Of joy and pain and find life fair?——

Wayfarers on a road where we
Set forth each day right valiantly,
Expectant, dauntless, blithe, content,
To make the great experiment.
> *Unknown.*

❧

Good, the more communicated, the more abundant grows.
> *Milton.*

❧

And many a discontented mourner
Is spending his days in Grumble Corner:
Sour and sad whom I long to entreat
To take a house in Thanksgiving Street.
> *Josephine Pollard.*

RAINBOWS — THE BOOK OF HOPE

HAPPINESS

*Joy is the grace
We say to God!*

Jean Ingelow

The world would be better and brighter if our teachers would dwell on the Duty of Happiness as well on the Happiness of Duty, for we ought to be as cheerful as we can, if only because to be happy ourselves is a most effectual contribution to the happiness of others.

Lord Avebury.

A Child's Laughter

All the bells of heaven may ring
All the birds of heaven may sing
All the wells on earth may spring
All the winds on earth may bring
  All sweet sounds together
    Algernon Charles Swinburne.

Requisite

Oh, leave me, Life, my laughter. Leave
  me but a feeble echo
  And I shall manage somehow, to **exist**
    the darkest day.
But bring the sprays of cypress and go
  dig a grave to hide me
  The moment that you take my laughter,
    every bit, away.

The Things That Count

Not what we have but what we use;
Not what we see but what we choose——
These are the things that mar or bless
The sun of human happiness.
    Clarence Urmy.

More on pg. 101

63

The Philosophy of an English Showman

"Good day" said 'e, "good day" said I
    "and 'ow do yer find things go
And what's the chance of millions when
    you runs a travellin' show?"
"I find," sez 'e "things very much as 'ow
    I've always found
For mostly they goes up and down or else
    goes round and round."
Said 'e, "The jobs the very spit o' wot it
    always were,
It's bread and butter mostly when the dog
    don't catch a 'are,
But looking at it broad, while it aint no
    merchant king's,
What's lost upon the roundabouts we
    pulls up on the swings . . ."
'E thumped upon the footboard and 'e
    lumbered on again
To meet a golden sunset down the twi-
    light in the lane
"For up and down and round and round"
    says 'e, "go all appointed things,
And losses on the roundabouts means
    profits on the swings."

                Patrick Chalmers.

※

There's one sad truth in life I've found,
    While journeying east and west—
The only folks we really wound
    Are those we love the best.
We flatter those we scarcely know,
    We please the fleeting guest,
And deal full many a thoughtless blow
    To those who love us best.

                Unknown.

Folks and Me

It is a funny thing, but true, that folks you don't like, don't like you. I don't know why this should be so, but just the same I always know if I am "sour", friends are few; if I am friendly, folks are too.

Sometimes I get up in the morn a-wishing I was never born. I make of cross remarks a few, and then my family wishes, too, that I had gone some other place, instead of showing them my face.

But let me change my little tune, and sing and smile, then pretty soon the folks around me sing and smile; I guess 'twas catching, all the while.

Yes, it's a funny thing, but true, that folks you like will sure like you.

                Anon.

※

As We Measure

True worth is in being, not seeming;
In doing each day that goes by,
Some little good——not in dreaming
Of great things to do bye and bye,
For whatever men say in blindness
And spite of the fancies of youth,
There's nothing so kingly as kindness,
And nothing so royal as truth.

We get back our mete as we measure:
We cannot do wrong and feel right;
Nor can we give pain and gain pleasure,
For justice avenges each slight.
The air for the wing of the sparrow,
The bush for the robin and wren,
But always the path that is narrow
And straight, for the children of men.

                Alice Cary.

Friends of Mine

Good-morning, Brother Sunshine,
  Good-morning, Sister Song,
I beg your humble pardon
  If you've waited very long.
I thought I heard you rapping,
  To shut you out were sin,
My heart is standing open,
  Won't you
    walk
      right
        in?

Good-morning, Brother Gladness,
  Good-morning, Sister Smile,
They told me you were coming,
  So I waited on a while.
I'm lonesome here without you,
  A weary while it's been,
My heart is standing open,
  Won't you
    walk
      right
        in?

Good-morning, Brother Kindness,
  Good-morning, Sister Cheer,
I heard you were out calling,
  So I waited for you here.
Some way, I keep forgetting
  I have to toil or spin
When you are my companions,
  Won't you
    walk
      right
        in?

James W. Foley.

The secret of success in conversation is to be able to disagree without being disagreeable.

Good Cheer

Good cheer is almost as essential to life as sunshine, air and water——and is quite as plentiful.

Cheerfulness has a dual value in life. First it helps you——then it helps you to help others——and it keeps on spreading out into the great throng of humanity, stirring the hearts of men as the gentle breeze stirs the leaves of the forest—— returning again and again to you in its endless course and all the while making the heavy load lighter and the dark road brighter for all.

Good cheer is one of the biggest little things among all the elements of Success.

G. W. H.

Hope

Never go gloomy, man with a mind,
  Hope is a better companion than fear;
Providence, ever benignant and kind,
  Gives with a smile what you take with
    a tear;
    All will be right,
    Look to the light.
Morning was ever the daughter of night;
All that was black will be all that is bright,
  Cheerily, cheerily, then cheer up.
Many a foe is a friend in disguise,
  Many a trouble a blessing most true,
Helping the heart to be happy and wise,
  With love ever precious and joys
    ever new.
    Stand in the van,
    Strike like a man!
This is the bravest and cleverest plan;
Trusting in God while you do what
    you can.
  Cheerily, cheerily, then cheer up.

What delightful hosts are they——
Life and Love!
Lingeringly I turn away,
This late hour, yet glad enough
They have not withheld from me
Their high hospitality.
So with face lit with delight
And all gratitude, I stay
Yet to press their hands and say,
"Thanks.——So fine a time! Goodnight."

James Whitcomb Riley.

A Hymn to Happiness

Let us smile along together,
Be the weather
    What it may.
Through the waste and wealth of hours,
Plucking flowers
    By the way.
Fragrance from the meadows blowing,
Naught of heat and hatred knowing,
Kindness seeking, kindness sowing,
    Not to-morrow, but to-day.

Let us sing along, beguiling
Grief to smiling
    In the song
With the promises of heaven
Let us leaven
    The day long,
Gilding all the duller seemings
With the roselight of our dreamings,
Splashing clouds with sunlight's gleam-
        ings,
Here and there and all along.

Let us live along, the sorrow
Of to-morrow
    Never heed.
In the pages of the present
What is pleasant
    Only read.

Bells but pealing, never knelling,
Hearts with gladness ever swelling,
Tides of charity upwelling
    In our every dream and deed.

Let us hope along together,
Be the weather
    What it may,
Where the sunlight glad is shining,
Not repining
    By the way.
Seek to add our meed and measure
To the old Earth's joy and treasure,
Quaff the crystal cup of pleasure,
    Not to-morrow, but to-day.

James W. Foley.

Mary White

She was the happiest thing in the
world. And she was happy because she
was always enlarging her horizon . . .
She loved to rollick; persiflage was her
natural expression at home.

Her humor was a continual bubble
of joy. She seemed to think in hyperbole
and metaphor. She was mischievous
without malice, as full of faults as an
old shoe. No angel was Mary White,
but an easy girl to live with, for she
never nursed a grouch five minutes in
her life.

A rift in the clouds in a gray day
threw a shaft of sunlight upon her coffin
as her nervous, energetic little body sank
to its last sleep.

But the soul of her, the glowing,
gorgeous, fervent soul of her, surely was
flaming in eager joy upon some other
dawn.

William Allen White.

66

Happiness

Happiness is the art of finding joy and satisfaction in the little privileges of life; a quiet hour in the sun, instead of a far-away journey; a little outing in the nearby woods, instead of long trips away; an hour with a friend, instead of an extended visit with relatives; a few pages of a book, instead of hours of reading at a time; a flash of sunset, a single beautiful flower, a passing smile, a kindly word, a little thoughtfulness here and there as the day slips by . . .

There's night and day, brother, both
    sweet things;
Sun, moon and stars, brother, all sweet
    things;
There's likewise a wind on the heath.
Life is very sweet, brother;
Who would wish to die?

George Barrow.

My Treasures

Nothing can erase the lovely things my
    life has known;
These treasures I shall always cherish as
    my very own.
The disappointments, unkind things,
    that have but touched my way
I brush aside, and quickly think upon the
    beauty of the day.
For each dawn brings a wonder I have
    not seen before.
And with that wonder comes the open-
    ing of still another door:
The blooming of a flower, the sunlight
    on the sea,
The kindness of a friend; all these are
    joys to me.

Marcella E. Minard.

Give because you love to give—as the flower pours forth its perfume.

Spurgeon.

The selfish man is not a complete man; he is not whole, normal, healthy. The truth is that he is sick.

Consider then the road by which a man moves out from this lamentable state toward health again!

He gains some surplus energy of thought to spend on some one besides himself. He feels in time a dawning capacity to be happy in the happiness of others. At length he eats and sleeps again with relish and delight, and sheds his returning radiance on all around. Rising within him like a tossing mill race, he feels returning vigor, fretting to be let loose upon some mill wheel.

He wants to do something for somebody. At last, his sickness gone, happily objective, not moodily subjective, thinking of others, not worrying about himself, spreading abroad his surplus vigor, not hoarding it greedily for his depleted strength, he goes out into life, a dynamic man come back to health again.

By as much as he expends himself, giving more than he gets, making his contributions offered greater than his contributions levied, he shows the marks of a well man. For selfishness is sickness, and overflowing usefulness is spiritual health and abounding life.

Harry Emerson Fosdick.

In the highest class of God's school of suffering we learn, not resignation nor patience, but rejoicing in tribulation.

J. H. Vincent.

The Desire

Give me no mansions ivory white
Nor palaces of pearl and gold;
Give me a child for all delight
　　Just four years old.

Give me no wings of rosy shine
Nor snowy raiment fold on fold
Give me a little boy all mine
　　Just four years old.

Give me no gold and starry crown
Nor harps, nor palm branches unrolled;
Give me a nestling head of brown
　　Just four years old.

Give me a cheek that's like the peach,
Two arms to clasp me from the cold;
And all my heaven's within my reach
　　Just four years old.

Dear God, You give me from Your skies
A little paradise to hold,
As Mary once her Paradise
　　Just four years old.
　　　　　　　Katharine Tynan.

❧

Some persons think God must be dead
or asleep or on a journey. They see such
stalking evils, such collapses of civilization, such ugly shadows over the fair
world, that they cannot hold their thin
clew of faith any longer. It has snapped
and left them standing alone in their dark
cave.

But He is there all the same, though
they see Him not nor know Him. He does
not vanish in the dark or in the storm.
There is much love working still in these
hard, dark days.
　　　　　　　Rufus M. Jones.

The air is full of whirring wings,
As if a thousand Springs
Swept earthward, heavenly whisperings
　　Of gladness to impart;

Oh, list, harmonious music rings!
Each bird a sweet hosanna sings,
And each from God a message brings
　　To cheer the human heart.
　　　　　　　I. S. T.

❧

Martin

When I am tired of earnest men,
Intense and keen and sharp and clever,
Pursuing fame with brush or pen,
Or counting metal disks forever,
Then from the halls of Shadowland,
Beyond the trackless purple sea,
Old Martin's ghost comes back to stand
Beside my desk and talk to me.

Still on his delicate pale face
A quizzical thin smile is showing
His cheeks are wrinkled like fine lace
His kind blue eyes are gay and glowing.
He wears a brilliant-hued cravat
A suit to match his soft grey hair
A rakish stick a knowing hat,
A manner blithe and debonair.

How good that he who always knew
That being lovely was a duty,
Should have gold halls to wander through
And should himself inhabit beauty.
How like his old unselfish way
To leave those halls of splendid mirth
And comfort those condemned to stay
Upon the dull and somber earth.

Some people ask: "What cruel chance
Made Martin's life so sad a story?"
Martin? Why, he exhaled romance,
And wore an overcoat of glory.
A fleck of sunlight in the street,
A horse, a book, a girl who smiled,
Such visions made each moment sweet
For this receptive ancient child.

Because it was old Martin's lot
To be, not make, a decoration,
Shall we then scorn him, having not
His genius of appreciation?
Rich joy and love he got and gave;
His heart was merry as his dress;
Pile laurel leaves upon his grave
Who did not gain, but was, success!

Joyce Kilmer.

Harvest

My neighbor hath a little field,
Small store of wine its presses yield,
And truly but a slender hoard
Its harvest brings for barn or board.
Yet tho' a hundred fields are mine,
Fertile with olive, corn, and wine,
Tho' Autumn piles my garners high,
Still for the little field I sigh.
For ah! methinks no otherwhere
Is any field so good and fair.
Small tho' it be, 'tis better far
Than all my fruitful vineyards are,
Amid whose plenty sad I pine——
"Ah, would the little field were mine!"

Large knowledge void of peace and rest,
And wealth with pining care possessed
These by my fertile lands are meant;
The little field is called Content.

Robertson Trowbridge.

Do It With a Song

Somehow the task seems lighter
    When we do it with a song;
It stills the heart's complaining
    And keeps the courage strong.
Somehow, though skies are gloomy,
    Or roads are rough and long,
He will not lack for comrades
    Who travels with a song.

Nellie Good.

The Spring Cleaning

Now open up the windows of the heart,
    And let the sunshine penetrate the
        gloom;
Clear out the fears and doubts that
        grimly start
    Like ghosts within the mind's dim
        haunted room.

Brush out the cobwebs that your malice
        wrought,
    And sweep away the grudges that
        you bear;
Replace each p e t t y and ungracious
        thought
    With one that is forgiving, true and
        fair.

And when the task is finished, you will
        find
    That happiness is destined to remain
Within the sunlit rooms of heart and
        mind,
    And know your work has not been
        done in vain.

Reynale Smith Pickering.

Thank God for the man who is cheerful
  In spite of life's troubles, I say;
Who sings of a bright tomorrow,
  Because of the clouds of today.
His life is a beautiful sermon,
  And this is the lesson to me——
Meet trials with smiles and they vanish;
  Face cares with a song and they flee.

Unknown.

❦

Beautifully the twin angels of life——memory and hope——mingle in the looking back to the old homestead and the looking forward to the Father's House on High.

Will Carleton does it finely:

Fare you well old house! You're naught
  that can feel or see
But you seem like a human being——a
  dear old friend to me;
And we never will have a better home
  if my opinion stands
Until we commence a-keepin' house in
  the House not made with hands.

❦

Do you wish to be free? Then above all things love God, love your neighbor, love one another, love the common weal; then you will have true liberty.

Savonarola.

'Tis sweet, as year by year we lose
Friends out of sight, to muse
How grows in Paradise our store.

Keble.

❦

Love is the open hand, nothing but that,
Ungemmed, unhidden, wishing not to
  hurt,
As one should bring you cowslips in a hat
Swung from the hand, or apples in her
  skirt,
  I bring you, calling out as children do;
"Look what I have!—And these are all
  for you."

Edna St. Vincent Milley.

Fast Manners

A few nights ago a man was hurrying along a street when another man rushed out of an alley and the two collided. One of them raised his hat and said, "My dear sir, I don't know which of us is to blame for this violent encounter, and I am in too great a hurry to investigate. If I ran into you, I beg your pardon; if you ran into me, don't mention it," and he tore away at redoubled speed.

E. J. Hardy.

❦

He is rich who does not desire more.
Persian Proverb.

RAINBOWS   THE BOOK OF HOPE

Heaven

Silently, one by one,
In the infinite meadows of heaven,
Blossom the lovely stars,
The forget-me-nots of the angels.

Longfellow

No Anchorage Here

Suppose that there were no changes, no disappointments, no wrecked and ruined hopes, no unrealized expectations, no shattered plans, no empty chairs, no wayside grave, no darkened hearths and homes, what then? Why we should be for staying here, and weaving our little nest in time, and there would be no such reaching out of hands towards the great unseen.

* * * *

It is because there is no anchorage here that will enable us to outride the final storm that we are encouraged to cast our anchor far within the veil. It is because the houses that we build, however solidly, must sooner or later totter into ruin and decay, that we are invited to become children in the "house not made with hands." It is because this world, with all its fashions and its lusts, is a passing and perishing splendour, that we are called to surrender ourselves to the "powers of the world to come."

Henry Howard.

This has been called *Richter's* unwritten beatitude: "Blessed are they that are homesick for they shall come at last to their father's house."

His Smile

He who came to earth to teach us the divine sense of humor showed us all that was lovely and beautiful in His character ——except one thing.

He showed us His power; He showed us His wisdom;

He showed us His melting kindness; He showed us His sorrow;

He showed us His tears. He showed us His forgiveness; but there was one thing He did not show. There was one thing He saved for Heaven that will make Heaven Heaven, and that was— His Smile.   *Fulton J. Sheen.*

❧❧

If there be none left on earth to bid us good cheer and sustain our hearts, there may be on the other side, and as we run our ordered course the Departed lean forward from the high places, rejoicing as we slip each weight, and forsake each sin, full of longing till we also reach the goal and receive the Crown.

Ian Maclaren.

De Glory Road

O De Glory Road! O De Glory Road!
I'm gwine ter drap mah load upon de
   Glory Road,
I lay on mah bed untell one erclock,
An' de Lawd come callin' all His faithful
   flock.
An' He call "Whoo-ee"! an' He call
   "Whoo-ee"!
An' I cry, "Massa Jesus is you callin' me?"
An' he call, "Whoo-ee!" an' he call
   "Whoo-ee!"
An' I riz up f'um mah pallet an' I cry
   "Hyahs me".

De Lawd sez "Niggah ain' I call yer thrice
Ter ride erlong behin' me up ter Paradise,
On de Glory Road, on de Glory Road?"
An' I clime up ter de saddle, an' I jined
   de load.

De hawse he wuz longer dan a thousan'
   mile;
His tail went lashin' an' his hoofs wuz wil'
His mane was flamin' an' his eyes wuz
   moons,
An' his mouth kep' singin' Halleluyah
   tunes!

De Lawd say, "Niggah why n'cher look
   erroun?"
An' dar we wuz flyin' over risin' groun'.
Powerful hills, an' mountains too
An' de earth an' de people wuz drapt
   f'um view.

And I hyahd all roun' me how de sperits
   sang,
And de Lawd sang louder dan de whole
   shebang!

De Lawd sez "Niggah why n'cher look
   ergin,"
An' dar wuz de Debbil, on de back uv
   Sin,
A hangin' on de critter wid his whip an'
   goad,
An' boun' he gwine ter kotch us, on de
   Glory Road!
"O Lawdy, it's de Debbil, comin' straight
   f'um Hell!
I kin tell him by his roarin' an' de brim-
   stone smell!"
But de Lawd sez, "Niggah, he ain' kotch
   us yit"!
An' He lashed an' He hustled an' He
   loosed de bit,

Den de Debbil crep' closuh, an' I hyahd
   him yell
"I'm gwine ter ketch a niggah, fur ter
   roas' in Hell!"
An' I cried, "Lawd Sabe me!" An' de
   Lawd cry, "Sho!"
And hyah it was Hebben, an' we shet
   de do'.

O Glory, Glory, how de angels sang!
O Glory, Glory, how de rafters rang!
An' Moses n' Aaron an' Methusalum,
Dey shout an' dey holler an' dey beat
   de drum.
King Solomon kissed me an' his thousan'
   wives,
Jes' like dey'd knowed me, durin' all dey
   lives:

An' de Lawd sez, "Niggah take a gran'-
   stan seat,
But I specks youse hungry; have a bite
   ter eat!"
An' de ravens fed me an' Elijah prayed,
An' de Sabed Ones gathered, while de
   organ played,
An' dey cry, "O Sinnah come an' lose
   yuh load
On de Glory Road, on de Glory Road.
An' come and dwell in de Lawd's abode."
Glory, Glory on de Glory Road!

Sez de Lawd, "No sinnah you mus' trabbel
   back
Ter he'p po' niggahs up the Glory rack;
Ter he'p old mo'ners an' de scoffin coons
By shoutin' loud Halleluyah tunes".

O come, mah breddren, won' you drap
   yuh load,
And ride ter Hebben up de Glory Road?
                Clement Wood.

Heaven and Hell

I walked through Hell.
No lake of fire was there
Nor gloating demons harrying their prey
Nor implements of torture
Nay, nor pain of any kind
But only dull despair.
Faces expressionless,
Eyes without light,
Spirits of stone,
Cold, hard and dead.
Suddenly I slipped on slag
Or slime of crawling thing
I slipped and fell
And strove to rise but could not
Hands pushed me back and down
And mirthless chuckles, fiendish cruel
Choked in that loathsome air.
This was the den of hate
The home of cruelty
Called Hell.

I walked through Heaven.
No gates of pearl, I saw,
Nor streets of gold
Nor jasper walls,
Nay, nor no harps of minstrelsy,
But only happy faces
Radiant with rapture indescribable
Alight with smiling welcome.
Suddenly I slipped upon some verdant
   green
I slipped but did not fall
For hands were out to help
And arms there were around me
And all the fragrant air was musical
With voices speaking sympathy and love.
This was the home of comradeship
The city of the kind
Called Heaven.
            George W. Humphreys.

So in true brotherhood and charity, with a smile in the thick of it, with a little music in the worst of it, we shall come at last where the rough wind and the east wind are hushed and for ever and for ever, and for ever broods the peace of God.

G. H. Morrison.

❧

It was Christ's glory to show the ascending scale of God's gifts. The devil ever gives his best first. Feasting with harlots, then famine with swine.

But the Master, on the other hand, is always giving something better. As the taste is being constantly refined, it is provided with more delicate and ravishing delights. That which you know of Him to-day is certainly better than that which you tasted when first you sat down at His board. And so it will ever be. The angels as His servants, have orders to bring in and set before the heirs of glory things which eye hath not seen, and man's heart has not conceived, but which are all prepared. The best of earth will be far below the simplest fare of heaven. But what will heaven's best be? If the wine in the peasant's house is so luscious what will be the new wine in the Father's Kingdom? What may we expect from the vintage of the celestial hills! What will it be to sit at the Marriage Supper of the Lamb? And for ever and ever, as fresh revelations and wonder break on our glad souls, we shall look up to the Master of the Feast, and cry, "Thou hast kept the best until now."

Frederick Brotherton Meyer.

The Better Land

Eye hath not seen it, my gentle boy!
Ear hath not heard its deep songs of joy;
Dreams cannot picture a world so fair——
Sorrow and death may not enter there;
Time doth not breathe on its fadeless
　bloom,
Far beyond the clouds and beyond the
　tomb,
It is there, it is there, my child.

Felicia D. Hemans.

My Ain Countree

"But now they desire a better
country, that is, an heavenly."

I'm far frae my hame, and I'm weary
　aftenwhiles,
For the langed-for hame-bringing and my
　father's welcome smiles;
I'll ne'er be fu' content, until my een
　doth see
The shining gates o' heaven and my ain
　countree.

The earth is flecked wi' flowers, mony-
　tinted fresh an' gay,
The birdies warble blythely, for my
　father made them sae;
But these sights and these sounds will
　as naething be to me,
When I hear the angels singing in my
　ain countree.

I've his gude word of promise that some
　gladsome day the King
To his ain royal palace his banished hame
　will bring:
W'een and wi' hearts runnin' owre we
　shall see
The King in his beauty in our ain
　countree.

74

My sins hae been mony, an' my sorrows
    hae been sair,
But there they'll never vex me, nor be
    remembered mair;
His bluid has made me white, his hand
    shall dry mine ee,
When he brings me hame at last, to my
    ain countree.

Like a bairn to its mither, a wee birdie
    to its nest,
I wad fain be ganging noo, unto my
    Saviour's breast;
For he gathers in his bosom, witless,
    worthless lambs like me,
And carries them himsel' to his ain
    countree.

He is faithfu' that hath promised, he'll
    surely come again,
He'll keep his tryst wi' me, at what hour
    I dinna ken:
But he bids me still to wait, an' ready
    ay to be,
To gang at ony moment, to my ain
    countree.

So I'm watchin' aye, an' singin' o' my
    hameland as I wait,
For the soundin' o' his footfa' this side
    the shinin' gate,
God gie his grace to ilka ane who listens
    noo to me,
That we may a'gang in gladness to our
    ain countree.

                Mary Lee Demarest.

The Cripple

When I get to heaven I
Shall dance upon my toes;
(Just what the winged ones will say
Only God knows.)

And only those who love a light
Moving without sound——
Only they will notice me
Pirouetting 'round.

And those who know the still spell
Of rhythm's loveliness,
The ecstasy that I shall feel
Only they can guess.

O, will it be a strange thing,
In Heaven, if I do
This thing that I never could
But always wanted to?
                Ruth E. Hopkins.

Earth Is Enough

We men of Earth have here the stuff
Of Paradise——we have enough!
We need no other thing to build
The stairs into the Unfulfilled——
No other ivory for the doors——
No other marble for the floors——
No other cedar for the beam
And dome of man's immortal dream.

Here on the paths of every-day——
Here on the common human way
Is all the stuff the gods would take
To build a Heaven, to mold and make
New Edens. Ours the stuff sublime
To build Eternity in time!
                Edwin Markham.

There no more parting, no more pain,
    The distant ones brought near,
The lost so long are found again,
    Long lost but longer dear:
Eye hath not seen, ear hath not heard,
    Nor heart conceived that rest,
With them our good things long deferred,
    With Jesus Christ our Best.
              Christina Rossetti.

For an Old Fisherman

When he goes home, dear Lord, may
    he be met
By some tanned crony of his fishing days,
His creel snugged on his back, his line
    still wet,
And thought of secret trout streams in
    his gaze.
There must be quiet woods for men like
    these.
What would they do upon a golden street
Who still hear April sauntering through
    the trees,
And feel the ground thaw under eager
    feet?
Give him a casting rod like that he lost——
He never found one like it, so he said;
A swirling pool of promise to be crossed,
And Thy eternal summers on his head,
And sometimes, margin for the truth,
    to say
How long the other one, that got away.

Eleanor Alletta Chaffee.

❧

But chiefly it is the echo of older steps
I hear—steps whose sound is long since
stilled—feet that have crossed the horizon
and have gone on journey for a while.
And when I listen I hear echoes that are
fading into silence.

Charles S. Brooks.

❧

Sir Cecil Spring-Rice was Britain's am-
bassador in Washington during the darkest hours of the First World War.
Shortly before his death in 1918 he wrote
a poem of two verses. The first voiced
his undying loyalty to his country and
the second his devotion to that wider
cause which we call the Kingdom of
God, which is served by higher means.
Here is the poem, wrought out in a time
of deep darkness:

I vow to thee, my country, all earthly
    things above,
Entire and whole and perfect, the service
    of my love:
The love that asks no question; the love
    that stands the test,
That lays upon the altar the dearest and
    the best;
The love that never falters, the love that
    pays the price,
The love that makes undaunted the final
    sacrifice.

And there's another country I've heard
    of long ago
Most dear to them that love her, most
    great to them that know;
We may not count her armies, we may
    not see her King;
Her fortress is a faithful heart, her pride
    is suffering:
And soul by soul and silently her shining
    bounds increase,
And her ways are ways of gentleness and
    all her paths are Peace.

'The River Path'

No bird-song floated down the hill,
The tangled bank below was still;
No rustle from the birchen stem,
No ripple from the water's hem.
The dusk of twilight round us grew,
We felt the falling of the dew.

For, from us, ere the day was done,
The wooded hills shut out the sun.
But on the river's farther side

76

We saw the hill-tops glorified,——
A tender glow, exceeding fair,
A dream of day without its glare.

With us the damp, the chill, the gloom;
With them the sunset's rosy bloom;
While dark through willowy vistas seen,
The river rolled in shade between.
From out the darkness where we trod,
We gazed upon those hills of God.

Whose light seemed not of moon or sun.
We spake not, but our thought was one.
We paused, as if from that bright shore
Beckoned our dear ones gone before;
And stilled our beating hearts to hear
The voices lost to mortal ear!

Sudden our pathway turned from night;
The hills swung open to the light.
Through their green gates the sunshine
    showed,
A long, slant splendor downward flowed.
Down glade and glen and bank it rolled;
It bridged the shaded stream with gold.

And borne on piers of mist, allied
The shadowy with the sunlit side!
"So" prayed we, "when our feet draw
    near
The river dark, with mortal fear,
"And the night cometh chill with dew,
O Father! let Thy light break through!

"So let the hills of doubt divide,
So bridge with faith the sunless tide!
"So let the eyes that fail on earth
On Thy eternal hills look forth;
"And in Thy beckoning angels know
The dear ones we have loved below!"

John Greenleaf Whittier.

Names

Names! . . . I hate the tyranny of names,
Harsh things inflexible as wooden frames,
From which each timid spirit must peer
    out
Upon his fellows, through a gilded doubt,
And wonder, sometimes, what his gaze
    might see
Of loveliness——but for that pedigree.
I hope that when I reach Heaven I shall
    meet
No pompous angel strutting down the
    street,
To introduce me to the other dead
With knowing words, much better left
    unsaid.
Such fragile things are souls——they need
    to be
Left to explore each other silently.

I'll want to walk around and simply stare,
Until I find one ghost whose special air
Appeals to me. Then I will dare to say:
"I think I saw your thoughts on earth
    one day;
Tree-shadow on a river was your smile;
I like your wings . . . shall we be friends
    awhile?"

Joan Dareth Prosper.

The Gentle Soul

I think the gentle soul of him
    Goes softly in some garden place
With the old smile time may not dim
    Upon his face.

He who was lover of the Spring
    With love that never quite forgets,
Surely sees roses blossoming
    And violets.

Now that his day of toil is through,
I love to think he sits at ease,
With some old volume that he knew
Upon his knees.

Watching, perhaps, with quiet eyes
The white cloud's drifting argosy;
Or twilight opening flower-wise
On land and sea.

He who so loved companionship
I may not think he walks alone,
Failing some friendly hand to slip
Within his own.

Those whom he loved aforetime, still
I doubt not, bear him company;
Yea, even laughter yet may thrill
Where he may be.

A thought, a fancy——who may tell?
Yet I who ever pray it so,
Feel through my tears that all is well;
And this I know——

That God is gentle to His guest,
And, therefore, may I gladly say,
"Surely the things he loved the best
Are his to-day."

Theodosia Garrison.

A Life-Lesson

There! little girl; don't cry!
They have broken your doll, I know;
And your tea-set blue,
And your play-house, too,
Are the things of the long ago;
But childish troubles will soon pass by——
There! little girl; don't cry!

There! little girl; don't cry!
They have broken your slate, I know;
And the glad, wild ways
Of your school-girl days
Are things of the long ago;
But life and love will soon come by——
There! little girl; don't cry!

There! little girl, don't cry!
They have broken your heart, I know;
And the rainbow gleams
Of your youthful dreams
Are things of the long ago;
But Heaven holds all for which you
sigh.——
There! little girl; don't cry!

James Whitcomb Riley.

We may perhaps fittingly offer as the final quotation (in this chapter) words by *Henry Van Dyke.* Having spoken of the ferry waiting to bear us hence when at last our names appear on the list of passengers, he concludes:-

"For what port? Methinks I know; for One who is worthy of all trust, my Pilot, hath spoken a name to me and told me not to be afraid.

But where it lies, that haven of salvaged ships and of forgiven failures, and when or on what course it will be approached, I know not, friend, any more than you. The guide posts of the sea are the stars. And all its mighty waters lie in the hollow of an Almighty Hand."

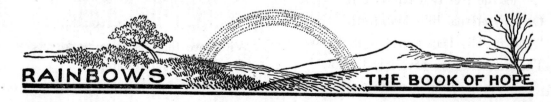

Humor

Imagination was given to man to compensate him for what he is not, and a sense of humor was provided to console him for what he is.

Humor is a tonic breeze from off the coasts of God. In this world
"Where smiles have only a fitful play
And hearts are breaking every day,"
we must laugh or we shall die.

Surely in Heaven humor shorn of satire will hold immortal place. Whatever else that City of your dreams may be, it must be a home of smiling faces.

The "Smilers" of this section are largely selected from the personal experiences of the editor.

No guarantee is given for the authenticity of the following.

It is related that a Mr. Du Bose was escorting home a young lady from a party one evening.

The girl had that peculiarity of speech known as lisping. Presently they came to a stile over which Mr. Du Bose gallantly helped the young lady, saying that his fee for such service would be a hug or a kiss.

And the reply? "O Mither Du Both!"

Dr. Samuel Upham, for many years professor at Drew Theological Seminary, possessed a fund and faculty of humor as sparkling and spontaneous as that of Lincoln or Bill Nye or Mark Twain. It may therefore be imagined how he appreciated the following incident.

He once came to speak at the Schuylkill Haven Church, in which I began my ministry in Methodism. It was quite an event to have so well known a man, and one of the leading members of the church was chosen to be chairman for the occasion. He was a Pennsylvania Dutchman, who handled the English language with some difficulty. For days before the meeting, one could see his lips moving as he was walking along the street, for he was memorizing the introduction: "Friends, this is Dr. Upham of the Drew Theological Seminary." When the moment arrived, however, and he looked over the crowded church, recollection faltered and the best he could do was, "Friends, this is Dr. Drew of the Upper Zoological Cemetery." It was three minutes before the convulsed Dr. Upham could utter a word.

❧

Blessed be mirthfulness. It is one of the renovators of the world. Men will let you abuse them if only you will make them laugh.

Beecher.

❧

Then there was the man who was unchivalrous enough to say, "She was so tired she could hardly keep her mouth open".

The two following incidents illustrate the familiar point that there are always two ways of doing anything.

A missionary was explaining Christianity to a native king. Very naturally he judged that the point most necessary to emphasize was that to become a Christian you must forgive your enemies.

The king said he had no enemies for he had had them all shot the day before.

Put that over against this:-

During the Civil War, President Lincoln was saying some kind words about the Confederates. A woman angrily asked how he could speak kindly words of his enemies when it was his duty to destroy them.

"Why, Madam," was the immortal answer, "do I not destroy my enemies when I make them my friends?"

❧

Some good stories have been told based on the fondness of the colored race for using long words without fitting very accurately, words and meanings.

Here is an authentic instance:-

A lady of Salisbury, Maryland, asked her colored cook who was about to make a cake one morning "Do you prefer granulated or pulverized sugar?"

The astonishing answer came "It's puffectly obnoxious to me ma'am whether it's graduated or paralyzed."

❧

There was a lady who used to bow low whenever the devil was mentioned.

On being asked to explain she said that civility costs nothing and—you never know.

"Getting" His Audience

An evangelist who was conducting nightly services announced that on the following evening he would speak on the subject of "Liars." He advised his hearers to read in advance the seventeenth chapter of Mark.

The next night he arose and said: "I am going to preach on 'Liars' and I would like to know how many read the chapter I suggested." A hundred hands were upraised.

"Now," he said, "you are the very persons I want to talk to—there isn't any seventeenth chapter of Mark."

※

The little boy unconsciously voiced a popular philosophy of life when he said to his sister, "If one of us would get out of this swing there would be more room for me."

※

Generosity

Then there is the story by Sydney Smith of the man who was so moved by a Charity sermon that he stole a sovereign from the man sitting by him in the pew and put it on the plate.

※

A man is like a horse. If he is down, you have to get his head up before he can rise. Until he gets his head up, his struggles are futile.

Once get the head up, you can stand aside, for unless his back is broken, he will get to his feet alone. Heads up!

Joseph B. Dunn.

Cheerfulness or joyfulness is the atmosphere under which all things thrive.

Richter.

Bashful

For quite some years in the old country a man had been calling on a farmer's daughter, but no progress seemed to be made.

He was of the most backward and bashful type and though he called on her nearly every evening, the monotonous programme never varied.

He sat on one chair and she on another opposite, and they talked of the weather, the crops and the cattle and then presently shook hands and he went home.

One day, however, he came to tell her that a railroad excursion was to be run the coming Friday to Bristol. Would she like to go with him?

The day came, they boarded the train and for a long while everything went as usual.

But presently the unlighted English train plunged into the deep darkness of the Severn tunnel.

He edged nearer, he took her hand and then in a wild burst of unbelievable courage, for the first time in his life he kissed her.

At that instant the train swept out into the light. In his embarrassment he began hurriedly to talk of the famous tunnel—the many years it took to construct——how many men worked on it——how much it cost . . . Then, his knowledge exhausted, he stopped.

"Yes John," she said softly, "and it's worth every cent of it!"

Spell It, Please

An Englishman, from London's East End, was having difficulty over the wire.

"Yes," he was shouting, "this is Mr. 'Arrison. . . . What, you can't 'ear? This is Mr. 'Arrison——haitch, hay, two hars, a hi, a hess, a ho, and a hen——'Arrison!"

❧

Two persons each of whom owned a canary were discussing the merits of their respective birds. The argument ranged the realm of pedigree and plumage and reached the subject of song.

"Talk about singing," said one of them, "my bird warbled 'Home Sweet Home' so pathetically that tears stood in its eyes."

"That isn't anything," the other broke in, "a few days ago my bird whistled 'The Village Blacksmith' so naturally that sparks flew out of his eyes and burned his cage up."

❧

No Desertion

Rastus after being reprimanded by the judge for deserting his wife, made answer thus:-

"Jedge, ef yo' knowed dat woman like ah does yo' wouldn't call me no deserter. Ah's a refugee."

❧

We have a friend who thinks he is persecuted for being good whenever he is laughed at for being foolish.

Here is one for the validity of which the editor vouches.

A year or so ago a high officer of the Civil War was being buried in Arlington Cemetery.

Of course the ceremony was accompanied by full military honors.

At the right time the order to fire was given and a volley from the muskets rang over the grave. The shock of the firing caused the aged widow of the deceased to faint completely and fall to the ground.

The hush that immediately followed was broken by the high piping voice of a little grandson 'Holy Gee they've shot grandma.'

❧

I had an elderly happy married couple in an early pastorate, and one day the husband told me the story of the ultimate strategy of his wooing. Time after time he had asked his girl to marry him, and as often she evaded a direct answer.

Finally, he found himself so worried about it that one afternoon, in the midst of work, he laid down his carpenter's tools, hitched his horse to the buggy, and drove to her home. He was in overalls and she in house dress. He said, "Lizzie, I want you to come with me just as I am and just as you are to the preacher to get married. It is now or never." She was in the buggy in fifty seconds without change of a stitch.

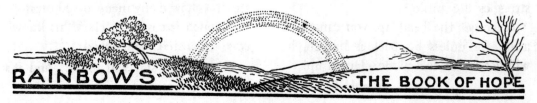

RAINBOWS   THE BOOK OF HOPE

Immortality

There is no thing I would not give,
There is no hour I dare not live,
There is no hell I'll not explore
To find a hidden heavenly door!
Irene Rutherford McLeod

A Stroll With Anne

Last week Anne and I went for a long walk in the deep woods that lie back of us. Hand in hand we walked. The spell of autumn was upon us.

It was a perfect day. We spoke of the dying year, the falling leaves, the natural process of the changing seasons, the Author of life and of death.

"Anne," I said on a note of great seriousness, "If you knew that you were going to die——that your life were over ——would you be frightened?" I waited breathlessly for her answer.

She pondered for a moment, then turned a trustful face to me. "No," she said. "I would not be afraid. I think people make entirely too much of death."

Her answer startled me a bit. It was so mature——such a grownup expression from such childish lips as though she had an insight that had gone beyond me.

Yesterday Anne came home from school, her eyes full of brooding mystery. "Mother," she said, "the little girl who lives just over the hill and goes my way to school died today. She was just as big as I, and she was the only little girl her mother had."

When supper was over we went to that house of grief. In another room the mother sobbed and wept and would not be comforted. I knew not what to say to her.

There in the little pink casket lay the child, just as big as Anne, the fair hair curled above her brow and the faint mysterious smile of death just touching the childish lips——what could I say to that mother——I, who had lost no child? The words of a kind old minister came to my mind: "There is no word of comfort as sweet as the warm clasp of a hand. If you find one in trouble sit by and give him your hand to hold in a firm, strong clasp. It will mean more than words."

The simple, direct prayer the mother uttered when she softly, with her own hands, covered the dead face of that loved child will ever remain in my memory because it is the prayer of my own heart every time a loved one passes from my life. Her words were these: "Dear God, take good care of her for me and please let her know me when I come."

"Please let her know me when I come!" The anguish and the longing in those words, and the pain of an exquisite hope! How we long to be recognized by those we have known and loved on earth. The human ties are so dear——the tendrils of life have bound us so close together.

Once during an illness, in some strange dream, a garden opened up to my vision —a garden of blossoming flowers, amid the stirring of gentle breezes. A beloved sister who had just died stood in the garden. She wore a flowering robe and a garland of flowers encircled her neck and fell below her waist. The breeze gently blew her robe and her hair. She smiled at me. Children played about her and beckoned to me. "Come," called the cherubs. The beauty of the place thrilled me, I forget all the earthly things I had to do. "I will come," I cried, Then Robin was speaking to me. "I believe you are a little delirious, Jenny," he said, and the vision was gone. I still remember the beauty of the garden of my dream and I believe that through the goodness of the Keeper of the Garden of Life our sainted ones will greet us in the loved personalities that we knew on earth.

Jenny Wrenn.

Beyond the Horizon

When men go down to the sea in ships,
'Tis not to the sea they go;
Some isle or pole the mariners' goal,
And thither they sail through calm and
    gale,
When down to the sea they go.

When souls go down to the sea by ship,
And the dark ship's name is Death,
Why mourn and wail at the vanishing
    sail?
Though outward bound, God's world is
    round,
And only a ship is Death.

When I go down to the sea by ship,
And Death unfurls her sail,
Weep not for me, for there will be
A living host on another coast
To beckon and cry, "All hail!"

Robert Freeman.

Rainbows

"I trace the rainbow through the rain
  And feel the promise is not vain
  That morn shall tearless be!"

George Matheson.

84

Over The Top

One of the most interesting soldiers in the British army during the last war was Donald Hankey, a lieutenant in the Royal Warwickshire Regiment. He was an Oxford man, a lover of the poor, and of Christ. It was he who gave us the unforgettable sentence, "True religion is betting your life that there is a God." Budd tells us in his simple story of Hankey's life that as he left England for his last campaign he wrote to a friend: "I feel singularly at ease. There is only one tragedy in life, and that is the loss of God's love; and of that I feel too confident to be afraid. There is no other tragedy."

On the twelfth of October, 1916, orders came to go "over the top." At two o'clock, just before the zero hour, Hankey asked the men in his section of the trench if he might pray with them. After the prayer he spoke these heartening words: "Remember men, if wounded, 'Blighty'; if killed, the resurrection." When he was last seen alive he was rallying his men, who had wavered under heavy machine-gun and rifle fire. He carried the waverers along with him, and was found that night close to the trench the winning of which cost him his life. For him it was the resurrection! In the same confidence we can know that death will for us yield only life, richer, more adventurous, eternal— through the power of the risen Christ.

❦

The glory is not in walking bravely to your Gethsemane or Calvary, but in walking to it happily.

Life

Life! we've been long together
Through pleasant and through cloudy
    weather,
'Tis hard to part when friends are dear—
Perhaps t'will cost a sigh, a tear;
Then steal away, give little warning,
Choose thine own time;
Say not Good-Night—but in some bright-
    er clime
Bid me Good-Morning.
Anna Letitia Barbauld.

❦

Palms and Willows

We speak sometimes of a man's "palmy days," and when we do so we invariably think of the days behind him. But really if we live wisely and faithfully the palmy days are before us. The great and glorious things are to come. The moon sets behind us; our face is to the sunrise. We have some slight knowledge of the palm now. God grants us this lest the spirit of man should fail before Him, and the souls that He has made; but in the main, this is the zone of the willow —the land of the palm is on the other side of the river. They are all palms there. No place for the willow. No more failure and defeat; all are conquerors with palms in their hands. No more exile; we have returned from Babylon to Zion. No more sickness and sorrow; the Lord God hath wiped away tears from all faces. No more death; buried in weakness, we are raised in power, and, like our Lord, we are alive forevermore. Palms everywhere, palms always, evergreens of everlasting spring!
W. L. Watkinson.

Lincoln Triumphant

Lincoln is not dead. He lives
In all that pities and forgives.
He has arisen, and sheds a fire
That makes America aspire.

Even now, as when in life he led,
He leads us onward from the dead:
Yes, over the whole wide world he bends
To make the world a world of friends.

Edwin Markham.

❧

Our friends are not lost. They have
marched out in the mist of the morning
and with trembling fingers have touched
a gate that swings only inward into the
light.

Frederick Spense.

❧

'Tis Dark

'Tis dark!
Nor is this cause for grief.
Look up and see the stars that shine,
And know these gems of night
Would not be yours to see—nor mine,
If still, 'twas light.
'Tis dark!
God made it so, dear heart.
He knows you could not do your best,
And always plod away,
He sends the darksome hours for rest
From toil of day.
'Tis dark!
Oh, yes, but light shall break!
Perchance not on these mortal eyes
Shall dawn the light of sun,
But glow shall come in heav'nly skies
When life is done.

Grant Colfax Tullar.

*Written by Mrs. Calvin Coolidge
after the loss of their son.*

You, my son,
Have shown me God.
Your kiss upon my cheek
Has made me feel the gentle touch
Of Him who leads us on.
The memory of your smile, when young
Reveals His face,
As mellowing years come on apace.
And when you went before,
You left the gates of Heaven ajar
That I might glimpse,
Approaching from afar,
The glories of His grace.
Hold, son, my hand,
Guide me along the path,
That, coming,
I may stumble not
Nor roam,
Nor fail to walk the way
Which leads us—Home.

❧

I am not satisfied now and here, but I
never suspected that such tethered words
as "now" and "here" were sufficient vo-
cabulary with which to express even me.
Now and here are not much. Now and
here would make a pessimist out of me
if my whole measure of life were circum-
vented by such cloistered words. Now is
a hard time. Here is a hard place. But I
am no permanent citizen of this now and
here. I look away. I am a pilgrim. I feel
the time-beat of my journey already in
my restless feet. I am an eternal pilgrim.
With such tireless facts in my biography
the short breath of now is gone, and the
tiny pilgrimage of here is surpassed.

M. S. Rice.

We may leave our dead in the love of God. There are a thousand questions a lonely heart will ask—there is but one answer—they are with God. For life as it now is, in the individual or the race, is but an unfinished symphony, a design sketched but not completed, a prophecy pathetically unfulfilled. Can death defeat God? I will not believe it. The dead, small and great, are with Him. He will finish His work.

Gaius Glenn Atkins.

Roofs

The road is wide and the stars are out and
    the breath of the night is sweet,
And this is the time when wanderlust
    should seize upon my feet.
But I'm glad to turn from the open road
    and the starlight on my face,
And leave the splendor of out-of-doors for
    a human dwelling place.

I never have seen a vagabond who really
    liked to roam
All up and down the streets of the world
    and not to have a home;
The tramp who slept in your barn last
    night and left at the break of day
Will wander only until he finds another
    place to stay.

A gipsy-man will sleep in his cart with can-
    vas overhead;
Or else he'll go into his tent when it is
    time for bed.
He'll sit on the grass and take his ease
    so long as the sun is high.
But when it is dark he wants a roof to
    keep away the sky.

If you call a gipsy a vagabond, I think you
    do him wrong.
For he never goes a-traveling but he takes
    his home along.
And the only reason a road is good, as
    every wanderer knows,
Is just because of the homes, the homes,
    the homes to which he goes.

They say that life is a highway and its
    mile-stones are the years,
And now and then there's a toll-gate
    where you buy your way with tears.
It's a rough road and a steep road, and it
    stretches broad and far,
But at last it leads to a golden Town
    where golden Houses are.

Joyce Kilmer.

No one will ever really know
Where I come from nor where I go.

This is not I, this body's mold
The hair that you touch, nor the hands
    you hold.
A voice to hear and a face to see
These are the outward sign of me.

Come close, come close, come near, come
    near
I am keeping a vigil here.

Here in a little house of clay
Something is now that will go away.
Something leaping and something light
To go like flame on a windy night.

To go like flame in a windy sky
O this is I, this is I.

Mabel Simpson.

87

The Vanishing Road

We are all treading the vanishing road of a song in the air, the vanishing road of the spring flowers and the winter snows, the vanishing roads of the winds and the streams, the vanishing road of beloved faces.

But in the great company of vanishing things there is a reassuring comradeship. We feel that we are units in a vast ever-moving army, the vanguard of which is in Eternity.

The road still stretches ahead of us. For a little while yet, we shall experience the zest of marching feet. The swift-running seasons like couriers bound for the front, shall still find us on the road, and shower on us in passing, their blossoms and their snows.

For a while the murmur of the running stream of time shall be our fellow-wayfarer—till, at last, up there against the sky-line, we too turn and wave our hands and know for ourselves where the road wends as it goes to meet the stars.

And others will stand as we today and watch us reach the top of the ridge and **disappear, and** wonder how it seemed to us to turn that radiant corner and vanish **with the rest** along the vanishing road.

Richard Le Gallienne.

❧

Life has given me of its best—
Laughter and weeping, labor and rest,
Little of gold, but lots of fun,
Shall I then sigh that all is done?
No, not I; while the new road lies
All untrodden, before my eyes.

Norah Holland.

"Because thou has been faithful over few things I will make thee ruler over many things." That was the joy and that was the reward, not singing praises in a heaven of idleness, but carrying on in unbroken service all the capacity that earth had shaped.

Nothing that we have fought for will be lost. Nothing we have striven for ignored. Every battle we have fought in secret will make the life beyond a grander thing. Every task that we have quietly done, when there were none to see and none to praise, will give us a heaven that is a sweeter place, and a service nearer the feet of the eternal.

Brethren, I know not how it be with you; but I know certainly how it is with me. No other thought of the beyond appeals to me. No other thought inspires me as does that. And of this I am sure, if I am sure of anything, that that is what Christ meant by life eternal.

G. H. Morrison.

Immortality

There are vague intimations of immortality that may be authentic, there are instincts that may be true, there are hopes that may prove valid, and there are dreams perhaps too beautiful to be unreal.

But the nearest thing to proof is the feeling that will not down that there are some from whom we cannot be finally parted.

. . . . I know
That somehow I shall follow when you go
To that still land beyond the evening star,
Where everlasting hills and valleys are
And silence may not hurt us any more,
And terror shall depart, and grief, and war.

His Soul Has Wings

"I knew that someday he would fly.
I saw the triumph in his eye
When, on his very first birthday
He poised, arms lifted, searched the way
From couch to chair—
Then back from there.
He did not seem to walk—he flew
Those baby steps as if he knew
He could not wait the usual way.
He must begin that very day
To climb up high.
He had to fly!

"When he was four, he had a swing
Made like a plane; a wooden thing
With places where his feet and hands
Could pump and guide to distant lands.
His eyes met mine.
'Twas in their shine
I glimpsed his rapture, saw his thrill;
Sensed his future, dauntless will.
His childish universe was bound
By clouds and air; the earth-caught
    ground
Was not his place

He must have space!
"He's flying now. He has his wings.
And tho' they're clever, man-made things,
He has another pair, bomb-proof—
His soul's been growing them since youth.
(I've watched them grow
For years, you know.)
Not feathered like the cherubim,
But oh, so much a part of him!
Not life nor death can stop his flight.
His soul has wings into the night.
Through dark—to dawn—
He shall fly on!"
                    Bessie Carrol Hicks.

Though my soul may sit in darkness,
it will rise in perfect light, I have loved
the stars too fondly to be fearful of the
night.   *Sarah Williams.*

❧

Our dear dead have travelled beyond
the sound of our voices, the boundaries
of our sight, the touch of our lips and
hands. They have not, will not, cannot
go beyond the call and reach of love.

They are not gone who pass
Beyond the clasp of hand
Out from the strong embrace.
They are but come so close
We need not grope with hands,
Nor look to see, nor try
To catch the sound of feet.
They have put off their shoes
Softly to walk by day
Within our thoughts, to tread
At night our dream-led paths of sleep.

They are not lost who find
The sunset gate; the goal
Of all their faithful years.
Not lost are they who reach
The summit of their climb,
The peak above the clouds
And storms. They are not lost
Who find the light of sun
And stars and God.
                    Hugh Robert Orr.

❧

I had ambition, by which sin
    The angels fell;
I climbed and step by step, O Lord,
    Ascended into Hell.
                    William Henry Davis.

The Meeting

After so long an absence
  At last we meet again:
Does the meeting give us pleasure,
  Or does it give us pain?

The tree of life has been shaken,
  And but few of us linger now,
Like the Prophet's two or three berries
  In the top of the uppermost bough.

We cordially greet each other
  In the old, familiar tone;
And we think, though we do not say it,
  How old and gray he is grown!

We speak of a Merry Christmas
  And many a Happy New Year;
But each in his heart is thinking
  Of those that are not here.

We speak of friends and their fortunes,
  And of what they did and said,
Till the dead alone seem living,
  And the living alone seem dead.
            Henry Wadsworth Longfellow.

❧

St. Agnes' Eve

Deep on the convent-roof the snows
  Are sparkling to the moon:
My breath to heaven like vapor goes:
  May my soul follow soon!
The shadows of the convent-towers
  Slant down the snowy sward,
Still creeping with the creeping hours
  That lead me to my Lord:
Make Thou my spirit pure and clear
  As are the frosty skies,
On this first snowdrop of the year
  That in my bosom lies.

As these white robes are soil'd and dark,
  To yonder shining ground;
As this pale taper's earthly spark,
  To yonder argent round;
So show my soul before the Lamb,
  My spirit before Thee;
So in mine earthly house I am,
  To that I hope to be.
Break up the heavens, O Lord! and far,
  Thro' all yon starlight keen,
Draw me, thy bride, a glittering star,
  In raiment white and clean.

He lifts me to the golden doors;
  The flashes come and go;
All heaven bursts her starry floors,
  And strews her lights below,
And deepens on and up! the gates
  Roll back, and far within
For me the Heavenly Bridegroom waits,
  To make me pure of sin.
The Sabbaths of Eternity.
  One sabbath deep and wide—
A light upon the shining sea—
  The Bridegroom with his bride!
            Alfred Tennyson.

❧

Baron von Hugel said, "I will wait for the breath of God. Perhaps He will call me today, tonight. I would live to finish my book, but if not, I shall live it out in the beyond."

            M. H. Lichliter.

❧

The Christian doctrine of immortality is not, properly speaking, an expectation of another life after death; it is a conviction of the deathlessness of life.

            Rockwell H. Potter.

Immortal

How living are the dead!
Enshrined, but not apart,
How safe within the heart
We hold them still—our dead
Whatever else be fled!

Florence Earle Coates.

❧❧

Felix Adler, in a brilliant passage, makes the point that though life is a tragedy if only because of death which all must face, yet at life's close and over life's ruins a glory shines.

"The hero strives after some high ideal carries in his breast some noble purpose. He fails but the fault is not in him, it is in his surroundings.

The time is not ripe for him, the people with whom he must deal are below his standard; and he fails but in failing he sets forth in high relief the grandeur to which he has aspired the greatness at which he aimed.

There are high powers at work, a great and noble strain is trying to express itself in things and in men, but conditions are not fit or adequate, and the greatness is constantly breaking down, the nobility failing, not because it ought to fail, but because conditions are insufficient, because the finite can not embody the infinite. Yet the failures only serve to set off the infiniteness in the tendency.

Work helps; sympathy helps; in all the ordinary circumstances of life, not to be sorry for one's self but to be sorry for others is the best help. But the thought that life is a grand tragedy, that over the ruins a glory shines, is to me the supreme help."

We shall build on!
We shall build on!
On through the cynic's scorning,
On through the coward's warning,
On through the cheat's suborning,
We shall build on!

Firm on the Rock of Ages,
City of saints and sages,
Laugh while the tempest rages,
We shall build on!

Christ, though my hands be bleeding,
Fierce though my flesh be pleading,
Still let me see Thee leading,
Let me build on!

Till through death's cruel dealing,
Brain wrecked and reason reeling,
I hear Love's Trumpets pealing,
And I pass on!

G. A. Studdert-Kennedy.

❧❧

To live in hearts we leave behind is not to die.   *Campbell.*

❧❧

I have too much invested in the other world to be careless about its existence.

There are too many little grassy mounds where I have buried a part of my heart to permit me to be unconcerned about the resurrection.

I turned away from those places once, comforting myself with the thought that it was only for a little while, that these few years of separation are short as compared with the eternities of reunion.

I have too much at stake to give up that faith. I shall cling to it to the last.

Clarence Edwin Flynn.

Song of Day and Night

Hear ye the dawn, with the music of
  morning?
Thundering over the hilltops—it comes!
Shivering silvers gleam bright in its
  baldric,
Crimson and scarlet beat alternate drums!
The mountains shout gladly and echo
  their greeting,
The valleys are bright with a yellowing
  ray;
Hear ye the dawn, with the music of
  morning?
It's morning, it's morning! Hear ye, 'tis
  day!

Walter F. Bowman.

❧

And still the soul a far-off glory sees,
  Strange music hears.
A something, not of earth, still haunts the
  breeze,
  The sun and spheres.

All things that be, all thought, all love,
  all joy
  Spell-bind the man
As once the growing boy,
  And point afar—

Point to some land of hope and crystal
  truth,
  Of life and light,
Where souls renewed in an immortal
  youth
  Shall know the infinite.

Eternal

The pure, the beautiful, the bright,
  That stirred our hearts in youth;
The impulse to a wordless prayer,
  The dream of love and truth,
The longings after something lost,
  The spirit's yearning cry,
The striving after better hopes—
  These things can never die.

Sarah Doudney.

❧

"There is not room enough for friendship to unfold itself in full bloom in such
a nook of life as this. Therefore I am, and
must, and will be, yours for ever William
Cowper."

QUOTED BY *Arthur Gossip.*

❧

The Christian therefore is always
bound to have a great advantage over the
modern pagan. Simply because he knows
where he is going whereas the modern
pagan knows nothing.

The pagan must always be the pessimist, for he must always feel that this life
is too short to give a man a chance, and
the Christian will always be the optimist,
for he knows that this life is long enough
to give a man a chance for eternity.

That is why the Christian can be joy-
ful. That is why the pagan is sad and de-
pressed. He has only one world, one life,
one earth and that will be taken away.

Fulton J. Sheen.

RAINBOWS   THE BOOK OF HOPE

KINDNESS

*Kindness is the golden chain
By which society is bound together.*

Goethe

How Beautiful

How beautiful a day can be
When kindness touches it!
As suddenly illumined as
A room that's newly lit.

In busy hours how grateful is
A little word of cheer,
So close it brings its tenderness
Its sympathy so near.

The weariness of heavy tasks
Is lost upon a day
When kind words bring their comfort,
    joy,
To any busy day.   George Elliston.

It takes so little to make us sad,
Just a slighting word, a careless sneer,
Just a scornful curl to another's lips
And our footsteps lag, though the goal
    seem near.
And we lose the courage and hope we had
So little it takes to make us sad.

It takes so little to make us glad,
Just a cheery clasp of a friendly hand.
Just a word from one who can understand
And we finish the task we long had
    planned.
And we lose the doubt and the fear we
    had
So little it takes to make us glad.

    Ida Goldsmith Morris.

My old friend, the poet and editor, Charles Hanson Towne, was strolling along Fifth Avenue recently when he observed a startlingly handsome woman standing at the curb. "She was middle aged," he told me, "and a stranger. But after a moment's hesitation, I said to her, 'I beg your pardon. I am an elderly man with only the best intentions, so perhaps you won't mind my telling you that you are one of the most beautiful women I have ever seen.'"

"She must have thought you were crazy," I laughed.

"I thought so myself," Charley answered, "but afterward I decided that I had never done anything more sensible. The woman flushed with pleasure. She had reached the time of life when all of us need a little bolstering. We begin doubting that anyone finds us interesting or attractive, and it's a good thing to have our faith lifted. What's really crazy is that most of us are so niggardly with these vitamins for the soul."

Channing Pollock.

Our Part

Not once in life perhaps, 'tis ours
   To reach a long-sought goal;
But we may pause beside the road
   To help another soul.
Not once to us may come the call
   To play the hero's part;
But we, perchance, may find some word
   Of courage to some heart.

❧❧

One gift well given is as good as a thousand; a thousand gifts ill given are hardly better than none.

Dean Stanley.

It's Better

It's better sometime to be blind
   To the faults of some poor fellow being,
Than to view them with visions unkind,
   When there's good we ought to be
     seeing.

It's better sometime to be dumb,
   Than to speak just to be criticizing,
Though it seems to be given to some
   To recall traits both mean and despising.

It's better sometime to be deaf,
   Than to hear only lying and pander,
For there's nothing so low as theft
   Of a good name destroyed by slander.
Unknown.

❧❧

Are you willing to stoop down and consider the needs and the desires of little children; to remember the weakness and loneliness of people who are growing old; to stop asking how much your friends love you, and ask yourself whether you love them enough; to bear in mind the things what those who live in the same house with you really want, without waiting for them to tell you; to trim your lamp so that it will give more light and less smoke, and to carry it in front so that your shadow will fall behind you; to make a grave for your ugly thoughts, and a garden for your kindly feelings, with the gate open?

Henry Van Dyke.

Kindness

Kindness has converted more sinners than zeal, eloquence or learning.

F. W. Faber.

94

Drop a pebble in the water,
  And its ripples reach out far;
And the sunbeams dancing on them
  May reflect them to a star.

Give a smile to some one passing
  Thereby make his morning glad;
It will greet you in the evening
  When your own heart may be sad.

Do a deed of simple kindness;
  Though its end you may not see,
It may reach, like widening ripples,
  Down a long eternity.

                    James W. Foley.

❦

The Perfect Guest

She answered by return of post
The invitation of her host.
She caught the train she said she would
And changed at junctions as she should
She brought a light and smallish box
And keys belonging to the locks.
She left no little things behind
Excepting loving thoughts and kind.

                    Rose H. Heaton.

❦

"Human history has always been just
an unfinished waiting. What for? The
proud say for empire, the greedy say for
wealth, the enslaved say for freedom, and
three-fourths of history has been a picture
of war-weary people waiting for peace.
Paul says the world is waiting for men
and women who live and act like God's
children; waiting for kindness, for glowing and creative good will, for human
brotherhood, for fields undesolated, cities
undimmed by human tears."

Your Garden

Kind hearts are the gardens,
Kind words are the roots,
Kind thoughts are the flowers,
Kind deeds are the fruits.
Take care of your garden
And keep out the weeds;
Fill it with sunshine,
Kind words, and good deeds.

                    Unknown.

❦

Politeness is to do and say
The kindest thing in the kindest way.

❦

If you were busy being kind,
Before you knew it you would find
You'd soon forget to think 'twas true
That someone was unkind to you.

If you were busy being glad,
And cheering people who are sad,
Although your heart might ache a bit,
You'd soon forget to notice it.

If you were busy being good,
And doing just the best you could,
You'd not have time to blame some man
Who's doing just the best he can.

If you were busy being true
To what you know you ought to do,
You'd be so busy you'd forget
The blunders of the folks you've met.

If you were busy being right,
You'd find yourself too busy, quite,
To criticize your neighbor long
Because he's busy being wrong.

                    Rebecca Foresman.

Funeral Oration

A lady died in our town:
Carve the wood, and grave the stone;
Stretch her straight and lay her down;
And here be words for her renown:

Though her body lieth low,
High and high her soul doth go.

She never said, "I told you so."

Her body lieth with the night,
Her soul disporteth in the light.

She never cried, "It served you right!"

Her body taketh earth's decay,
But her soul walketh heaven's way.

She never whispered, "Well they say
                              ."

Marie De L. Welch.

❧

I cannot omit an incident I have long cherished. A young minister had come to the close of his pastorate in a small town. He had three young children, and the salary had been pitifully insufficient. And of that meager stipend the church owed him one hundred dollars. As that church had allowed previous pastors to leave without being paid in full, his chances were slim.

He was in debt to the local physician to the extent of fifty dollars. The young man told the doctor the circumstances, adding that he was going to a larger church and a better salary, and asking if it would be all right if he sent a small sum each month till his debt was liquidated.

The doctor firmly replied that he must pay his bill in full before leaving, or legal action would be brought. So the minister laid the matter before the officials of the church. They felt it would never do to have anything like that happen, especially, I suppose, as it involved their delinquency. So they paid him all that was owning. He hurried to the doctor with the fifty dollars. "Put it in your pocket, man," said the physician. "I wouldn't touch a cent of it. But I knew your only chance of getting your money from that church was by my threatening to sue you."

That sort of a church is rare, but that kind of a physician is not rare.

G. W. H.

❧

Sunshine

The thing that really matters is the "something else" you do,

Besides the getting dollars all your whole life through.

It's just the touch you're giving to others day by day,

The sunshine that you scatter all along your way.

The kindly deed you're doing when some one needs a friend;

The service that you render, the helping hand you lend.

It brings a joy that's lasting, which money cannot do—

To know that someone's gladness is just because of you.

Sidney J. Burgone.

Little Things

Oh, it's just the little homely things,
the unobstrusive, friendly things, the
"won't-you-let-me-help you" things, that
make our pathway light.

And it's just the jolly, joking things,
the "never-mind-the-trouble" things, the
"laugh-with-me-it's funny" things that
make the world seem bright.

For all the countless famous things, the
wondrous record-breaking things, those
never-can-be-equaled things, we often
read about, aren't like the little human
things, the every-day-encountered things,
the "just-because-I like-you" things, that
drive the worries out.

So here's to all the little things, the
done-and-then-forgotten things, those
"Oh-it's-simply-nothing" things, that
make life worth the fight.

Grace Haines.

❦

A metropolitan newspaper offered an
award for the best answer to the question:
"What would you do if you had only one
more year to live?" Mary Davis Reed of
Hagerstown, Maryland, was given the
award. Her answer was the following:

If I had but one year to live;
One year to help; one year to give;
One year to love; one year to bless;
One year of better things to stress;
One year to sing; one year to smile;
To brighten earth a little while;
One year to sing my Maker's praise;
One year to fill with work my days;

One year to strive for a reward
When I should stand before my Lord,
I think that I would spend each day,
In just the very self-same way

That I do now. For from afar
The call may come to cross the bar
At any time, and I must be
Prepared to meet eternity.

So if I have a year to live,
Or just one day in which to give
A pleasant smile, a helping hand,
A mind that tries to understand
A fellow-creature when in need,
'Tis one with me. I take no heed,
But try to live each blessed day
In just a plain, unselfish way.

❦

My Daily Wish

My daily wish is that we may
See good in those who pass our way:
Find in each a worthy trait
That we would gladly cultivate;
See in each one passing by
The better things that beautify—
A softly spoken word of cheer,
A kindly face, a smile sincere.

I pray each day that we may view
The things that warm one's heart anew:
The kindly deeds that can't be bought—
That only from the good are wrought,
A burden lightened here and there,
A brother lifted from despair,
The aged ones freed from distress;
The lame, the sick, brought happiness.

Grant that before each sun has set
We'll witness deeds we can't forget:
A soothing hand to one in pain,
A sacrifice for love—not gain;
A word to ease the troubled mind
Of one whose fate has seemed unkind.
So, friend, my wish is that we may
See good in all who pass our way.

Phil Perkins.

A New Start

I will start anew this morning with a
    higher, fairer creed;
I will cease to stand complaining of my
    ruthless neighbor's greed;
I will cease to sit repining while my duty's
    call is clear;
I will waste no moment whining, and my
    heart shall know no fear.

I will look sometimes about me for the
    things that merit praise;
I will search for hidden beauties that
    elude the grumbler's gaze.
I will try to find contentment in the paths
    that I must tread;
I will cease to have resentment when an-
    other moves ahead.

I will not be swayed by envy when my
    rival's strength is shown;
I will not deny his merit, but I'll strive
    to prove my own;
I will try to see the beauty spread before
    me, rain or shine;
I will cease to preach your duty, and be
    more concerned with mine.

                  Unknown.

The Gift

Most of us have been taken so frequently by hard luck stories which have
no foundation in fact, that we are apt to
grow discouraged and lose faith in the
essential integrity of human nature.

At any rate, so far as those who seek
financial help are concerned.

However there are still some who feel
they would rather be deceived a hundred
times than turn down a deserving case
once.

And the following authentic incident
would serve to encourage them: Some
years ago a rather well known pastor was
called upon by a stranger who frankly ad-
mitted he had just served a jail term and
with further frankness stated that his own
mother had lost faith in him and, indeed,
he had lost faith in himself.

He asked money from the minister for
train fare to take him away from all who
knew him.

The pastor handed him a five dollar
bill saying: "You may perhaps take this
money from me and use it to get drunk
and I shall not blame you, but I am a
minister of Christ who would like me to
tell you that He believes in you still."

Presently the man rising to go said, "I
thank you, Sir, for the money. I shall not
try to thank you for the other gift."
"What gift is that?" "The gift of hope,"
he said with breaking voice.

Have you had a kindness shown?
Pass it on!
Let it travel down the years
Let it wipe another's tears
Till in Heaven the deed appears—
Pass it on!

                  Henry Burton.

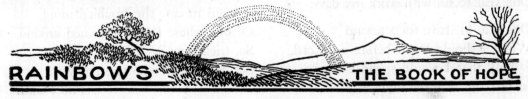

RAINBOWS   THE BOOK OF HOPE

LIFE

For when the one great scorer comes
To write against your name
He marks—not that you won or lost,
But how you played the game.

Grantland Rice

The ultimate test is our ability to finish. In one of our Federal prisons today is a man who for fifty years with unblemished reputation lived a life of probity and honor in his own community, Then, as a government servant, he went to France during the war and mishandled funds. Only that will be remembered about him. The half century of fine living is blotted out. He was not able to finish.

Even when the problem presents itself in less dramatic terms, it still is there. All biography is a commentary on the necessity of seeing life through.

Harry Emerson Fosdick.

Recompense

The gifts that to our breasts we fold
  Are brightened by our losses;
The sweetest joys a heart can hold
  Grow up between its crosses.
And on life's pathway many a mile
  Is made more glad and cheery,
Because, for just a little while,
  The way seemed dark and dreary.

Nixon Waterman.

"There is no way to the highest except through the high."

Victor Hugo.

On a Spiteful Letter

Here, it is here—the close of the year,
  And with it a spiteful letter.
My fame in song has done him much
    wrong,
  For himself has done much better.

O foolish bard, is your lot so hard,
  If men neglect your pages?
I think not much of yours or of mine:
  I hear the roll of the ages.

This fallen leaf, isn't fame as brief?
  My rhymes may have been the stronger.
Yet hate me not, but abide your lot;
  I last but a moment longer.

O faded leaf, isn't fame as brief?
  What room is here for a hater?
Yet the yellow leaf hates the greener leaf,
  For it hangs one moment later.

Greater than I—isn't that your cry?
  And I shall live to see it.
Well, if it be so, so it is, you know;
  And if it be so—so be it!

O summer leaf, isn't life as brief?
  But this is the time of hollies.
And my heart, my heart is an evergreen:
  I hate the spites and the follies.

                    Alfred Tennyson.

❧

Out of the dusk a shadow,
  Then, a spark;
Out of the cloud a silence,
  Then, a lark;
Out of the heart a rapture,
  Then, a pain;
Out of the dead, cold ashes,
  Life again.

                    John B. Tabb.

"I, too, will turn my face to the wind,
and cast my handful of seed on high."

                    Gaelic Saying.

❧

We are not merely a chip off the old block as we used to say. We are chips off many blocks and the art of life is to personalize every chip.

We are to keep open minds and open hearts to garner eagerly every blessing that life has to offer and then presently send out those blessings, touched and tinged by the soul.

Here is a young man fresh from the schools with his medal, his diploma, his degree.

Can he take the medal and personalize it—transmute it into coin to enrich some other life?

Can he take his diploma and make the dry, dusty parchment live?

Can he weave his personality through and through it—make it tell the great story of the cross?

He has been graduated. Can he graduate—the hopeless into hope, the weak into strength, the foolish into wisdom. The bad into goodness?

What is his personal force? This is the supreme factor.

The woman of Samaria came to the well a mere drawer of water. She went out from the presence of Christ an exhaustless fountain springing up into everlasting life.

It is on the flood tide of personalities that history is lifted through the ages.

                    Gardner S. Eldridge.

The Things That Count

Not what we have, but what we use;
Not what we see, but what we choose—
These are the things that mar or bless
The sum of human happiness.

The things near by, not things afar;
Not what we seem, but what we are—
These are things that make or break,
That give the heart its joy or ache.

Not what seems fair, but what is true;
Not what we dream, but good we do—
These are the things that shine like gems,
Like stars, in Fortune's diadems.

Not as we take, but as we give;
Not as we pray, but as we live—
These are the things that make for peace,
Both now and after Time shall cease.

Clarence Urmy.

By Contract

A classmate of mine in the Nottingham Congregational Seminary, England, was called following graduation to the pastorate of a rural church. The one-hundredth anniversary nearing, the minister and officials ventured to ask Dr. Joseph Parker, then in his heyday at the London City Temple, to deliver the sermon. Yes, he would come on the Sunday evening and preach for twenty-five pounds—about one hundred and twenty-five dollars. The suggested honorarium was agreed to, and Dr. Parker arrived safely by train and was met at the nearest station.

Soon after arrival, a terrific storm swept the entire community. It was impossible for the people to hitch up and drive in, so that only a handful living near by could attend. The offering naturally, was correspondingly small.

After the service, the few men present anxiously considered the problem of the preacher's payment. Finally, they asked the pastor if, under the circumstances, he would suggest more lenient terms to Dr. Parker. Rather timidly, the young man broached the matter to the famous preacher, who asked, "What did you men agree to pay me?" "Why, twenty-five pounds, sir." "Then," was the answer, "twenty-five pounds is the amount I want." After the ultimatum reached the officials, one of them said he would give his check and they could repay as the money came in.

On the following Wednesday my friend received a note from Dr. Parker which said, "I enclose a donation of fifty pounds for your church." And then, in large letters, "Keep your men to their word." **G. W. H.**

No wind serves him who has no destined port. *Montaigne.*

To be Alive in such an age—
   To live to it,
   To give to it,
Rise, soul, from thy despairing knees,
What if thy lips have drunk the lees?
Fling forth thy sorrow to the wind,
And link thy hope with human kind;
The passion of a larger claim
Will put thy puny grief to shame.
Breathe the world thought, do the world
   deed,
Think hugely of thy brother's need.

Angela Morgan.

Sin

Sin has binding power and the grip of its habits is tremendous. Sin has blinding power and eyes once perverted by it do not easily regain the grace of seeing straight. Sin has multiplying power, and each sin spawns other sins like fish in the sea until it seems impossible to be rid of them. Sin has hardening power; it callouses the soul until the spiritual touch which once would have roused us leaves us dead. To get out of sin once you are in it is a terrific process. When therefore mastered by evil habit, walking at large, a moral freeman, one wonders if he half appreciates the splendor of his opportunity.

So many sermons have been preached on the glory of the prodigal's return; so few upon the glory of his chance before he went away at all.

Harry Emerson Fosdick.

❧

No other poem, perhaps, presents so vividly the Christ who intrudes Himself upon our pleasures and lures us from the world to Himself as Laurence Housman's remarkable one titled "Sweet Tempter Christ."

Oh, tempt me not! I love too well this
    snare
Of silken cords.
Nay Love, the flesh is fair
So tempt me not! This earth affords
Too much delight;
Withdraw Thee from my sight,
Lest my weak soul break free
And throw me back on Thee!

Thy face is all too marred. Nay Love,
    not I—
I did not that! Doubtless Thou hadst to
    die;
Others did faint for Thee; but I faint not.
Only a little while hath sorrow got
The better of me now; for Thou art
    grieved,
Thinking I need Thee. O Christ lest I
    fall
Weeping between Thy feet, and give
    Thee all;
Oh, Christ, lest love condemn me unre-
    prieved
Into Thy bondage, be it not believed
That Thou hast need of me!
Dost Thou not know
I never turned aside to mock Thy woe?
I had respect to Thy great love for men;
Why wilt Thou, then,
Question of each new lust—
"Are these not ashes and is this not
    dust?"

O, Love Thou hast not eyes
To see how sweet it is.
Each for himself be wise
Mock not my bliss!

Ere Thou cam'st troubling, was I not
    content?
Because I pity Thee, and would be glad
To go mine own way, and not leave Thee
    sad,
Is all my comfort spent?

Go Thine own ways, nor dream Thou
    needest me!
Yet if again Thou on the bitter tree
Wert hanging now, with none to suc-
    cour Thee
Or run to quench thy sudden cry of thirst,
Would not I be first?—

Oh, Love, the prize!—
To lift one cloud of suffering from Thine
    eyes!
Oh, Christ, let be!
Stretch not Thine ever-pleading hands
    thus wide,
Nor with imperious gesture touch Thy
    side!
Past is Thy Calvary. By the life that died
Oh, tempt not me!
Nay if Thou weepest, then must I weep
    too,
Sweet Tempter Christ! Yet what can I
    undo,
I, the undone, the undone
To comfort Thee, God's Son?
Oh, draw me near, and, for some lowest
    use
That I may be
Lost and undone in Thee
Me from mine own Self loose!

※

If we do our best, if we do not magnify
trifling troubles; if we look resolutely, I
will not say at the bright side of things,
but at things as they really are; if we avail
ourselves of the manifold blessings which
surround us, we can not but feel that life
is indeed a glorious inheritance.

Lord Avebury.

※

It's good to have money and the things
that money can buy, but it's good too, to
check up once in a while and make sure
you haven't lost the things that money
can't buy.

George Horace Lorimer.

Sin never does work out as expected.
It never keeps faith. It promises so much,
and performs so little. It shows us the
sparkling cup, but conceals the lurking
serpent till we have drained the draught.
It leads us into flowery meads; and when
we have taken our fill of the forbidden
sweets, and fain would fling ourselves
upon the fragrant sward and steep our
senses in forgetfulness, it not only opens
up a Vesuvius beneath our feet, but
thrusts us into the sulphurous throat to
suffer the tortures of the damned, and
then, like the wily Vivien of the Idylls,
makes all the forest echo with the hate-
ful name of "Fool!"

Henry Howard.

※

My Rule of Life

To let no thought go unexpressed
    That might give some one pleasure;
To say no word I might regret
    In later hours of leisure;

To do the kindly, little deeds
    That make life worth the living;
To overlook another's faults
    Nor fail to be forgiving;

To strive to leave each task well done
    And make a joy of duty;
Unceasingly to give God thanks
    For life and love and beauty;

To honor God and, loving Him,
    Love, as myself, my neighbor.
This, the high test of perfect love—
    The goal toward which to labor.

Ella Colter Johnston.

My Creed

To live as gently as I can;
To be, no matter where, a man;
To take what comes of good or ill
And cling to faith and honor still;
To do my best, and let that stand
The record of my brain and hand;
And then should failure come to me,
Still work and hope for victory.

To have no secret place wherein
I stoop unseen to shame or sin;
To be the same when I'm alone
As when my every deed is known;
To live undaunted, unafraid
Of any step that I have made;
To be without pretense or sham
Exactly what men think I am.

To leave some simple mark behind
To keep my having lived in mind;
If enmity to aught I show,
To be an honest, generous foe,
To play my little part, nor whine
That greater honors are not mine.
This, I believe, is all I need
For my philosophy and creed.

Edgar A. Guest.

❧❧

Two Ways

Young man, life is before you. Two voices are calling you—one coming out of the swamps of selfishness, where success means death; and the other from the hilltops of justice and progress, where even failure brings glory.

Two lights are seen on your horizon—one the fast fading marsh light of force, and the other the slowly rising sun of human brotherhood.

Two ways lie open for you—one leading to an ever lower and lower plain, where are heard the cries of despair and the curses of the poor, where manhood shrivels and possession rots down the possessor; and the other leading to the highlands of the morning, where are heard the glad shouts of humanity and where honest effort is rewarded with immortality.

John P. Altgeld.

❧❧

My Resolve

To cherish dreams of loveliness, of silver
    and of blue,
To find the trail of fairyland, where all
    the paths are new;
To make a garden blossom with old for-
    gotten flowers;
To find a gleam of beauty as I watch the
    passing hours;

To find a better pattern for the warp that
    I must weave;
To know that life is always good, though
    sometimes I must grieve;
To read a shining splendor in the tales
    the far stars tell;
To laugh through weeping raindrops and
    to feel that all is well;

To look for golden rainbows, to love the
    simple things,
The dream-blue of the summer sky, the
    song the robin sings;
To dare to send my ships to sea, but find
    a gallant crew;
To keep their crimson sails afloat . . . this
    I resolve to do.

Helen Welshimer.

"The Salutation of the Dawn"

Listen to the exhortation of the dawn!
Look to this day! For it is life,
The very life of life!
In its brief course lie all the verities
And realities of existence:
The bliss of growth,
The glory of action,
The splendor of beauty.
For yesterday is but a dream,
And tomorrow is only a vision;
But today, well lived,
Makes every yesterday a dream of happiness,
And every tomorrow a vision of hope.
Look well therefore to this day!
Such is the salutation of the dawn.

From the Sanscrit.

Life

Life is a day,
With morning, noon, and coming night;
The morning with its hopes life high,
The noontide with its heavens bright,
And evening when we die.
Life is a road
That winds up hills with rocks and steep,
And down the cliffs where torrents flow
Through valleys where smooth rivers creep.
Life is the road we go.

Life is a fight
Against the enemy without;
The demon that resides within
With faithful heart we put to rout
And conquer every sin.

Ray Burgess.

Every moment of this strange and lovely life, from dawn to dusk, is a miracle. Somewhere, always, a rose is opening its petals to the dawn. Somewhere, always, a flower is fading in the dusk. The incense that rises with the sun, and the scents that die in the dark, are all gathered, sooner or later, into the solitary fragrance that is God. Faintly, elusively, that fragrance lingers over all of us.

Beverley Nichols.

When Is a Man Educated?

Joseph Fort Newton, famed clergyman of Philadelphia, gives answer: "When he can look out upon the universe, now lucid and lovely, now dark and terrible, with a sense of his own littleness in the great scheme of things, and yet have faith and courage. When he knows how to make friends and keep them, and above all, when he can keep friends with himself. When he loves flowers, can hunt the birds without a gun and feel the stir of a forgotten joy in the laugh of a child. When star-crowned trees, and the glint of sunlight on flowing waters, subdue him like the memory of one much loved and long dead.

"A man is educated when he can be happy alone, and high-minded amid the meaner drudgeries of life. When he can look into a wayside puddle and see something besides mud, and into the face of the most forlorn mortal and see something beyond sin. When he knows how to live, how to love, how to hope, how to pray—glad to live and not afraid to die, in his hand a sword for evil, in his heart a bit of song."

When Nature Wants a Man

When nature wants to drill a man
And thrill a man,
And skill a man,
When nature wants to mould a man
To play the noblest part;
When she yearns with all her heart
To create so great and bold a man
That all the world shall praise—
Watch her method, watch her ways!
How she ruthlessly perfects
Whom she royally elects;
How she hammers him and hurts him
And with mighty blows converts him
Into trial shapes of clay which only Na-
    ture understands—
While his tortured heart is crying and he
    lifts beseeching hands!—
How she bends, but never breaks,
When his good she undertakes . . .
How she uses whom she chooses
And with every purpose fuses him,
By every art induces him
To try his splendor out—
Nature knows what she's about . . .

When nature wants to name a man
And fame a man
And tame a man;
When nature wants to shame a man
To do his heavenly best . . .
When she tries the highest test
That her reckoning may bring—
When she wants a god or king!
How she reins him and restrains him
So his body scarce contains him
While she fires him
And inspires him!
Keeps him yearning, ever burning for a
    tantalizing goal—
Lures and lacerates his soul.

Sets a challenge for his spirit,
Draws it higher when he's near it—
Makes a jungle, that he clear it;
Makes a desert, that he fear it
And subdue it if he can—
So doth Nature make a man.
Then to test his spirit's wrath
Hurls a mountain in his path—
Puts a bitter choice before him
And relentlessly stands o'er him.
"Climb, or perish!" so she says . . .
Watch her purpose, watch her ways! . . .

Then doth Nature show her plan
When the world has found—a man!

                Angela Morgan.

Lord, make me an instrument of Thy
    peace!
Where there is hatred . . . let me sow
    love.
Where there is injury . . . pardon.
Where there is doubt . . . faith.
Where there is despair . . . hope.
Where there is darkness . . . light.
Where there is sadness . . . joy.

O Divine Master, grant that I may not so
    much seek
To be consoled . . . as to console,
To be understood . . . as to understand,
To be loved . . . as to love;

            For
It is in giving . . . that we receive;
It is in pardoning . . . that we are par-
    doned;
It is in dying . . . that we are born to
    eternal life.

              St. Francis of Assisi.

The dear Lord's best interpreters
Are humble human souls;
The Gospel of a life like hers
Is more than books or scrolls.

From scheme and creed the light goes
out,
The saintly fact survives;
The blessed Master none can doubt
Revealed in holy lives.

John Greenleaf Whittier.

Success

He has achieved success who has lived well, laughed often, and loved much; who has gained the respect of intelligent men and the love of little children; who has filled his niche and accomplished his task; who has left the world better than he found it, whether by an improved poppy, a perfect poem or a rescued soul; who has always looked for the best in others and given the best he had; whose life was an inspiration; whose memory a benediction.

J. L. Stanley.

"One ship drives east and one drives west
By the very same wind that blows,
'Tis the set of the sails and not the gales
That tells which way she goes.

Like the waves of the sea are the gales
which blow
As we journey together through life,
'Tis the set of the soul determines the
goal
And not the storm and strife."

Ella Wheeler Wilcox.

Great nations have tried to make a civilization by selfishness; by greed; by the self-sufficiency that leads to violence, or the self-sufficiency that shuts itself in callous isolation, but these things which the vanity of small minds account to be wisdom have only been the marsh-lights that led, and will lead, into the swamps.

What is needed now is the red light that can come only from religion. Mankind will be saved not by Mars nor by Mammon but by Jesus Christ. Redemption will come, not from the mailed fist nor from the clutch of avaricious fingers, but only from the touch of the wounded hands.

W. Russell Bowie.

Edwin Markham, commenting on The Rubaiyat of Omar Khayyam says after speaking of its masterly construction, the freshness of its phrases, its ringing epigrams:—"But I cannot speak so warmly of its . . . glorification of pleasure as the chief end of our existence . . . WE ARE NOT HERE TO ENJOY OURSELVES BUT TO BEHAVE OURSELVES. There is something higher than pleasure—higher even than happiness—and that higher thing is Blessedness.

This is the high satisfaction that descends upon a man when, through self-surrender or other heroic action, he has put self aside and performed some difficult duty that confronted him.

As Thomas Lake Harris says there is a sorrow that is richer than the world's joy, and a burden that is easier than its rest."

Home

A home is where
A heart can stay
When hand and foot
Are far away,
A home is where
A child can play.

A home is where
A fire bright
Reminds the traveller
In the night
That somewhere there are
Rest and light.

A home is where
Old age, content
Remembers what
A life has meant
A home is riches
Never spent.

Anon.

Parties must tell that all may know
Towards what goals they wish to go,
But man, at life's adventurous start,
Must write his platform on his heart;
Must tell himself in silent hours
To what he'll dedicate his powers;
To what high aim his strength he gives,
And for what purposes he lives.

Edgar A. Guest.

Life's Mirror

There are loyal hearts, there are spirits
    brave,
  There are souls that are pure and true;
Then give to the world the best you have,
  And the best will come back to you.

Give love, and love to your life will flow,
  A strength in your utmost need;
Have faith, and a score of hearts will show
  Their faith in your word and deed.

Give truth, and your gift will be paid in
    kind,
  And honor will honor meet;
And a smile that is sweet will surely find
  A smile that is just as sweet.
For life is a mirror of king and slave;

  'Tis just what we are to do;
Then give to the world the best you have,
  And the best will come back to you.

Madeline S. Bridges.

There is no short-cut, no patent tram-road, to wisdom. After the centuries of invention, the soul's path lies through the thorny wilderness which must still be trodden in solitude, with bleeding feet, with sobs for help, as it was trodden by those of olden time.

George Eliot.

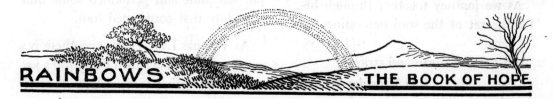

RAINBOWS   THE BOOK OF HOPE

He had lived out his life
But not outlived his love.
William Croswell Doane

Mary

That day the small Christ hurt his hand
Upon a rusty nail,
Joseph could never understand
Why Mary grew so pale.

And why she sat with drooping head
And eyes gone dark with pain,
Long after he was comforted,
And sent to play again—

And why long after day was done
And all the household slept,
She knelt beside her little Son
And clasped her hands and wept.

Sara Henderson Hay.

Love ever gives—
Forgives—outlives—
And ever stands
With open hands.
And while it lives,
It gives.
For this is Love's prerogative—
To give—and give—and give—

John Oxenham.

She's one o' them things as looks the brightest on a rainy day, and loves you the best when you're most i' need on't.

George Eliot.

A Day

What does it take to make a day?
A lot of love along the way;
It takes a morning and a noon
A father's voice, a mother's croon;
It takes some task to challenge all
The powers that a man may call
His own; the powers of mind and limb;
A whispered word of love; a hymn
Of hope—a comrade's cheer,
A baby's laughter and a tear;
It takes a dream, a hope, a cry
Of need from some soul passing by;
A sense of brotherhood and love;
A purpose sent from God above;
It takes a sunset in the sky,
The stars of night, the winds that sigh;
It takes a breath of scented air
A mother's kiss, a baby's prayer.
This then it takes to make a day:
A lot of love along the way.

William L. Stidger.

❦

It is not while beauty and youth are thine
　　own,
　　And thy cheeks unprofaned by a tear,
That the fervor and faith of a soul can
　　be known,
　　To which time will but make thee more
　　dear;
No, the heart that has truly loved never
　　forgets,
　　But as truly loves on to the close,
As the sunflower turns on her god, when
　　he sets,
　　The same look which she turned when
　　he rose.

Thomas Moore.

It is a continuation of that sublime transaction in which Christ says: "you give Me your humanity and I will give you My divinity. You give Me your time and I will give you My eternity. You give Me your bonds and I will give you My freedom. You give Me your nothingness, I will give you My all."

And the consoling thought throughout the whole process is that it does not require much time to make us saints; it requires only much love.

Fulton J. Sheen.

❦

Poets

Among men the poets alone have really understood Jesus: and in the category of the poets must be included the saints, whose religion has always been interpreted to them through the imagination. *The poets have understood; the theologians rarely or never.* Thus it happens that men, being the general and accepted interpreters of Christ, have all but wholly misinterpreted Him. The lyric passion of that life, and the lyric love which it excites, has been to them a disregarded music. They have rarely achieved more than to tell us what Christ taught; they have wholly failed to make us feel what Christ was. But Mary Magdalene knew this, and it was what she said and felt in the Garden that has put Christ upon the throne of the world. Was not her vision after all the true one? Is not a St. Catherine a better guide to Jesus than a Dominic? When all the strident theologies fall silent, will not the world's whole worship still utter itself in the lyric cry:

　　Jesus, Lover of my soul,
　　　　Let me to Thy bosom fly.

W. J. Dawson.

Marriage Morning

Light so low upon earth,
   You send a flash of the sun.
Here is the golden close of love,
   All my wooing is done.
O the woods and the meadows,
   Woods where we hid from the wet,
Stiles where we stay'd to be kind,
   Meadows in which we met!
Light, so low in the vale,
   You flash and lighten afar:
For this is the golden morning of love,
   And you are his morning star.
Flash, I am coming, I come,
   By meadow and stile and wood:
O lighten into my eyes and my heart,
   Into my heart and my blood!
Heart, are you great enough
   For a love that never tires?
O heart, are you great enough for love?
   I have heard of thorns and briers.
Over the thorns and briers,
   Over the meadows and stiles,
Over the world to the end of it
   Flash for a million miles.

Alfred Tennyson.

❧❦

I have long since given up hope of solving the problem of pain. Yet in all pain is the promise of the possibility of cure. Pain comes always from nature's effort to heal.

In many a case you know the end is near and hope is gone when the patient says, "I feel no pain today." No pain because nature has given up the struggle to cure.

While there's pain there's hope.

G. W. H.

We have been followed by the "Love that will not let us go." Step for step it has pursued us with insistent feet, never for one moment missing our track until, overtaking us, it has bent over us with infinitely more than even a mother's tenderness—

To heal the bleeding wounds, and soothe the pain,
And bring back life and hope and strength again.

God never waits for us to take the first step. He is always first in the field, with healing for our wounds and pardon for our sin. This is the Father's privilege—to forgive. It is Love's grand prerogative—to seek and even suffer that it may save.

Henry Howard.

❧❦

"The world waits
For help. Beloved, let us love so well,
Our work shall still be better for our love,
And still our love be sweeter for our work,
And both commended, for the sake of each,
By all true workers and true lovers born."

Elizabeth Barrett Browning.

The Prison and the Angel

Self is the only prison that can ever bind
   the soul;
Love is the only angel who can bid the
   gates unroll:
And when he comes to call thee, arise and
   follow fast;
His way may lie through darkness, but it
   leads to light at last.

Henry Van Dyke.

The night has a thousand eyes
And the day but one;
Yet the light of the bright world dies
With the dying sun.

The mind has a thousand eyes
And the heart but one;
Yet the light of the whole life dies
When love is done.

Francis William Bourdillon.

❧

Some pray to marry the man they love;
My prayer; will somewhat vary;
I humbly pray to heaven above
That I love the man I marry.

Rose Pastor Stokes.

❧

The Blue Flower

Long years I sought it—but in vain
I searched for it where clouds let silver
    rain
Fall on the hidden vales and shadowed
    rills,
I searched the endless caverns of the hills,
And where the sapphire, flashing cascades
    fell
Down mountainside; and in cool, leafy
    dell,
I searched where beauty over all held sway
Beside an emerald sea, at break of day.
In crumbling temples of past deities
Where lingered still a lotus laden breeze.
I hoped to find it by a sylvan pool
Where, o'er its crystal depths, the forest
    cool
Stretched forth its verdant arms in silent
    prayer.
. . . The flower born of dreams . . . it
grew not there.

I turned from nature to humanity,
In dark despair. "How shall I ever find
So frail a flower, blooming near mankind,
With all its suffering, bitterness and pain,

Wild strife and ceaseless turmoil," I
    would fain
Give up the quest, but hope burned
    bright within.
I searched the hearts of men beneath
    their sin,
And hoped, in glorious youth to find my
    dream.
But, when at last I saw the glory gleam,
'Twas not in man nor youth I found the
    flower—
But in a dim cathedral, twilight hour,
When kneeling, lifting up my heart in
    prayer,
I found it, blooming in celestial sod,
Formed by man's love for the Eternal
    God!

Victoria B. Demarest.

❧

I doubt that any man and woman can
live together indefinitely and amicably on
terms of friendship. It is possible only
on terms of affection.

❧

Love and Light

There are many kinds of love, as many
    kinds of light,
And every kind of love makes a glory in
    the night.
There is love that stirs the heart, and love
    that gives it rest,
But the love that leads life upward is the
    noblest and the best.

Henry Van Dyke.

112

Window With a Star

This small, still house a woman keeps.
See all the lights.
A woman's house, where no man sleeps
These nights.

A house without a man in charge
Stays neat from pride;
But the frying pans are all too large
And the bed too wide.

The attic floors are known to creak
In a winter gale.
The clock ticks seven nights a week
Till the next mail.

The woman in this house can wait,
Keep the fire going,
With one fresh-laundered towel hung
    straight
And a star showing.

Betty Bridgman.

❧❧

There is a very gripping story told of
a Roman Catholic nun who saw one of
the girls she helped to teach and train
slipping into sin.

All endeavours and pleas proved of no
avail. Then the nun began flogging herself heavily each day saying she would
keep it up till death came or until the
girl had given up her sin. Inevitably in
the presence of such love, the girl had
to forsake the sin.

There is a deep sense in which this story
reveals the heart of Calvary. For Sin still
crucifies Him afresh. While you sin He
still must suffer.

The Turk

In the course of the Armenian atro-
cities a young woman and her brother
were pursued down the street by a Turkish solder, cornered in an angle of the
wall, and the brother was slain before his
sister's eyes. She dodged down an alley,
leaped a wall, and escaped. Later, being
a nurse, she was forced by the Turkish
authorities to work in the military hospital. Into her ward was brought, one day,
the same Turkish soldier who had slain
her brother. He was very ill. A slight inat-
tention would insure his death. The
young woman, now safe in America, con-
fesses to the bitter struggle that took place
in her mind. The old Adam cried, "Ven-
geance;" the new Christ cried, "Love."
Equally to the man's good and to her
own, the better side of her conquered,
and she nursed him as carefully as any
other patient in the ward. The recogni-
tion had been mutual and one day, unable longer to restrain his curiosity, the
Turk asked his nurse why she had not let
him die, and when she replied, "I am a
follower of Him who said 'Love your
enemies and do them good,'" he was silent for a long time. At last he spoke: "I
never knew there was such a religion. If
that is your religion tell me more about
it, for I want it."

Harry Emerson Fosdick.

❧❧

Here's a sigh to those who love me,
And a smile to those who hate;
And whatever sky's above me,
Here's a heart for every fate.

Lord Byron.

113

Abou Ben Adhem

Abou Ben Adhem (May his tribe in-
  crease!)
Awoke one night from a deep dream of
  peace,
And saw within the moonlight of his
  room,
Making it rich and like a lily in bloom,
An angel writing in a book of gold.
Exceeding peace had made Ben Adhem
  bold,
And to the presence in the room he said:
"What writest thou?"—The vision raised
  its head,
And, with a look made of all sweet accord,
Answered, "The names of those who love
  the Lord."

"And is mine one?" said Abou. "Nay, not
  so,"
Replied the angel.—Abou spoke more low,
But cheerily still; and said, "I pray thee,
  then,
Write me as one that loves his fellow-
  men."

The angel wrote, and vanished. The next
  night
It came again, with a great awakening
  light,
And showed the names whom love of
  God had blessed,—
And lo! Ben Adhem's name led all the
  rest!

                              Leigh Hunt.

※

"We should always conduct ourselves
toward an enemy as if he were one day to
be our friend."

Gilbert Chesterton says in one of his
essays, "If Americans can be divorced for
incompatibility of temper I cannot con-
ceive why they are not all divorced.

. . . For a man and woman as such are
incompatible. The whole aim of marriage
is to fight through and survive that instant when incompatibility becomes un-
questionable."

Now, Mr. Chesterton, in spite of his interesting habit of brilliant exaggeration, is
generally sufficiently right in any state-
ment to make it worth thinking through,
after you have caught your breath again.

There is an inherent difference between
men and women, not merely in instincts
and aptitudes, but in basic standards.
Thus an incompatibility of viewpoint is
often inevitable.

Probably, however, a better and surer
method than to "fight through" the crisis
is to love through. For, differ as men and
women may, there is no situation so dark
but that out of it love can light the path.

※

Fare thee well! and if forever,
Still forever, fare thee well.

                              Lord Byron.

※

Love of God and love of country are
the two noblest passions in the human
heart. A man without a country is an
exile in the world, and a man without
God is an orphan in eternity.

                              Henry Van Dyke.

114

Mary Magdalene

At The Door of Simon the Pharisee.

Mary has left a festal procession, and is ascending by a sudden impulse the steps of the house where she sees Christ. Her lover has followed her and is trying to turn her back.

"Oh loose me! See'est thou not my Bride-
        groom's face
    That draws me to Him? For His feet
        my kiss,
My hair, my tears He craves today:—and
        oh!
    What words can tell what other day
        and place
Shall see me clasp those blood-stained
        feet of His?
    He needs me, calls me, loves me: let
        me go!"

Dante Gabriel Rossetti.

❧

True sympathy should always bring men to a Love which never lets them go and which never lets them off; a Love which faces the fact that life is full of thorns, but which can show us how to do what Jesus did—wear those thorns as a crown.

Leslie D. Weatherhead.

❧

And I, for one, do not believe that the love of Christ has become, in our day, a spent force. On the contrary, I am confidently expecting that it will become a more powerful force than it has yet been. When the full meaning of His gospel is made known to the world; when the good news of social salvation is proclaimed with as much passion and contagious enthusiasm as was the good news of individual salvation; when men begin to sing about the new Chicago as men once sang about the new Jerusalem; when they begin to pray for the coming of the city of God with as much earnestness as they once prayed for the salvation of their own souls, then I believe, the love of Christ will become in human hearts a passion so powerful that the gates of hell will not be able to prevail against it.

Ernest Fremont Tittle.

❧

But a Fraction

Whatever is best in the treasured lives of heroic men and the serene unwritten lives of innocent women; whatever is best in the loyalty of human hearts and the unwearying sweetness of a mother's love; whatever is noble in the sacrificing care of a father and the devotion of an unselfish friend, is but the dim reflection, the far off echo, the faint shadow of that which in God is perfect.

We are but enjoying a two-billionth part of the light and heat which streams from the sun, and it may equally be that we are receiving even a smaller fraction of the Love and Life and Truth which is in God . . . If a human heart has the power to thrill us and exalt then what must be the great Heart of Hearts! If the Spark is so bright, oh, what must be the Flame.

Fulton J. Sheen.

115

My April Lady

When down the stairs at morning
  The sunbeams round her float,
Sweet rivulets of laughter
  Are rippling in her throat;
The gladness of her greeting
  Is gold without alloy;
And in the morning sunlight
  I think her name is Joy.

When in the evening twilight
  The quiet book-room lies,
We read the sad old ballads,
  While from her hidden eyes
The tears are falling, falling,
  That give her heart relief;
And in the evening twilight,
  I think her name is Grief.

My little April lady,
  Of sunshine and of showers
She weaves the old spring magic,
  And breaks my heart in flowers!
But when her moods are ended,
  She nestles like a dove;
Then, by the pain and rapture,
  I know her name is Love.

Henry Van Dyke.

❧

Men live for something; for what did Jesus live? And the answer that leaps upon us like a great light from every page of the Gospels is plain; He lived for love. If He did not care for praise or honour; if He regarded even the preservation of His teachings with a divine carelessness, it was because He had a nobler end in view, the love of men. He could not live without love, and His supreme aim was to make Himself loved. And yet it was less a conscious aim, than the natural working out of His own character. Fishermen by the sea saw Him but once; instantly they left their boats and followed Him. A man sitting at the receipt of custom, a hard man we should suppose, little likely to be swayed by sudden emotions, also sees Him once, and finds his occupation gone. A beautiful courtesan, beholding Him pass by, breaks from her lovers, and follows Him into an alien house, where she bathes His feet with tears and wipes them with the hairs of her head. Mature women without a word spoken or a plea made, minister to Him of their substance, and count their lives His.

When He sleeps wearied out upon a rude fishing-boat there is a pillow for His head, placed there by some unknown adorer. The men He makes apostles, all but one, count His smile over-payment for the loss of home, of wife, of children. Countless throngs of ordinary men and women forget their hunger, and are content to camp in desert places only to listen to the music of His voice. Wild and outlawed men, criminals and lepers and madmen, become as little children at His word, and all the wrongs and bruises inflicted on them by a cruel world are healed beneath His kindly glance. *Does it matter greatly what He taught? This is how He lived.* He lived in such a way that men saw that love was the only thing worth living for, that life had meaning only as it had love. And this is the imperishable tradition of Jesus:
This is His divinity,
This His universal plea,
Here is One that loveth thee.

W. J. Dawson.

Need of Loving

Folk need a lot of loving in the morning;
  The day is all before, with cares beset—
The cares we know, and they that give
    no warning;
  For love is God's own antidote for fret.

Folk need a heap of loving at the noon-
    time—
  In the battle lull, the moment snatched
    from strife—
Halfway between the waking and the
    croontime,
  While bickering and worriment are
    rife.

Folks hunger so for loving at the night-
    time,
  When wearily they take them home to
    rest—
At slumber song and turning-out-the-
    light-time—
  Of all the times for loving, that's the
    best.

Folk want a lot of loving every minute—
  The sympathy of others and their
    smile!
Till life's end, from the moment they
    begin it,
  Folks need a lot of loving all the while.

Strickland W. Gillilan.

❧❧

Example

Suppose Jesus had not lived above con-
ventional ideals but had simply lived ac-
cording to the conventions we respect?

Suppose He had smitten His enemies
with leprosy as Elisha did; that He had
sanctioned the stoning of the adultress

taken in sin or that He had branded
Simon Peter for his perfidy?

Then He would no longer attract us,
still less win our hearts . . . Dare we question that a world governed wholly by the
ideals of Jesus would be a far happier
world than this we know? Love, as the
one necessary law of life, clearly stands
justified in Jesus since it has produced the
most adorable character in history. If we
admit this, it is foolish to speak of Christ's
ideals as impracticable. What we approve
in another's life we cannot wholly repudi-
ate in our own. Let it be added also, that
a life lived by one is always a life that
others can live. We may seek to cover our
failure, and the world's failure, to repro-
duce the life of Jesus, by the plea of in-
competence, but against our plea Jesus
records His verdict, "Behold I have left
you an example."

From that verdict there is no appeal.

W. J. Dawson.

❧❧

A soul like mine—as rich as poor—
Knocks both at Hell's and Heaven's door.

It cries all night, it seeks all day
And never finds the faith to pray;

But flutters on its feeble wings
Searching about for precious things.

To have had some dreams my heart has
    had
I think might make an angel glad;

So I believe, if God there be
His love is given to fools like me.

Julia Wickham Greenwood.

117

The House of Pride

I lived with Pride; the house was hung
With tapestries of rich design.
Of many houses, this among
Them all was richest, and 'twas mine.
But in the chambers burned no fire,
Though all the furniture was gold:
I sickened of fulfilled desire,
The House of Pride was very cold.

I lived with knowledge; very high
Her house rose on a mountain's side
I watched the stars roll through the sky,
I read the scroll of Time flung wide
But in that house, austere and bare,
No children played, no laughter clear
Was heard, no voice of mirth was there,
The House was high but very drear.

I lived with Love; all she possest
Was but a tent beside a stream.
She warmed my cold hands in her breast,
She wove around my sleep a dream.
And one there was with face idvine
Who softly came when day was spent,
And turned our water into wine,
And made our life a sacrament.

William J. Dawson.

The Mark of Royalty

When one day Saint Martin of Tours
was in his cell a knock came at the door
and a kindly visitor entered, "Who are
you?" asked the Saint. "I am the Saviour." "Where then are the prints of
the nails?" And the devil vanished.

"Hath he marks to lead to him,
If he be my guide?
In His hands and feet are wound prints,
And His side."

I loved you, Evelyn, all the while!
My heart seemed full as it could hold;
There was place and to spare for the frank
    young smile,
    And the red young mouth, and the
    hair's young gold.
So, hush,—I will give you this leaf to
    keep;
    See, I shut it inside the sweet cold
    hand!
There, that is our secret: go to sleep!
    You will wake, and remember, and
    understand.

Robert Browning.

❧

A life without love in it is like a heap
of ashes upon a deserted hearth—with the
fire dead, the laughter stilled and the light
extinguished. It is like a winter landscape
with the sun hidden, the flowers frozen,
and the wind whispering through the
withered leaves.

God knows we need all the unselfish
love that can come to us . . . Do you
remember William Morris and how his
life was lived, his fortune spent, his hands
busied—in the service of others? . . . After
he was gone, his life began to grow in
radiance and power like a beacon set high
upon a dangerous shore.

In the twilight of his days he wrote
what I like to think was his creed—and
mine. "I'm going your way, so let us go
hand in hand. You help me and I'll help
you. We shall not be here very long for
soon death, the kind old nurse, will come
back and rock us all to sleep. Let us help
one another while we may."

Frank P. Tebbets.

My Job

I see it now.
O, God, forgive my pettish row!
I see your job. While ages crawl,
Your lips take laboring lines, your eyes
    a sadder light,
For man, the fire and flower and center
    of it all—
Man won't come right!
After your patient centuries,
Fresh starts, recastings, tired Geth-
    semanes
And tense Golgothas, he, your central
    theme,
Is just a jangling echo of your dreams.
Grand as the rest may be, he ruins all.
Why don't you quit?
Crumple it all and dream again! But no;
Flaw after flaw, you work it out, revise,
    refine—
Bondage, brutality and war and woe,
The sot, the fool, the tyrant and the
    mob—
Dear God, how you must love your job!
Help me, as I love mine.

               Badger Clark.

Sheep and Shepherd

The shepherd's work was done
The sheep were safe
Within the fold—
Ninety-and-nine, and one.

But he had paid the cost
Of climbing step—
Of daring flood and frost.

The sheep were safe
Within the fold;
The Shepherd? . . . He was lost.

               Egbert Sandford.

In our personal relations, moreover, disappointments frequently come to us. Friends do not measure up to what we expect of them; even our families, it may be, are less loyal or less devoted than we feel they should be. When, in any time of intimate associations of life, one accepts such a disappointment as final, then that association suffers grave damage, if not indeed complete severance. But when, with patience and sympathy, we take a long view of the years ahead in which we may still enjoy this precious contact if now we but show forbearance and maintain a forgiving spirit, then the very intensity of our own loyalty will sooner or later overcome the lack in those whom we love, and a relationship more blessed and more fruitful than ever we enjoyed in the past will succeed this temporary setback to our affections.

               Russell Henry Stafford.

The trumpet was blown and the Heavenly archangel made announcement:—"The sheep will now be separated from the goats. The sheep to stand on the right hand of the throne and the goats on the left. And those on the right shall be welcomed into the Kingdom, but those on the left shall be accursed and flung into everlasting fire.

"Is there any appeal from this sentence?" A brief pause in Heaven. Then forward One stepped with lifted hand in which nail prints were visible. "The goats," He said, "The goats are also Mine."

               G. W. H.

The Rich Young Man

It seemed so mad a way to do—
To grieve so deep; to suffer, too,
For men He never even knew!

A life so lonely, meek, and bare!
I wonder why He made a prayer
For them that mocked and nailed Him
   there!

Vast wealth is mine; why do I see
My golden hoard without avail?
Why turns no man with love to me?
Why did He triumph, and I fail?

Poor—and despised! how strange a thing
That mighty hosts, with worshipping
In endless praise His name should sing!

Oh, 'tis a grievous mystery—
That mankind never looks to me
As to that spent and broken Christ
That drooped on Calvary!

> *Laura Simmons.*

Behold Him now where He comes!
   Not the Christ of our subtle creeds,
But the Lord of our hearts, our homes,
   Of our hopes, our prayers, our needs;
The Brother of want and blame,
   The lover of women and men,—
With a love that puts to shame
   All passion of mortal ken.

> *Richard Watson Gilder.*

As through the land at eve we went,
   And pluck'd the ripen'd ears,
We fell out, my wife and I,
O we fell out I know not why,
   And kiss'd again with tears.
And blessings on the falling out
   That all the more endears,
When we fall out with those we love,
   And kiss again with tears!
For when we came where lies the child
   We lost in other years,
There above the little grave,
O there above the little grave,
   We kiss'd again with tears.

> *Alfred Tennyson.*

The Little Word

If any little word of mine
May make a life the brighter,
If any little song of mine
May make a heart the lighter,
God help me speak the little word
And take my bit of singing,
And drop it in some lonely vale
To set the echoes ringing.

If any little love of mine
May make a life the sweeter,
If any little care of mine
May make a friend's the fleeter
If any lift of mine may ease
The burden of another,
God give me love and care and strength
To help my toiling brother.

RAINBOWS   THE BOOK OF HOPE

Memories

Beauty will mold each thought that lives
with me—
I shall remember only lovely things.
Willa Hoey

The Origin of the Forget-Me-Not

When to the flowers so beautiful
The Father gave a name
Back came a little blue-eyed one
All timidly it came;
And standing at its Father's feet
And gazing in His face
It said in low and trembling tone
"Dear God, the name Thou gavest me
Alas! I have forgot!"
Kindly the Father looked Him down
And said "For-get-me-not."

Emily Bruce Roelofson.

The Secret Heart

Across the years he could recall
His father one way best of all.

In the stillest hours of night
The boy awakened to the light.

Half in dreams, he saw his sire
With his great hands full of fire.

The man had struck a match to see
If his son slept peacefully.

He held his palms each side the spark
His love had kindled in the dark.

His two hands were curved apart
In the semblance of a heart.

He wore, it seemed to his small son
A bare heart on his hidden one.

A heart that gave out such a glow
No son awake could bear to know.

It showed a look upon a face
Too tender for the day to trace.

One instant, it lit all about
And then the secret heart went out.

But it shone long enough for one
To know that hands held up the sun.

Robert P. Tristram Coffin.

Lest Thou Forget

Lest thou forget in the years between
The beautiful things thine eyes have seen:
The light of the sun and the silver sheen
Of cobwebs over a field of green.

The light of love on a destined day
When blossomed the first sweet flowers
  of May
And sunlight flooded the wistful way;

The vows we took and the prayers we said
When the urge of love to the altars led
And the mystical marriage rites were read;

The sacrament scenes of death and birth
The tragedies testing human worth—
These are the timeless things of earth!

Reverence, worship, and love and prayer,
Kneeling alone at the altar stair
Hearing the Infinite whisper there.

William L. Stidger.

After long experience of the world, I affirm before God I never knew a rogue who was not unhappy.

Junius.

Curly-Head

There was no band, no flags, no ceremonial. It wasn't even dramatic. A car honked outside and he said: "Well, I guess that's for me." He picked up his little bag, and his mother said: "You haven't forgotten your gloves?"

He kissed his mother and held out his hand to me. "Well, so long," he said. I took his hand but all I could say was "Good luck."

The door slammed and that was that—another boy gone to war.

After the door closed behind him I went upstairs. I went to what had been his room. It was in worse chaos than usual. His bureau was littered—an incredible collection of things, letters, keys, invitations to parties he would not attend.

Clothing was scattered about.

I went then to my room. On the wall was a picture of a little boy, his toothless grin framed in tawny curls—the same boy who had just taken my hand and said: "Well, so long."

Suddenly a queer thing happened. Objects came alive—whispered to me. The house was full of soft voices. They led me to the attic—to a box of toy soldiers, a broken music rack, a football helmet, a home made guitar, school books, class pictures, a stamp album, a penny bank with the lid pried off . . . telegrams, passports, a baptismal certificate, a ribbon won in a track meet, faded photographs—

one taken on the memorable first day of long pants,—a bit of golden hair.

Well, curly-head—you're a man now, bearing your bright new shield and spear. I hated to see you go out of my house and close the door behind you; but I think I would not have halted you if I could. I salute you, sir. I cannot pretend that I am not sad; but I am proud, too. So long.

Howard Vincent O'Brien.

❧

The Homeland

My land was the west land; my home was
    on the hill.
I never think of my land but it makes
    my heart to thrill;
I never smell the west wind that blows
    the golden skies,
But old desire is in my feet and dreams
    are in my eyes.

My home crowned the high land; it had
    a stately grace.
I never think of my land but I see my
    mother's face;
I never smell the west wind that blows
    the silver ships
But old delight is in my heart and mirth
    is on my lips.

My land was a high land; my home was
    near the skies,
I never think of my land but a light is
    in my eyes;
I never smell the west wind that blows
    the summer rain—
But I am at my mother's knee, a little
    lad again.

Dana Burnet.

Lovely Things

Let me remember only lovely things;
    The scattered smiles of children at their
        play,
The sapphire of the sea, a star adrift,
    The spreading glory of the dying day;
The friendliness of those who light my
    soul,
    Like crystals woven into winter snow;
The clear, blue sky that follows summer
    rain,
    Sweet warbled notes, and sunset's after-
        glow.
Thus shall I keep the storehouse of my
    mind
    Barred to the gloom that memory often
        brings;
Beauty will mold each thought that lives
    with me—
    I shall remember only lovely things.

Willa Hoey.

❧

Be a good forgetter. Life is too short to remember that which prevents one from doing his best, "Forgetting the things that are behind, I press forward," said a brave old man in the first century: The successful man forgets. He knows the past is irrevocable. He lets the dead past bury its dead. He is running a race. He cannot afford to look behind. His eye is on the winning post: The magnanimous man forgets. He is too big to let little things disturb him. He forgets quickly, and forgets easily. If any one does him wrong, he keeps sweet. It is only the small man who cherishes a low revenge: Be a good forgetter. Business dictates it, and success demands it.

The Secret Pack

My memory hath a secret pack
   Wherein I store the loveliest things;
And in my heart, not on my back,
   My dear and guarded treasure swings.
With every passing year it grows,
   And as it grows life fairer gleams;
And lesser weigh my daily woes,
   And brighter, rarer shine my dreams.

My memory hath a secret pack;
   It steads me, cheers me all the while.
Within it enters nothing black,
   But each kind word, each loving smile.
It matters not if darkness fall,
   I never let my heart be dumb
For love knows not until it call
   What faithful echoes back will come.

My memory hath a secret pack
   When I am sad I open it
And soon of solace I've no lack,
   And all my soul with joy is lit;
And over land, and over sea,
   My thought flies swifter than a dove,
For are not those who smiled on me
   Still keeping bright the lamp of love?
         Samuel Minturn Peck.

❦

On the Bank of the James River, a husband erected a tombstone in memory of his wife, one of those 100 maidens who had come to Virginia in 1619 to marry the lonely settlers. The stone bore this legend:

"She touched the soil of Virginia with her little foot and the wilderness became a home."
        Eudora Ramsey Richardson.

Salvage

Time to collect my salvage. Let me see:
Hot-water bottles, papers; what can be
Inside this box? A lot of rubber rings;
And here, my old flatirons—heavy things.

How many miles I've traveled to and fro
From stove to table, tired to death and
   slow,
Pressing wee petticoats and dresses small,
Pink ones and blue and white, with frills
   on all,

And stiffly starched. My girlies looked
   so sweet
In them. His shirts—he always did look
   neat
On Sunday when he went with us to
   church.
I'm reminiscing. That's no way to search

For salvage. Here's a stable lantern old.
Why, when I left the farm, was it not
   sold?
Strange how I keep unneeded, intimate
   things
And how they play upon long-muted
   strings

Of memory. How it all comes back to
   me:
The supper set—roast pork, there'd have
   to be,
Hot fried potatoes, catchup, homemade
   bread.
(Mine was the best he ever ate, he said.)

Beside the window I'd quite often stand
And watch him come. The lantern in his
   hand
Making strange lights and shadows on the
   snow.
Oh, that was all so many years ago!

Here's our old clock. Its brass and springs
    of steel
Are needed for the war. How strange I
    feel.
I seem to hear it yet—the night he died—
Ticking so loudly, not a sound beside.

He was so young! But they are young
    who go
To fight for us in this mad war; and so
Christ, too, was young, and dearly He
    loved life.
Dear God, for His sake end this awful
    strife.

Here's someone coming. Oh; she must
    not see.
The girls are such fuss-budgets over me.
She'll tell her mother she found grannie
    crying.
This hunting salvage has been rather
    trying.

        Evelyn E. Peacock.

Memories

They told me, Heraclitus, they told me
    you were dead;
They brought me bitter news to hear
    and bitter tears to shed.
I wept as I remembered how often you
    and I
Had tired the sun with talking and sent
    him down the sky.

And now that thou art lying, my dear old
    Carian guest,
A handful of grey ashes, long, long ago
    at rest,
Still are they pleasant voices, thy night-
    ingales awake;
For Death he taketh all away, but them
    he cannot take.

        William Cory.

Old Lace

The old, old elm has put on clouds of
    lace
Delicate as a bride's. A dawn-like grace
Covers a million dark-twigged memories,
A dryad gaiety is in her face;
And, light as lilac-spray against the skies,
New wonder is upborne by ancient stress,
I marvel at a mortal thing so wise
To weave herself enchantment for a dress,
And heal the feud of Time with Loveli-
    ness.

        Karle Wilson Baker.

❧

I had a lady in one of my churches whose disposition was more variable than weather vanes or political prophesies. Within the same half hour she could play the North Pole or the Tropics.

After I had preached my final sermon in that pastorate as we shook hands she said, "Remember me at my best." I am glad I had just enough sense and grace to say "I certainly shall, for our better selves are our true selves."

George Eliot declared that we are always underestimating or overestimating each other and that only God sees us as we are.

It is, however, a safe conclusion to arrive at, that we are apt to under-rate rather than over-rate and that people as a whole are considerably better and bigger than we rate them to be. The Lord Christ's immense faith in man could be offered as evidence and might well be accepted as sufficient proof.

        G. W. H.

A Child Goes to Church

First of all the people sing and then—
　they say
"Our Father," just as I do every day;
It makes me feel so proud, because I, too,
Know how to pray the words that Grown-
　Ups do.

Right after that, four men march down
　the aisles—
(My Uncle Joe is one; he always smiles
On week days—but on Sundays, what a
　change!
Church seems to make him look so stern
　and strange.)

They all pass silver plates, and each one
　there
Must put in money, like you pay a fare.
I carry my own purse, and when it's time
For me to pay, put in a brand-new dime.

I like this part of church, but later, when
The man in robes begins to talk, why
　then,
My thoughts, like birds, go flying any-
　where—
(But God, who lives here in this house,
　won't care

So long as I sit still). The sun shines
　through
Three stained glass windows just above
　our pew;
One of them shows a shepherd with a
　lamb
Cuddled close to his shoulder. Oh I am
So fond of him! Within that kind, strong
　arm
No little lamb could ever come to harm.
A lovely lady in a queer blue gown
From out the second window frame
　smiles down,

Holding her Baby—'twould be great if He
Should climb down from her lap and play
　with me!
The middle picture is the best of all;
A bearded Man, tall as my father's tall—
Stands underneath a great, big, spreading
　tree,
And little children gather 'round His
　knee—
They seem to talk together like dear
　friends—
His face is beautiful. When service ends,
The organ plays a lively tune, as though
It meant to tell us "hurry up and go."
So everybody crowds to reach the door.
But I turn back to look at them once
　more—
The Shepherd and the Lady and the
　Man—
And say good-bye as often as I can!
Their eyes all follow me—they cannot
　speak—
But church will be locked up a whole
　long week,
And they'll be lonely till next Sunday,
　when
They know I'll come to see them all
　again!

　　　　　　　　　　　Mazie V. Caruthers.

Sometimes

Across the fields of yesterday
He sometimes comes to me,
A little lad just back from play
The lad I used to be.

And yet he smiles so wistfully
Once he has crept within,
I wonder if he hopes to see
The man I might have been.

　　　　　　　　　　　Thomas S. Jones, Jr.

126

Christmas

O Christmas, merry Christmas!
  Is it really come again?
With its memories and greetings,
  With its joy and with its pain.
There's a minor in the carol
  And a shadow in the light.
And a spray of cypress twining
  With the holly-wreath tonight.
And the hush is never broken
  By laughter, light and low,
As we listen in the starlight
  To the "bells across the snow."

O Christmas, merry Christmas!
  'Tis not so very long
Since other voices blended
  With the carol and the song!
If we could but hear them singing
  As they are singing now,
If we could but see the radiance
  Of the crown on each dear brow,
There would be no sighs to smother,
  No hidden tear to flow,
As we listen in the starlight
  To the "bells across the snow."

O Christmas, merry Christmas!
  This never more can be
We cannot bring again the days
  Of our unshadowed glee.
But Christmas, happy Christmas,
  Sweet herald of goodwill,
With holy songs of glory
  Bring holy gladness still.
For peace and hope may brighten
  And patient love may glow,
As we listen in the starlight
  To the "bells across the snow."

Frances Ridley Havergal.

Memories of a Modern Fisherman

Certain places become dear with memory. *Henry Van Dyke* had some such place in mind when he visited one of his old haunts and saw in memory the lad who once accompanied him:

"Well, the fireplace is still standing. The butternut tree spreads its broad branches above the stream. The violets and the bishop's-caps and the wild anemones are sprinkled over the banks. The yellow-throat and the water-brush and the vireos still sing the same tunes in the thicket. And the elder of the two lads often comes back with me to that pleasant place and shares my fisherman's luck beside the Swiftwater.

"But the younger lad?

"Ah, my little Barney, you have gone to follow a new stream—clear as crystal —flowing through fields of wonderful flowers that never fade. It is a strange river to Teddy and me; strange and very far away. Some day we shall see it with you; and you will teach us the names of those blossoms that do not wither. But till then, little Barney, the other lad and I will follow the old stream that flows by the woodland fire-place—your altar. Rue grows here. Yes there is plenty of rue. But there is also rosemary, that's for remembrance! And close beside it I see a little heart's ease."

❦

A noble nature can alone attract the noble, and alone knows how to retain them.

Goethe.

127

Lou Gehrig Was My Friend

Lou Gehrig is dead. Those of us who knew him cannot express our sorrow.

He was a man, and I tell you his true stature could not be appreciated unless you knew him as a favored few of us knew him.

You will read of Lou Gehrig's epic achievements. Of his incredible record of 2130 consecutive games over a span of 14 years and 11 months; of his .361 batting average in seven World Series; of his 494 home runs, four in one game and 23 with the bases filled; of his 184 runs batted in for one season.

And I tell you mere statistics, which will be inscribed in the record books as long as baseball is played, cannot begin to tell of Lou Gehrig's infinite courage and his tremendous inspirational force as a competitor.

Joe McCarthy said everything, simply and succinctly, when he called Lou Gehrig the most valuable ball player of all time.

But today I want to remember Lou Gehrig as I will see him always. I want to remember him as a magnificent athlete, a professional playing his game more cleanly and gallantly than any amateur played any game and above all, as a man I was lucky to call a friend.

I want to listen to him gagging, yelling encouragement and thumping his glove when a pitcher was faltering . . . giving a pep talk to a teammate in a slump . . . shouting hello the first time he saw you in the locker room at St. Pete . . . and meaning it.

I want to keep before me the unforgettable picture of Lou Gehrig putting his great shoulders into a pitch when the Yankees needed a base-hit in the clutch . . . the ball etched high against the sky when he met the ball on the sweet spot of his bat . . . the fights with bad throws at first base . . . the look of intense concentration on his face when the Yankees were losing . . . And his happy smile when they won.

I want to recall his overwhelming pride in his profession and the Yankees, his first and only major league team . . . how he piped down boisterous teammates when they were attracting undue attention in hotel lobbies and dining cars . . . how he worked at his job of team captain on and off the field . . . the quick word of praise he invariably had for an opposing player.

I like to think of Lou Gehrig going to McCarthy and voluntarily taking himself out of the lineup to help the team . . . and appointing himself a one-man cheering section for his successor, Babe Dahlgren . . . how he insisted on appearing in uniform every day in 1939 when disease already was gnawing at him . . . how he refused to accept a sinecure with the Yankees because he wanted to pull his own weight . . . and how he continued to appear every day at his office in the Parole Commission long after he was unable to walk without assistance and when every move he made meant agony.

I want to remember Lou Gehrig crying unashamed on July 4, 1939, when 60,000 fans filled the Stadium to pay him homage . . . and his affectionate reunion with Babe Ruth . . . the last time I saw his tired face wreathed in smiles . . . the wonderfully courageous grin he tried to give you when he knew his number was up.

I want to remember Lou Gehrig coming back after getting knocked unconscious by a pitch in Norfolk seven years ago and hitting three straight triples in Washington the next day . . . I want to remember him disregarding broken fingers, broken toes, broken ribs, ugly spike wounds because he remembered he had a job to do . . . I want to recapture the thousand thrills he gave me.

They say Lou Gehrig is dead. I say Lou Gehrig always will be with us who knew him as an enduring, shining symbol of devotion to duty, pride in achievement and worthwhile friendship.

I hope there is a uniform with a No. 4 on the shirt, a bat, a ball, a pitcher and a rightfield fence where Lou Gehrig has gone. He would like that.

Stanley Frank.

"Afterwards"

Fling wide the gates of memory
And call them home once more,
The dear dead dreams of yesterday
That clamor at your door.

The gay glad hours which once were
    yours,
The hope of joys to be,
The many-cargoed ships that sailed
And sank on some wild sea.

When all the songs of life are sung
And all Life's tales are told,
Fling wide the gates of memory
To treasures loved of old.

Marjorie D. Turner.

Youth

I shall remember then,
At twilight time or in the hush of dawn
Or yet mayhap, when on a straying wind
The scent of lilac comes, or when
Some strain of music startles and is gone.

Old dreams, old roses, all so far behind,
Blossoms and birds and ancient shadow-
    trees,
Whispers of sunset, the low hum of bees,
And sheep that graze beneath a summer
    sun,
Will they too come, they who in yester-
    year
Walked the same paths and in the first
    of spring;
And shall I hear
Their distant voices murmuring?

I shall remember then
When youth is done,
With the dim years grown gray;
And I shall wonder what it is that ends,
And why they seem so very far away—
Old dreams, old roses . . . and old friends.

Thomas S. Jones, Jr.

Memories of Mother

Among the influences we may waste, desecrate, but can never quite lose—are the memories of parental piety. Thomas Carlyle after fifty years were gone bore testimony to the power of his mother's prayer. "The highest whom I knew on earth, I here saw bowed down with awe unspeakable, before a Higher in Heaven. Such things, especially in infancy, reach inwards to the very core of your being."

Sunday Service

They tell me I've no longer need to go
To church, come Sabbath morn; that,
    now the Lord
Has time and station on the radio,
The old can sit at home and hear the
    Word.
So in my best black silk, I draw a chair
Up to the carven case . . . A famed
    quartet,
Or soloist, sings; someone leads in prayer;
The preaching's wonderful—and yet—and
    yet—

There are no children after Sunday
    school;
No choir for looking at; no ushers, as
They smilingly show folks to pews and
    pass
The plates . . . and afterwards, no ves-
    tibule
For talk, or chance to shake the pastor's
    hand,
And say, "Your sermon, Brother, was just
    grand."

Ethel Romig Fuller.

❧

The Surgeon

Now he begins, his fingers feel
The tiny burning bits of steel;
They move, obedient to a star
Unseen by us; his sure hands are
So swift that the swift hands of death
Are held; there is one slender breath
Between the two, so delicate
No calipers can measure it
Save those he holds—I think there is
No deed so near to God as his.

Wilfred J. Funk.

Twilight

Twilight it is, and the far woods are dim,
    and the rooks cry and call.
Down in the valley, the lamps, and the
    mist, and a star over all,
There by the rick, where they thresh, is
    the drone at an end
Twilight it is, and I travel the road with
    my friend.

I think of the friends who are dead, who
    were dear long ago in the past,
Beautiful friends who are dead, though I
    know that death cannot last;
Friends with the beautiful eyes that the
    dust has defiled,
Beautiful souls who were gentle when I
    was a child.

John Masefield.

A Lynmouth Widow

He was straight and strong and his eyes
    were blue
As the summer meeting of sky and sea,
And the ruddy cliffs had a colder hue
Than flushed his cheek when he married
    me.

We passed the porch where the swallows
    breed,
We left the little brown church behind
And I leaned on his arm, though I had
    no need,
Only to feel him so strong and kind.

One thing I never can quite forget;
It grips my throat when I try to pray—
The keen salt smell of a drying net
That hung on the churchyard wall that
    day.

He would have taken a long, long grave—
A long, long grave, for he stood so tall . . .
Oh, God, the crash of a breaking wave,
And the smell of the nets on the church
        yard wall.

Amelia Josephine Burr.

He'd nothing but his violin
I'd nothing but my song,
But we were wed when skies were blue
And summer days were long;
And when we rested by the hedge
The robins came and told
How they had dared to woo and win
When early spring was cold.

We sometimes supped on dewberries
Or slept amid the hay,
But oft the farmers' wives at eve
Came out to hear us play;
The rare old songs, the dear old times—
We could not starve for long
While my man had his violin
And I my sweet love song.

The world has aye gone well with us
Old man, since we were one
Our homeless wanderings down the
        lanes—
They long ago were done.
But those who wait for gold or gear,
For houses or for kine
Till youth's sweet spring, grows brown
        and sere
And love and beauty pine
Will never know the joy of hearts
That met without a fear
When you had but your violin
And I my song—my dear.

Mary Kyle Dallas.

Remember

Always remember to forget
    The things that made you sad,
But never forget to remember
    The things that made you glad.

Always remember to forget
    The friends that proved untrue,
But never forget to remember
    Those that have stuck to you.

Always remember to forget
    The troubles that passed away
But never forget to remember
    The blessings that come each day.

Levi Forbush.

Old Songs Are Best

Old songs are best—how sweet to hear
The strains to home and memory dear!
Old books are best—how tale and rhyme
Float with us down the stream of time!

Clarence Urmy.

Remember

Remember me when I am gone away,
Gone far away into the silent land;
When you can no more hold me by the
        hand,
Nor I half turn to go yet turning stay.
Remember me when no more, day by day,
You tell me of our future that you
        planned:
Only remember me; you understand
It will be late to counsel then or pray.
Yet if you should forget me for a while
        *   *   *   *
Better by far you should forget and smile
Than that you should remember and be
        sad.

Christina Rossetti.

I Remember, I Remember

I remember, I remember
  The house where I was born,
The little window where the sun
  Came peeping in at morn:
He never came a wink too soon,
  Nor brought too long a day;
But now, I often wish the night
  Had borne my breath away.

I remember, I remember,
  The roses, red and white;
The violets and the lily-cups,
  Those flowers made of light!
The lilacs where the robin built,
  And where my brother set
The laburnum on his birthday,—
  The tree is living yet!

I remember, I remember,
  Where I was used to swing;
And thought the air must rush as fresh
  To swallows on the wing:
My spirit flew in feathers then,
  That is so heavy now,
And summer pools could hardly cool
  The fever on my brow!

I remember, I remember,
  The fir trees dark and high;
I used to think their slender tops
  Were close against the sky:
It was a childish ignorance,
  But now 'tis little joy
To know I'm farther off from heaven
  Than when I was a boy.
                    Thomas Hood.

"All the Trees of the Wood Rejoice"

"All the trees of the wood rejoice"—
An ancient prophecy finds voice
In the sun-steeped, mist-wrapped autumn
      days;
One chant of color, one shout of praise
From a thousand hills they flame with
      pride,
For the trees of the wood have no fears
      to hide.
Schooled in the faith of the open sky
They flaunt brave boughs as the winds
      sweep by:
They read no sorrow, they own no grief
In the winging flight of the shrivelled leaf,
For only the cringing spirit clings
With frantic hands to the wornout things.
White roots grow deeper than frosts can
      reach,
So maple and elm and oak and beech,
"The trees of the wood" with one accord
"Rejoice together before the Lord!"
                    Molly Anderson Haley.

❧

And when Christmas Day is almost done
When they all grow sleepy one by one,
I shall sit alone by the fire and see
Ghosts of you come close to me.
For the dead and the absent always stay
With the ones they love on Christmas
      Day.
                    Aline Kilmer.

RAINBOWS · THE BOOK OF HOPE

MOTHERHOOD

One good mother is worth a hundred school-
masters. In the home she is a lode-stone to
all hearts and a lode-star to all eyes.
George Herbert

For a First Night in Heaven

You see, dear Lord, Miss Sally never
    married,
And though she rocked many a babe to
    sleep,
They were merely loaned, they were not
    hers
To look upon with mother pride, and
    keep.

She nursed new babies fully forty years—
She loved them when they smiled and
    when they cried.
I know tonight she'll miss her little ones,
For just an hour ago Miss Sally died.

She was my friend, and sensing how she
    feels,
I thought I'd write a note to tell you this;
So if you see her weeping you will know
She wants a little one to soothe and kiss.

On her first night in Heaven, please dear
    Lord,
Give her a tiny one to rock to sleep—
She'd rather have it than a golden harp;
She'll understand it's not her own to
    keep.
Rosa Zagnoni Marinoni.

"There is a sea—a quiet sea—
Beyond the farthest line,
Where all my ships that went astray
Where all my dreams of yesterday
And all the things that were to be
Are mine."

A. E. Housman.

❧❧

Rock Me to Sleep

Backward, turn backward, O time, in your
flight,
Make me a child again just for tonight!
Mother, come back from the echoless
shore,
Take me again to your heart, as of yore;
Kiss from my forehead the furrows of care
Smooth the few silver threads out of my
hair;
Over my slumbers your loving watch
keep,
Rock me to sleep, mother, rock me to
sleep.

Backwards, flow backward, O tide of the
years!
I am so weary of toil and of tears—
Toil without recompense, tears all in
vain—
Take them and give me my childhood
again!
I have grown weary of dust and decay—
Weary of flinging my soul-wealth away;
Weary of sowing for others to reap;
Rock me to sleep, mother, rock me to
sleep.

Tired of the hollow, the base, the untrue,
Mother, O mother, my heart calls for you!
Many a summer the grass has grown green
Blossomed and faded our faces between;

Yet, with strong yearning and passionate
pain,
Long I tonight for your presence again.
Come from the silence so long and so
deep;
Rock me to sleep, mother—rock me to
sleep.

Over my heart in the days that are flown
No love like mother-love ever has shone;
No other worship abides and endures—
Faithful, unselfish and patient like yours,
None like a mother can charm away pain,
From the sick soul and the world-weary
brain.
Slumber's soft calm o'er my heavy lids
creep;
Rock me to sleep, mother—rock me to
sleep.

Come, let your brown hair, just lighted
with gold,
Fall on your shoulders again, as of old;
Let it drop over my forehead tonight,
Shading my faint eyes away from the
light;
For with its sunny-edged shadows once
more
Haply will throng the sweet visions of
yore;
Lovingly, softly, its bright billows sweep—
Rock me to sleep, mother, rock me to
sleep.

Mother, dear mother, the years have been
long
Since I last listened to your lullaby song.
Sing, then, and unto my soul it shall seem
Womanhood's years have been only a
dream.
Clasped to your heart in a loving embrace,
With your light lashes just sweeping my
face,

Never hereafter to wake or to weep—
Rock me to sleep, mother, rock me to
  sleep.

Elizabeth Akers Allen.

Mothers With Little Sons

O Mothers with little sons
  And burning hearts to teach,
You are the chosen ones—
  Give hearing, I beseech!
The world is a ghastly place
  Since war has slain our men;
But yours is the gift and yours is the grace
  To bring love back again.

Mothers, I beg you, heed
  What hate's dark hand has done;
How the hearts of the people bleed
  Till peace and right are won.
How the maimed and halt and blind
  And the dread ones hidden away
Are a challenge to all mankind
  To fashion a better way.

Mothers with little sons,
  As you hold them to your breast,
Teach them to hate the guns—
  That love and faith are best;
Show how the tyrant war
  Destroys but does not win,
How the goals men battle for
  Are lost with the world's great sin.

Strip from the monster's frame
  His glittering robe of lies;
Show him in all his shame
  To your children's visioning eyes;
Show how the lust to kill
  Is the jungle's law of might,
And shells dropped down on a helpless
  town
  Are murder in God's sight.

O mothers with little sons,
  Who stand with lifted faces,
All of earth's helpless ones
  Cry from the lonely places;
And the dead men plead their cause
  And the crippled men implore:
"Go, fashion the future's laws
  That war shall be no more."
For war is a knave's design
  And a coward's brutal scheme,
And men whose courage is divine
  Shall foster a nobler dream.

O mothers with little sons,
  The years lie in your hands;
You are the chosen ones;
  Men wait for your commands;
Not till your lips declare,
  "Our sons no more shall fight,"
Shall the crimson soil be fair
  And the ravaged earth be right.

Angela Morgan.

Mothers in War Time

We must remember to read fairy tales
To buy small boats with brightly colored
  sails.
To bake plump crunchy men of
  gingerbread
And press a warm kiss on a sleepy head.

These are the things no mother's heart
  will shirk;
The need for singing blithely at her work,
Of saving just a bit of garden space
For daffodils, to light a little face.

She'll keep gay ribbons tied and soft hair
  curled,
While we march staunchly toward a
  better world.

Geraldine Ross.

135

Motherhood

The night throbs on; O let me pray dear
    Lord!
Crush off his name a moment from my
    mouth,
To Thee my eyes would turn, but they
    go back,
Back to my arm beside me where he lay,—
So little, Lord, so little and so warm!

I cannot think that Thou hadst need of
    him!
He was so little, Lord, he cannot sing,
He cannot praise Thee; all his life had
    learned
Was to hold fast my kisses in the night.

Give him to me—he is not happy there!
He had not felt this life; his lovely eyes
Just knew me for his mother, and he died.

Hast Thou an angel there to mother him?
I say he loves me best—if he forgets,
If Thou allow it that my child forgets
And runs not out to meet me when I
    come—

What is my curse to Thee? Thou hast
    heard
The curse of Abel's mother, and since
    then
We have not ceased to threaten at Thy
    throne,
To threat and pray Thee that Thou hold
    them still

In memory of us. See Thou tend him
    well,
Thou God of all mothers. If he lack
One of his kisses—Ah, my heart, my heart,
Do angels kiss in Heaven? Give him back!

Forgive me, Lord, but I am sick with
    grief,
And tired of tears and cold to comforting.
Thou art wise, I know, and tender, aye,
    and good;
Thou hast my child and he is safe with
    Thee.

And I believe—Ah, God my child shall go
Orphaned among the angels! All alone,
So little and alone! He knows not Thee,
He only knows his mother—give him back.

[The angels have no arms and cannot
    soothe
But Thou hast arms, so tender and so
    strong,
And he is with Thee. Father, hold him
    close.
And now 'tis dark. Kiss him goodnight
    for me.]

        Josephine Dodge Daskam.
    The last verse added by the editor.

Never Done

Tired fingers so worn, so white,
Sewing and mending from morn 'til
    night.
Tired hands and eyes that blink,
Drooping head, too tired to think.

Tired arms that once had pressed
A curly head to a mother's breast.
Tired voice so soft, so dear
Saying "Sleep well, darling, mother's
    near."

Tired fingers so worn, so true.
Sewing and mending the whole day
    through,
From break of dawn 'til setting sun,
"A Mother's Work Is Never Done."
                  Anon.

For Me the Hills

For me the hills—no winding valley ways
Hemming me in and sheltering my days;
For me the effort, the vast far flung goal,
Great draughts of beauty for my thirsting
    soul.

From far above, the mists that drift below
Drown in soft azure beauty sin and woe;
And oh, the joy of conquest, looking
    back to say
"My feet are bruised, but I have climbed
    today."

Helen Koch.

Sure I love the dear silver that shines in
    your hair,
And the brow that's all furrowed and
    wrinkled with care.
I kiss the dear fingers so toil-worn for me,
Oh, God bless you and keep you, Mother
    Machree.

Rida Johnson Young.

A mother's love and work is indeed the
golden link that binds youth to age; and
he is still but a child, however time may
have furrowed his cheek or silvered his
brow, who can yet recall with a softened
heart the fond devotion, or the gentle
chidings, of the best friend that God
ever gives us.

Bovee.

What God will do for us under all
circumstances is the very same that a good
mother would do if she had the power
and wisdom.

E. P. Brown.

Mostly a word, a sermon, a book, a
home or a life must be valued by the love
that is in it.

In making the point that motherhood
is spiritual rather than physical Anne
Shannon Monroe goes so far as to say
that it doesn't much matter who does the
"borning"—it's the loving that counts.

No less an authority than the Lord
Christ seems to endorse that view. His
emphasis was never on the fact that God
created us but on the fact that God loves
us.

And in the home of Bethany when
forced to take sides He seems to give the
palm to Mary who spent herself in loving
rather than to Martha who spent herself
in doing.

It is too bad that one so seldom finds
the two—serving and loving to a high
degree of quality and quantity in one
person.

Efficiency can be so frightfully cold
that it exasperates rather than inspires.

Whatever it is you are doing, warm it
up with a bit of love.

"Thou see'st how closely, Abba, when at
    rest
My child's head nestles to my breast;
And how my arm her little form enfolds
Lest in the darkness she should feel
    alone
    And how she holds
My hand, my hands, my two hands in
    her own?
A little easeful sighing
And restful turning round
And I too, on Thy love relying,
Shall slumber sound."

Nancy Hanks

If Nancy Hanks
Came back as a ghost,
Seeking news
Of what she loved most
She'd ask first
Where's my son?
What's happened to Abe?
What's he done?

Poor little Abe
Left all alone
Except for Tom,
Who's a rolling stone;
He was only nine
The year I died
I remember still
How hard he cried.

Scraping along
In a little shack
With hardly a shirt
To cover his back,
And a prairie wind
To blow him down
Or pinching times
If he went to town.

You wouldn't know
About my son
Did he grow tall?
Did he have fun?
Did he learn to read?
Did he get to town?
Do you know his name?
Did he get on?

Rosemary and Stephen V. Benet.

Prayer for a New Mother

The things she knew, let her forget
again—
The voices in the sky, the fear, the cold,
The gaping shepherds, and the queer old
men
Piling their cumbrous gifts of foreign
gold.

Let her have her laughter with her little
one;
Teach her the endless, timeless songs to
sing;
Grant her her right to whisper to her son
The foolish names one dare not call a
king.

Keep from her dreams the rumble of a
crowd,
The smell of rough-cut wood, the trail
of red,
The thick and chilly whiteness of the
shroud
That wraps the strange new body of the
dead.

Ah, let her go, kind Lord, where mothers
go
And boast his pretty words and ways; and
plan
The proud and happy years that they shall
know,
Together, when her son is grown a man.

Dorothy Parker.

RAINBOWS — THE BOOK OF HOPE

O let me leave the plains behind,
And let me leave the vales below:
Into the headlands of the mind,
Into the mountains let me go.

        William Watson

Over the Hills

Over the hills my friends are going,
Over the hills and far away,
To a place beyond my knowing—
Ah! one more has gone today.

They are all like comrades straying
Far from home on darkened nights;
Yet some voice they are obeying,
And they see strange, distant lights.

No! it is not dark out yonder;
It is all a sunlit way.
Glad are those called forth to wander
Over the hills and far away.

        Charles Hanson Towne.

And here stands the Lord of Life, saying, "Follow thou me." If we do follow Him, will moral reenforcement be given us? Has the love of Christ given men power for overcoming? It has. It has turned drunkards into sober men, thieves into honest men, Pharisees into humble men, and domestic tyrants into kind husbands and fathers. It has enabled literally millions of human beings to climb out of mud and slime and selfishness onto glorious sunlit heights where their souls were washed clean by the winds of God, and their eyes opened to the beauty of the world, and their hearts were sustained by deathless hopes.

        Ernest Fremont Tittle.

The Secrets of Life

We would miss the fleecy vapor,
If the skies were always blue
We would miss the pearly sparkles
If there never was a dew;
We would long for shade and darkness
Were the hours like brighest day;
We would sigh for hills and valleys
Were our path a level way.

Thus it is on life's brief journey—
There must be both night and day;
There must come the rain and sunshine,
On our rough uneven way;
There must be some days of sorrow,
Where the heart is crushed with grief,
When the tears will flow in silence,
And their falling brings relief.

We must learn life's secret lesson—
Blending bitter with the sweet,
Sending sunshine with the raindrops
Bringing to us cold and heat.
We must learn the art of blending;
We must needs pass through the deep
Ever pressing onward, forward,
Till we climb the mountains steep.

N. P. Neilson.

❧

Everybody needs to take that vow—that he will not sell out. We ministers need to take it. Men in politics and women in society, and those who live under the terrific pressure of self-interest in the business world need to make that vow their own, that they will not sell out. What is finer in history than a soul that is not for sale.

Harry Emerson Fosdick.

The greatest lesson of life has been learned when one has accepted the fact that, whatever his other activities, he can best aid the coming of the Kingdom of God by loyalty to the near duties which once seemed small but which somehow loom large with advancing years—the maintenance of a fearless soul in the maze of common life, the steady cultivation of a living faith in a loving God who holds and controls the destiny of man, and the jealous safeguarding of inner peace which is the just heritage of a quiet conscience.

Charles Henry Brent.

❧

To seek is our destiny. Irrevocably we are pilgrims. There is but one quest and one goal but we must follow the gleam:—

"There is a quest that calls me
In nights when I am alone,
The need to ride where the ways divide
The known from the unknown.

"I mount what thought is near me
And soon I reach the place
The tenuous rim where the Seen grows
    dim
And the sightless hides its face.

"I have ridden the wind
I have ridden the sea
I have ridden the moon and stars,
I have set my feet in the stirrup seat
Of a comet coursing Mars.

"And everywhere
Thro' the earth and air
My thought speeds, lightning-shod
It comes to a place where checking pace
It cries 'Beyond lies God'."

Cale Young Rice.

Round by Round

Heaven is not reached at a single bound;
But we climb the ladder by which we
rise
From the lowly earth to the vaulted
skies,
And we mount to its summit, round by
round.

I count this thing to be grandly true:
That a noble deed is a step toward
God,—
Lifting the soul from the common clod
To a purer air and a broader view.

We rise by the things that are under feet;
By what we have mastered of good and
gain;
By the pride deposed and the passion
slain,
And the vanquished ills that we hourly
meet.

We hope, we aspire, we resolve, we trust,
When the morning calls us to life and
light,
But our hearts grow weary, and, ere
the night,
Our lives are trailing the sordid dust.

We hope, we resolve, we aspire, we pray
And we think that we mount the air
on wings
Beyond the recall of sensual things,
While our feet still cling to the heavy
clay.

Wings for the angels, but feet for men!
We may borrow the wings to find the
way—
We may hope, and resolve, and aspire,
and pray;
But our feet must rise, or we fall again.

Only in dreams is a ladder thrown
From the weary earth to the sapphire
walls;
For the dreams depart, and the vision
falls;
And the sleeper wakes on his pillow of
stone.

Heaven is not reached at a single bound;
But we build the ladder by which we
rise
From the lowly earth to the vaulted
skies,
And we mount to its summit, round by
round.

J. G. Holland.

To be strong and true; to be generous
in praise and appreciation of others; to
impute worthy motives even to enemies;
to give without expectation of return; to
practice humility, tolerance and self-re-
straint, to make the best use of time and
opportunity; to keep the mind pure and
the judgment charitable; to extend intelligent sympathy to those in distress; to
cultivate quietness and non-resistance; to
seek truth and righteousness; to work,
love, pray and serve daily, to aspire greatly, labor cheerfully, and take God at His
word—this is to travel Heavenward.

Grenville Kleiser.

"Sometimes it seems to me I must
Just quit the city's din and dust,
For field of green and skies of blue;
And say! How does it seem to you?"

Anon.

A Clean Wind Blowing

God, keep a clean wind blowing through
    my heart,
Night and Day,
Cleanse it with sunlight, let the silver
    rain
Wash away
Cobwebs and the smouldering dust that
    years
Leave, I pray.
Bitterness can have no place in me,
Nor grief stay,
When the winds of God sweep through
    and wash
Them away.
God, keep a clean wind blowing through
    my heart
Night and day.

***

I toil, but I must also climb;
What soul was ever quite at ease
Shut in by earthly boundaries?

I am not glad till I have known
Life that can lift me from my own:
A loftier level must be won,
A mightier strength to lean upon.

And heaven draws near as I ascend;
The breeze invites, the stars befriend:
All things are beckoning towards the Best:
I climb to Thee, my God, for rest.

Lucy Larcom.

Mountains

"I am homesick for the mountains—
My heroic mother hills—
And the longing that is on me
No solace ever stills.

"I would climb to brooding summits
With their old untarnished dreams,
Cool my heart in forest shadows
To the lull of falling streams.

"I need the pure strong mornings,
When the soul of day is still,
With the touch of frost that kindles
The scarlet on the hill.

"Lone trails and winding wood roads
To out-looks wild and high,
And the pale moon waiting sundown
Where ledges cut the sky.

"My eyes dim for the sky line
Where purple peaks aspire
And the forges of the sunset
Flare up in golden fire.

"Where cloud-mists from the warm earth
Roll up about their knees,
And hang their filmy tatters
Like prayers upon the trees."

***

Saviour, where'er Thy steps I see,
Dauntless, untired, I follow thee;
O let Thy hand support me still,
And lead me to Thy holy hill.

Count Zinzendorf.

RAINBOWS   THE BOOK OF HOPE

PEACE

"Come unto me . . ."

To understand that God has not merely a programme for your life but that you are an integral part of God's great universal plan, is to be at peace.

"Be Still and Know That I Am God"

All beauty whispers to the listening heart:
   Love does not shout, and ecstasy is still;
The friendly silence of infinity
   Forever broods above a lifted hill.

A flower leaps to life—the quiet clod
   Has uttered music; noiselessly a tree
Flings forth green song; the snow breathes
      soundless prayers;
   And stars are vocal with tranquillity!
            Mary Hallet.

On the stone marking the grave of Mark Twain's daughter, Olivia Susan Clemens:

Warm summer sun, shine kindly here;
   Warm southern wind, blow softly
      here;
Green sod above, lie light, lie light;
   Good night, dear heart, good night,
      good night.

❧

The joys and sorrows of others are as much ours as theirs, and in proper time as we feel this and learn to live so that the whole world shares the life that flows through us, do our minds learn the Secret of Peace.
            Annie Besant.

143

The Day Is Done

The day is done, and the darkness
  Falls from the wings of night,
As a feather is wafted downward
  From an eagle in his flight.

I see the light of the village
  Gleam through the rain and mist,
And a feeling of sadness comes o'er me
  That my soul cannot resist:

A feeling of sadness and longing,
  That is not akin to pain,
And resembles sorrow only
  As the mist resembles the rain.

Come, read to me some poem
  Some simple and heartfelt lay,
That shall soothe this restless feeling,
  And banish the thoughts of day.

Not from the grand old masters,
  Not from the bards sublime,
Whose distant footsteps echo
  Through the corridors of Time.

For, like strains of martial music,
  Their mighty thoughts suggest
Life's endless toil and endeavor;
  And to-night I long for rest.

Read from some humbler poet,
  Whose songs gushed from his heart,
As showers from the clouds of summer,
  Or tears from the eyelids start;

Who, through long days of labor,
  And nights devoid of ease,
Still heard in his soul the music
  Of wonderful melodies.

Such songs have power to quiet
  The restless pulse of care,
And come like the benediction
  That follows after prayer.

Then read from the treasured volume
  The poem of thy choice,
And lend to the rhyme of the poet
  The beauty of thy voice.

And the night shall be filled with music,
  And the cares, that infest the day,
Shall fold their tents, like the Arabs,
  And as silently steal away.
      Henry Wadsworth Longfellow.

The Hills of Rest

Beyond the last horizon's rim,
  Beyond adventure's farthest quest,
Somewhere they rise, serene and dim,
  The happy, happy, Hills of Rest.

Upon their sunlit slopes uplift
  The castles we have built in Spain—
While fair amid the summer drift
  Our faded gardens flower again.

Sweet hours we did not live go by
  To soothing note, on scented wing:
In golden-lettered volumes lie
  The songs we tried in vain to sing.

They are all there; the days of dream
  That build the inner lives of men;
The silent, silent sacred years we deem
  That might be or that might have been.

Some evening when the sky is gold
  I'll follow day into the west;
Nor pause, nor heed, till I behold
  The happy, happy Hills of Rest.
      Albert Bigelow Paine.

For the thoughts that I think toward you, saith the Lord, are thoughts of peace . . . to give you hope.
      Jeremiah 29:11.

A Song of the Hills

The wind whips over the hills tonight,
  Whips hard my beloved hills,
And it tells of a storm surging on its way,
That threatens to maim or destroy or slay,
And my heart is heavy, my strength at
    bay,
  While the wind whips over my hills
    tonight.

The lightnings flash on the hills tonight,
  And they sting my beloved hills,
While the thunders pound like a can-
    non's roar,
And the barrelling rains in floods outpour,
And my heart is troubled and weak and
    sore,
  While it storms on my hills tonight.

The moon peeps over my hills tonight,
  Lighting up my beloved hills
With a halo from God of His loving care
That watches and guards His own every-
    where,
And my heart is uplifted in grateful prayer
  For the peace on my hills tonight.
                    L. Bradley Spaun.

❧

And His that gentle voice we hear,
Soft as the breath of even,
That checks each fault, that calms each
    fear,
And speaks of Heaven.
                    Harriet Auber.

❧

Oh, the little birds sang east, and the
    little birds sang west,
And I smiled to think God's greatness
    flowed around our incompleteness,—
Round our restlessness, His rest.
            Elizabeth Barrett Browning.

Vacation

I find it quite impossible
  To hie away and rest;
Away from cares and troubles,
  To distant mountain crest.

So I shall stay at home this year
  And send my cares away
Upon a long vacation,
  While I enjoy each day!
                    Ruth Smeltzer.

❧

That is one effect of the influence of
Christ upon us, to deepen the meaning
of all great words. Love, faith, goodness,
duty, salvation—they all grow richer as
we walk with God, like pearls, which are
said to take their quality from the wearer
on whose breast they lie.

"New occasions teach new duties, time
    makes ancient good uncouth,
They must upward still and onward, who
    would keep abreast of truth."

Lowell was pointing out a very common danger—the danger of luxuriating in
the light of the past, instead of walking
in the light of the present, as it falls upon
some fresh citadel to be stormed for God,
or some bit of "No-man's Land" to be
charted and brought under the harrow
and the plough of His will. We are pilgrims—that is the point. Our truly Christian hymns are marching songs. Our only
rest is in moving with the unfolding
purpose. Our only peace is walking in the
challenging light.
                    James Reid.

Woodrow Wilson

Memorial Day 1925

There will be those today who weep their
    own
  Who fell in battle or upon the sea;
And those who, when they mourn, will
    think of all
  America's brave dead. Well, as for me,
I too have tears and sad remembering
  For every man of them, named or un-
    known.
Yet from the throng one gray, gaunt face
    appears
  Of him who battled, at the last, alone.

Condemn him if you will; his is the place
  Of honor in our land due every man
Whose soul has glimpsed ideals and
    whose **heart**
    Has fought to prove them true. Lone
    veteran
Of visions was his role unto the last.
  Repudiated, still he dared to face
The world, head up, and loyal unto death
    To his great plan of peace for all the
    race.

He was lone outpost for that world-old
    hope
  Humanity can never quite release:
He gave his heart, his life, his soul, to
    hold
    Our eyes upon the gleam of lasting
    peace.
If he was right (God knows he may have
    been!)
    Come, bring heart-laurel for his sleep-
    ing head!
If he was wrong, still true his heart and
    brave
    His fight: His place is with our soldier
    dead.   *S. Omar Barker.*

Sweet and Low

Sweet and low, sweet and low,
  Wind of the western sea,
Low, low, breathe and blow!
  Wind of the western sea!

Over the rolling waters go,
Come from the dying moon, and blow,
  Blow him again to me;
While my little one, while my pretty one
    sleeps.

Sleep and rest, sleep and rest,
  Father will come to thee soon;
Rest, rest, on mother's breast
  Father will come to thee soon;

Father will come to his babe in the nest,
  Silver sails all out of the west
Under the silver moon:
  Sleep, my little one, sleep, my pretty
    one, sleep.   *Tennyson.*

Soldier, rest! thy warfare o'er,
  Sleep the sleep that knows not break-
    ing;
Dream of battled fields no more,
  Days of danger, nights of waking.
In our isle's enchanted hall,
  Hands unseen thy couch are strewing,
Fairy strains of music fall,
  Every sense in slumber dewing.
Soldier, rest! thy warfare o'er,
  Dream of fighting fields no more;
Sleep the sleep that knows not breaking
  Morn of toil, nor night of waking.
    Sir Walter Scott.

Penitence

She lived alone, but peace lay in her
    eyes—
Her slender hands found helpful things
    to do;
Her feet were winged by mercy; she was
    wise
In counsels, and the ways of children, too.

No one had ever asked her aid in vain
Through darkest night or hottest noon-
    day sun—
Untiring always, yet a flash of pain
Would sometimes cross her face, and
    then be gone.

One day she did not wake . . . I helped
    prepare
The lovely body for its last, long rest;
And working tenderly (I'd grown to care
So much for her), I found hid in her
    breast,
A flat, gold locket holding this one scene—
The Christ forgiving Mary Magdalene.
                Virginia Eaton.

Peace in the Home

As your husband has changed a woman into a wife, it is your duty to change
a house into a home.

And a house is transformed into a
home by the spirit of restfulness and
comfort that broods about it. No man
can stand a spring-cleaning program kept
up through the whole year.

There are more important tributes to
earn than the comment of callers, "How
immaculately your house is kept."

Cleanliness may be next to godliness,
but an obsession for cleanliness may turn
the husband from a saint into a sinner.

To be cozy is at least as important as
to be clean. And the continuous moaning of an electric sweeper is certainly no
benediction to a tired man's spirit.

                G. W. H.

Dr. Fosdick says: "Every man has a
date with adversity which he must keep
and which adversity does not forget. One
notes the evidence of this in every normal
maturing life. As children we wanted
happiness and were impatient lacking it.
Our cups of pleasure easily brimmed and
overflowed. A Christmas tree or a birthday party—and our hearts were like sun-
parlors on cloudless days with all the
windows open to the light.

But the time comes to all when happiness like this is not our problem; we recognize that it has gone; our Edens are behind us with flaming angels at the gate.
We have had friends and lost them and
something has gone from our hearts that
does not return; we have won success
which we do not estimate as highly in
possession as we did in dreams, and it
may be have lost what little we achieved;
we have sinned, and though forgiven, the
scars are still upon us; we have been
weathered by the rains and floods and
winds.

Happiness in the old fashion we no
longer seek. We want peace.

. . . We Want Peace . . .

We have joined the human procession
that moves out into the inevitable need
of comfort.

And it is here that Christ comes in. It
is here He is at His best. He specializes
in comforting."

Contrasts

If all the skies were sunshine
   Our faces would be fain
To feel once more upon them
   The cooling plash of rain.

If all the world were music,
   Our hearts would often long
For one sweet strain of silence,
   To break the endless song.

If life were always merry,
   Our souls would seek relief,
And rest from weary laughter
   In the quiet arms of grief.

         Henry Van Dyke.

Though Augustine to his mother sailed
   long since the death-wave o'er
Still his word sweeps down the ages like
   the surging of the sea;
"Bless Thee Lord, that we are restless,
   till we find our rest in Thee."

         Lucy Larcom.

I know the beds of Eastern princes and the luxurious couches of Occidental plutocrats, but under the rafters of a farmhouse where the mud-wasp's nest answers for a Rembrandt and the cobweb takes the place of a Murillo, there is a feather-bed into which one softly sinks until his every inch is soothed and fitted, and settling down and farther down falls into sweet unconsciousness, while the screech-owl is calling from the moonlit oak and the frost is falling upon the asters.

Stocks may fluctuate and panic seize the town, but there is one man who is in peace.

         Robert T. Morris.

Resurrection

It came so quietly—the first gray light
That touched the open tomb that Easter
   dawn
Long years ago. There, where the weight
   of night
And death had laid a dark despair upon
Each sorrowing heart, came morning, a
   bird's voice,
And cypress trees showed sunrise trickling
   through.
The day that bade the whole wide world
   rejoice
Was born where lilies in a garden grew.

It will come quietly. There will be bread,
Water for long-parched lips. The hurt-
   filled breast
Will sense a healing comfort, void of
   dread.
Slowly earth's war-torn peoples will have
   rest.
And, with its life, its light, its sweet
   release,
Like that first Easter morning, will come
   peace.

         Ida Norton Munson.

RAINBOWS   THE BOOK OF HOPE

PRAYER

God of the hidden purpose,
Let our entreaties be
The prayers of proud men asking
Not to be safe, but free.

We cannot tell how often as we pray
For some hurt one bewildered and dis-
tressed
The answer comes, but many times those
hearts
Find sudden peace and rest.
Someone had prayed, and faith, a reach-
ing hand
Took hold of God and brought Him
down that day—
So many, many hearts have need of
prayer—
Oh, let us pray.

Anon.

Each day I pray high God to give me
strength anew
To do the task I do not wish to do;
To love and own the truth and scorn
the lie,
To yield obedience, not asking why;
To cheer for those who pass me in the
race,
To look a cold world in the face;
To bear my burdens daily, unafraid,
To lend a hand to those that need my aid;
To measure what I am by what I give.
God, give me strength that I may rightly
live.

Anon.

149

Prayer in a June Garden

Dear God, Your roses bloom so very
    sweetly—
Your shadows lie so softly on the grass!
The very singing winds that try to pass
Must linger in this lovely place . . .
    Completely
Your presence here is felt, this tender
    garden
Is all Your Own, each fragrant flower
    head
Is rising like Your voice. Each mossy bed
Is like a psalm that breathes of peace and
    pardon.

Dear Father, You, Who made the tender
    showers,
Who made the sunlight coming after
    rain,
Have made new hope, to follow after
    pain!
Life must be formed of alternating hours,
Some fair, some dim . . . some wonderful
    with grace . . .
We, who are pilgrims, only ask You this—
That we may know, at times, the utter
    bliss
Of walking with You, in some garden
    place.

                                    Amen.

Gilead

The heart is cold that has not chilled
    With fear that love could pass away.
The soul is dry that does not thirst
    For clear refreshment day by day.
And eyes are dim that in the light
    Have never seen the need to pray.

                    Mary Brennan Clapp.

There was a prayer they used to pray in Scottish homes, and I do not know whether it has fallen out of use; but I have seen a gray head bowed, and seemed to hear the accent of the prayer; "Lord, help us to live every day as we will wish we had done when we come to die." It is not a poor prayer, and it is not a cowardly prayer.

                    John Watson.

He Cannot

Could not Christ have saved Lazarus from dying? Could not Christ have saved you or me from perplexity or temptation or doubt? He could, because the power of life and death was in Him . . . But if it were best for Lazarus to die, then Christ could not have caused that he should not have died. That is a sublime incapacity; to stand with the gift of life in the all-powerful hands, to see the cry for life in the eager eyes, to hear it in the dumb appeal of the terrified lips, and yet to say, "No, not life but death is best," and so to be unable to give life,—that is a sublime, a divine incapacity.

Could not Christ have answered your prayer? No, He could not; not because the thing you asked for was not in His treasury, but because behind the question of His giving or refusing it there lay the fundamental necessity of His nature and His love, that He should do for you only the absolutely best. The thing you asked for was not absolutely best, therefore He could not give it. Back of how many unanswered prayers lies that divine impossibility!

                    Phillips Brooks.

A Prayer

These are the gifts I ask of thee—
Spirit serene,
Strength for the daily task,
Courage to face the road,
Good cheer to help me bear the traveler's
    load,
And for the hours of rest that come be-
    tween,
An inward joy in all things heard and
    seen.

These are the sins I fain would have you
    take away—
Malice and cold disdain,
Hot anger, sullen hate,
Scorn of the lowly, envy of the great,
And discontent that casts a shadow gray
On all the brightness of a common day.

Henry Van Dyke.

❦

Prayer really does things. It cannot
change God's intention, but it does
change God's action. God had long intended Isaiah to be his prophet. When
Isaiah said, "Here am I, send me," he did
not alter in the least the divine purpose,
but he did release it. God could do then
what before He could not. God had long
intended that Africa should be evange-
lized. When Livingstone cried, "O God,
help me to paint this dark continent
white," he did not alter God's intention,
but he did alter God's action.

Power broke loose that before had
been pent; the cooperation of a man's
prayer, backed by his life, opened a way
for the divine purpose.

Harry Emerson Fosdick.

Gardener's Prayer

Grant me this prayer, oh Lord!
That when my eyelids close
In last long sleep,
I may awake
To find my hand upon a garden gate,
And, passing through,
Feel in my face
The scent of Mignonette.

To wander down a garden path
Bordered with those dear growing things
I loved so well in life—
The simple, homely flowers—
Gay Zinnias, tall Phlox, and Marigold;
And, bending for the perfume from a
    Rose,
To drop upon my knees
Before unfolding beauty of white Violets.

There could I rest content,
My trowel in my hand.

Nancy Allen.

❦

Lord, I have laid my heart upon Thy altar,
    But cannot get the wood to burn;
It hardly flares ere it begins to falter,
    And to the dark return.
Old sap, or night-fallen dew, has damped
    the fuel;
    In vain my breath would flame pro-
        voke;
Yet see—at every poor attempt's renewal
    To Thee ascends the smoke!
'Tis all I have—smoke, failure, foiled en-
    deavor,
    Coldness and doubt, and palsied lack:
Such as I have I send Thee; perfect Giver,
    Send Thou Thy lightning back!

George Macdonald.

The Little Boy's Baby Prayer

Dear God I need you awful bad
I don't know what to do;
My papa's cross, my mamma's sick,
I haint no fren' but you.

Them keerless angels went and brung
'Stid of the boy I ast,
A ween-chy, teen-chy baby girl.
I don't see how they dast.

Dear God I wish you'd take her back
She's just as good as new;
Wont no one know she's second-hand,
But 'cept-in-' me and you.

An, pick a boy, dear God, yourself,
The nicest in your fold;
But please don't choose him quite so
    young;
I'd like him five years old.

S. Marie Talbot.

Heritage

A highway runs beside my door—
Just a broad, straight road and nothing
    more—
Except when the westering sun droops
    low
Till the dust in the air takes a golden glow
Like a veil or a web, and within its sheen
The present fades as the past is seen.

Then like a dream down the broad high-
    way
Pass women of old and of yesterday;
Spartan mother, a jeweled queen,
Peasant martyr and Magdalene;
Fair young faces unmarked by years,
Sad eyes faded and dimmed from tears;
Brave, strong shoulders unbent by loss,

Old backs, bowed from a long-borne cross.
Rank on rank a mighty throng,
They march to the beat of an unheard
    song:
Mothers of men they have toiled and
    wept
That a dream might live and a flame be
    kept.

Then from afar, like the whir of wings,
A voice in majestic paeon sings:
"These are they who have journeyed
    through,
They have kept the faith, they have
    builded true.
And the way will never be quite so long
Because they have wrought so fair and
    strong."

The vision fades . . . and the road once
    more
Is only a road by my open door.
Through a mist of tears I lift mine eyes
To the first faint star in the twilight skies,
And breathe my prayer on the evening
    breeze:
"Thank God for my heritage from these!"

Lytton Cox.

Dr. Hyslop, Superintendent of Bethlehem Royal Hospital, at the annual
meeting of the British Medical Association in 1905, said: "As an alienist, and
one whose whole life has been concerned
with the sufferings of the mind, I would
state that of all hygienic measures to
counteract disturbed, sleep-depressed
spirits, and all the miserable sequels of a
distressed mind, I would undoubtedly
give the first place to the simple habit of
prayer."

Washerwoman's Prayer

Lord, I can't pray the words the preach-
    ers pray;
    And all I know is clothes and soap and
      dirt;
But here I bring this badly laundered
    day.
    It won't come clean—just like the mis-
      ter's shirt.
I soaked it in my tears, Lord, rubbed each
    cuff
    Against the hard board of experience;
But all that I could do was not enough—
    The spots still show across my neigh-
      bor's fence.

You gave me all I needed—a whole sky
    Of cloudy soapsuds and Your heaven's
      own
Bottle of bluing, and to whip it dry,
    Upon this day Your choicest winds
      have blown;
But there it hangs still streaked with sin
    and sorrow
    Lord, could I try another day tomor-
      row?

Helen Frazee-Bower.

❧

Prayer in its simplest meaning is the
habit of talking to God with the same
friendly familiarity we use toward the
loved ones of earth.

To say naturally on awakening, "Good
Morning, Father," or on closing the eyes
for sleep, "Father, Good Night."

It is not a matter of "practising the
presence," for practice of any kind im-
plies effort, it is the spontaneous greeting of a friend who is always near.

A Business Man's Prayer

Dear Lord, I do not hesitate
To thank Thee for things truly great;
The universe is Thine, and all
Accomplishment is at Thy call.
Lord of each mountain art Thou, still—
Lord art Thou of each little hill.

It pleases me to know I may
Receive Thy backing every day
In all the larger things of life,
Howe'er tremendous be the strife;
But this thought pleases best of all—
Lord art Thou of the very small.

No matter how great may be my goal,
'Tis little tasks make up the whole
And the sure knowledge that Thou art
The Lord of each gives to my heart
The strength to face them one by one
Until the larger task is done.

When 'tis completed, I agree
The finished product's due to Thee:
I thank Thee for it as a whole,
But deep down in my toiling soul
My gratitude the greater clings
To Thee as Lord of little things.

William Ludlum.

❧

How silverly the echoes run!
Thy will be done,—thy will be done.

So oft the doing of God's will
    Our foolish wills undoeth!
And yet what idle dream breaks ill,
    Which morning-light subdueth?

And who would murmur and misdoubt,
When God's great sunrise finds him out?

Elizabeth Barrett Browning.

And This I Ask

The "Now I lay me's" floated in.
Rare eloquence, that once more sin
Be pardoned, shamed the sunset's glow,
And clouds grew thick with thanks.
    Below,
Earth held up hands for Heaven to fill.

God leaned against His window sill
In pensive brooding . . . Through the
    noise
A sob cut clearly. Then a boy's:
"If Rags should die before I wake,
I pray Thee, Lord, his soul to take."

God's hand, past priest and pedagogue,
Reached out to heal a small boy's dog.
                    May Howard McEachern.

❧❧

A Nurse's Prayer

Because the day that stretches out for me
Is full of busy hours, I come to Thee
To ask Thee, Lord, that Thou wilt see
    me through
The many things that I may have to do.
Help me to make my beds the smoothest
    way.
Help me to make more tempting every
    tray.
Help me to sense when pain must have
    relief.
Help me to deal with those borne down
    by grief.
Help me to take to every patient's room
The Light of Life to brighten up the
    gloom.
Help me to bring to every soul in fear
The sure and steadfast thought that Thou
    art near.

And if today, or, if tonight, maybe,
Some patient in my care set out to sea
To face the great adventure we call death,
Sustain them, Father, in their parting
    breath.
Help me to live throughout this live-long
    day
As one who loves Thee well, dear Lord,
    I pray;
And when the day is done, and evening
    stars
Shine through the dark above the sunset
    bars,
When weary quite, I turn to seek my rest,
Lord, may I truly know I've done my best.
                    Ruth Winant Wheeler.

❧❧

I Do Not Ask

I do not ask of life that it be free
From illness or from friends untrue,
From loss of loved ones who are dear
    to me
Long hours of toil or irksome tasks to do
All days of sunshine, without cloud or
    rain
Besetting enemies or base desire . . .
'Tis winter makes the summer come again
The metal gets its temper through the
    fire.

I only ask that God will point the way
'Twere best for me to tread while I am
    here
And give me strength and courage to
    obey,
To do my part to bring His Kingdom
    near.
That I may finish every task begun
And at the end deserve to hear "Well
    done."
                    L. Bradley Spaun.

154

"I that still pray at morning and at eve,
Loving those roots that feed us from the
    past,
And prizing more than Plato things I
    learned
At that best Academe, a mother's knee,
Thrice in my life perhaps have truly
    prayed,
Thrice, stirred below my conscious self,
    have felt
That perfect disenthralment which is
    God."

Rufus M. Jones.

❧

The Twentieth Century

Not unto us, O Lord, the praise
For what is wrought by sea or coast,
Through babel shouts and words that
    boast
Of conquest, comes the master phrase—
        "Not unto us."

Along the wires the currents fret
Or fly where there is none to guide;
The railway climbs the Great Divide,
And liners sail secure—but yet
        "Not unto us."

Factory, office, mine and mill—
The shuttles shift, the threads remain:
The garments still are Love and Pain
When woven. Therefore, say we still,
        "Not unto us."

From confident material ways,
From civilized complacent word,
From this our age, O save us, Lord,
And give not unto us the praise—
        "Not unto us."

E. A. Havelock.

A Prayer

Give me a good digestion, Lord,
And also something to digest.
Give me a healthy body, Lord,
With sense to keep it at its best.

Give me a healthy mind, good Lord,
To keep the good and pure in sight,
Which, seeing sin, is not appalled,
But finds a way to set it right.

Give me a mind that is not bored,
That does not whimper, whine or sigh,
Don't let me worry overmuch
About the fussy thing called I.

Give me a sense of humor, Lord,
Give me the grace to see a joke.
To get some happiness from life,
And pass it on to other folk.

Found in Chester Cathedral.

❧

There is no solid hindrance to prayer
except ourselves. We ourselves raise the
barriers and set up the obstacles. Still
as of old the soul finds what it undi-
videdly seeks, it gets what it persistently
asks for, it brings open the door at which
it unremittingly knocks. Everywhere in
the universe the soul may have what it
wants. If it hungers and thirsts for God,
it will be fed with the bread of life and
supplied with the water that satisfies. The
difficulty is not objective; it is subjective.
We so often do not really pray. We only
say over words and call it "prayer." Let us
instead learn to pray.

Prayer

We pray for Light
But when it shines and makes our duty
    clear,
Then, faltering, we hide our eyes in fear.
Nor bear the sight.

For Love we pray
Believing it is sweet,
    A happy thing;
Yet when it brings us pain and suffering
Our Love we slay.

We offer prayer
    For Opportunity
Yet when it knocks upon our doors
Heedless, we turn the locks,
    All unaware.

Father in heaven
Teach us to understand
    For what we pray
That we may turn Thine answers not
    away
    When they are given.

❧

I do not pray that Thou
    Shouldest grant me victory;
Enough to know that from my foe
    I have no will to flee.
Beaten and bruised and banned,
    Flung like a broken sword,
Grant me this thing for conquering—
    Let me die fighting, Lord!
            Theodosia Garrison.

❧

My Father, this I ask of Thee;
Knowing that Thou wilt grant the plea,—
For this, and only this, I pray,
Strength for today—just for today.

Strength for each trial and each task,
What more, my Father, should I ask?
Just as I need it, day by day,
Strength for my weakness—this I pray.
            Eben E. Rexford.

❧

As Thou hast made the world without
    Make Thou more fair the world within;
Shine through its lingering clouds of
    doubt;
    Rebuke its haunting shapes of sin;
Fill, brief or long, my granted span
    Of life with love to Thee and man;
Strike when Thou wilt the hour of rest,
    But let my last days be my best!
            Whittier.

❧

Here, O my Lord, I see Thee face to face;
    Here would I touch and handle things
    unseen,
Here grasp with firmer hand the eternal
    grace,
    And all my weariness upon Thee lean.

Here would I feed upon the bread of
    God,
    Here drink with Thee the royal wine
    of heaven;
Here would I lay aside each earthly load,
    Here taste afresh the calm of sins
    forgiven.

This is the hour of banquet and of song;
    This is the heavenly table spread for me;
Here let me feast, and feasting, still
    prolong
    The brief bright hour of fellowship
    with Thee.
            Horatius Bonar.

The Source

No rain for weeks . . . a burning sun
   . . . scorched grass . . .
And dust . . . And yet a clump of zinnias
   still
Unfolding brilliant colors from their dry
Brown stalks—their sustenance a mystery!

And then one morn, when early dawn
   outlines
Black velvet shadows with a touch of grey,
I looked into the garden. Sparkling dew
Like trembling diamonds clung to every
   leaf
And withered stem. The zinnias stood
   with heads
Uplifted, drinking in the cool night air
And dew. In vibrant silence, storing
   strength
To meet the day . . . I thought of One
   upon
A lonely mountain-top, retreating for
A few brief hours from men, soul hungry
   throngs
That He must feed . . . "And He con-
   tinued" (there
Alone—alone with God) "all night in
   prayer!"
          Isla Paschal Richardson.

I, Too, Have Known

I too, have known Gethsemane
   In lonely tryst,
I have broken bread with Peter . . .
   By Judas kissed.

And grim frustration I have known
   Of cherished plans,
Met Thomas-doubts instead of trust
   In many lands.

I, too, have known the rabble throng,
   Their taunts and jeers,
I, too, have borne the heavy cross
   'Mid scornful sneers.

But oh, I've reached the heights sublime
   At dawn of day,
Known glorious triumphs when the stone
   Was rolled away.
          Marguerite George.

If He turn His face away,
   Never answering a word,
When for some ill boon we pray . . .
Blessed be His name for aye
   For the prayers He hath not heard.
          Katharine Tynan Hinkson.

Prayer at Christmas

God, give us peace,—peace to endure,
While the sweet seasons come and go,—
The seed, the bud, the fruit, the snow . . .
Peace whole, and widespread, and secure.

Your Saviour Son was Prince of Peace,
Who brought a sword, that men might
   be
Guarded in cordial amity,
And that hate's dominance must cease.

The wealth we waste in useless war,
The pain and tears and death we bring,
Might make the lands and oceans sing
Paeans to peace, the conqueror.

God, give us peace,—peace to outlast
Hate, and all things of lesser worth;
That over all the blossoming earth
His kingdom will stand firm and fast!
          Clement Wood.

Unanswered Prayers

I thank Thee, Lord, for mine unan-
    swered prayers,
    Unanswered, save Thy quiet, kindly
    "Nay,"
Yet it seemed hard among my heavy cares
That bitter day.

I wanted joy, but Thou didst know for
    me
    That sorrow was the lift I needed most,
And in its mystic depths I learned to see
    The Holy Ghost.

I wanted health; but Thou didst bid me
    sound
    The secret treasuries of pain,
And in the moans and groans my heart
    oft found
Thy Christ again.

I wanted wealth; 'twas not the better part;
    There is a wealth with poverty oft
    given,
And Thou didst teach me of the gold
    of heart,
Best gift of Heaven.

I thank Thee, Lord, for these unanswered
    prayers,
    And for Thy word, the quiet, kindly
    "Nay."
'Twas Thy withholding lightened all my
    cares
    That blessed day.

                    Ella Wheeler Wilcox.

So many of our prayers we could answer without troubling God by drawing
upon resources within us or about us.

During a drought in the New Hebrides,
John G. Paton amused the natives by
digging for water. Laughingly they said
water always came down from Heaven,
not up through the earth. But Paton
proved that the answer to their need was
beneath their very feet.

We need to learn the kindness of unanswered prayer.

St. Augustine in his confessions tells
of his mother praying all through one
night that God would not let her son sail
for Italy.

She wanted her son to be a Christian
—here at home she could surround him
by holy influences and share her deep
faith with him. But in Italy how could he
stand against temptation and overcome
world and flesh and devil.

Yet even as she prayed that her boy
might not go to Italy he set sail for those
shores. There he came under the powerful spiritual influence of Ambrose, Bishop
of Milan, and Augustine became a Christian in the very place from which his
mother's prayers would have kept him.

Who rises from prayer a better man,
his prayer is answered.

                    George Meredith.

158

SERVICE

Hold thy lighted lamp on high
Be a star in someone's sky.

Henry Burton

To be alive in such an age,
To live in it.
To give in it.
Rise, soul, from thy despairing knees,
What if thy lips have drunk the lees?
The passion of a larger claim
Will put thy puny grief to shame:
Fling forth thy sorrow to the wind,
Breathe the world-thought, do the world-
    deed,
Think highly of thy brother's need.
Give thanks with all thy flaming heart,
Crave but to have in it a part,
Give thanks, and clasp thy heritage—
To be alive in such an age!

             M. H. Lichliter.

He found my house upon the hill
I made the bed and swept the floor
And labored solitary till
He entered at the open door.

He sat with me to break my fast,
He blessed the bread and poured the
    wine,
And spoke such friendly words
I knew not were they his or mine.

But only when he rose and went
And left the twilight in the door
I found my hands were more content
To make a bed and sweep the floor.

             Gerald Gould.

Across the Street

Cross the street:
You never know
But what the beggar passing there
May be a King, with gifts to share—
Gifts to set your heart aglow.
You never know.
Cross the street:
You never know

But what the little child you see
May someday rich and famous be—
But now he's crying and his need
Is for your help, so help. Indeed,
You never know

But what someday,
Lonely down some distant way,
Your child may tread a rocky road
And some kind friend may share his load.
You never know.
Cross the street:
You never know

But what the friend who's there today,
Tomorrow may have moved away—
Today's the day to do—
It's still your privilege to
Advance!
For this may be your final chance—
Your soul, tonight, to God may go,
You never know!

Marcella Hooe.

Fading away like the stars of the morning
Losing their light in the glorious sun,
Thus shall we pass from the earth and
its toiling,
Only remembered by what we have done.

When Darkness Gathers

When darkness gathers dismally about,
Then must I have these candles I can
light:
The candle of my faith, unwavering,
bright,

To banish every evil spell of doubt;
The candle of courageousness, to rout
Weakness and shrinking, shallowness and
fright;
And, ah, the candle of my love, to smite
All hate and selfishness, and drive them
out.

Nor would I be equipped without a small
Candle of laughter to combat my tears,
And one of song for lighting any minute.
I shall not mind the darkness, so, with all
These lovely flames like beacons for the
years—
Darkness is beautiful with candles in it!

Elaine V. Emans.

The Little Words

We are weary of little words,
They seem so very small;
And yet they weave the river-song
Brook-ripple and bird-call.

No proud philosophy has found
A straighter trail to God
Than all the faithful followers
Of worn old words have trod.

For "love" and "home" are little words;
And "flower" and "sea" and "star"
And yet they help the heart to find
Where God and glory are!

Edith Daley.

160

Heritage

There's never a rose in all the world
But makes some green spray sweeter;
There's never a wind in all the sky
But makes some bird's wing fleeter;
There's never a star but brings to heav'n
Some silv'ry radiance tender;
There's never a cloud that murks the sky
But crowns the sunset splendor.
There's never a robin but thrills some
    heart,
His dawn like gladness voicing—
God gives us all some small, sweet way
To set the world rejoicing.

These are the ringing words of *Bernard
Shaw* who at 90 years of age is still carrying on so valiantly: "I want to be thor-
oughly used up when I die, for the harder
I work, the more I live. I rejoice in life
for its own sake. Life is no brief candle
to me. It is a sort of a splendid torch
which I have hold of for the moment and
I want to make it burn as brightly as possible before handing it on to future generations."

Finely said, for it is yourself that you
bequeath to immortality. Your life with
its influences for good or ill is the legacy
you leave.

Seldom can the heart be lonely,
If it seek a lonelier still;
Self-forgetting, seeking only
Emptier cups of love to fill.

          Frances Ridley Havergal.

The Garden

A man there was of simple kind
Who to the Lord gave all his mind
For naught he cared, naught craved he
Save his Lord's servant for to be
And e'en his garden plot kept fair
Because, he said, the Lord walked there.

Of this his friends made many a jest
Yet he toiled on with heart at rest.
The years went by. His head grown gray,
Still he believed Christ passed that way.
Then came a time when he was left
Of loving wife and child bereft
He will doubt now the scoffers said
When wife and child and love are dead.
But all their words he heeded not
And tended still the garden plot
At last himself lay at death's door
To love, believe and work no more.
His pitying friends stood by his bed
And this is what to them he said:

O bury me not in the church-yard mound
But lay me in my garden ground
From loving dust it needs must be
That flowers will spring more fair to see.
And Christ will know, in my last sleep
For Him I still the garden keep.
        Gretchen Warren.

Waste is not merely nor chiefly in those
things we fling away. It is rather in the
money we do not give, the kindness we
do not show, the love we do not share,
the battle we do not wage, the service
we do not render.

Nothing that is given is wasted.

" 'Business is business,' the little man
        said,
    'A battle where everything goes,
Where the only gospel is "Get ahead,"
    And never spare friends nor foes.
"Slay or be slain" is the slogan cold,
        You must struggle and slash and
        tear,
For business is business, a fight for gold
    Where all you do is fair.'
" 'Business is business,' the big man said,
    'A battle to make of earth
A place to yield us more wine and
        bread,
    More pleasure and joy and mirth;
There are still some bandits and
        buccaneers
    Who are jungle beasts of trade,
But their number dwindles with
        passing years
    And dead is the code they made.'
" 'Business is business,' the big man said,
    'But it's something that's more, far
        more;
For it makes sweet gardens of deserts
        dread
        And cities it built now roar,
Where the deer and the gray wolf ran
        From the pioneer's swift advance;
Business is magic that toils for man;
    Business is true romance.'
" 'And those who make it a ruthless fight
    Have only themselves to blame
If they feel no whit of the true delight
    In playing the bigger game,
The game that calls on heart and the
        head
        The best of man's strength and
        nerve;
Business is business,' the big man said,
    'And that business is to serve.' "
                        Berton Braley.

Wreckers

I watched them tearing a building down,
A gang of men in a busy town,
With a ho-heave-ho and a lusty yell,
They swung a beam and the side wall fell.
I asked the foreman, "Are these men
        skilled,
And the men you'd hire if you had to
        build?"
He gave a laugh and said, "No, indeed!
Just common labor is all I need.
I can easily wreck in a day or two
What builders have taken a year to do."
I thought to myself as I went my way,
Which of these roles have I tried to play?
Am I a builder who works with care,
Measuring life by the rule and square?
Am I shaping my deeds to a well-made
        plan,
Patiently doing the best I can?
Or am I a wrecker, who walks the town,
Content with the labor of tearing down?
                        G. S. Harp.

❧

Out of the Leaf-Falls

These are the things to cherish:
    A seed, and a dream, and a child;
Else must the nations perish,
    And earth fall away to the wild.

These are the things to nourish:
    The budding of trees and youth;
So shall the grown things flourish—
    Manhood and beauty and truth.

Out of the leaf-falls that perish,
    Retrieved from the waste and the wild,
These are the things to cherish:
    A seed, and a dream, and a child.

Somebody Else

The Lord had a job for me, but I had
    so much to do.
I said: "You git somebody else, or wait
    till I git through."
I don't know how the Lord came out, but
    he seemed to git along—
But I felt kind o' sneakin' like—knowed
    I'd done God wrong!
One day I needed the Lord myself—
    needed Him right away—
An' He never paid no heed at all—an' I
    could hear him say
Down in my accusin' heart: "Niggah, I'se
    got too much to do;
You git somebody else," He said, "Or
    wait till I git through."
Now when the Lord has work for me,
    I never tries to shirk;
I drops what I'se on hand right now, an'
    does the good Lord's work,
An' my own things can run along, or wait
    till I gits free.
No one else can do the job the Lord's
    marked out for me!

Paul Laurence Dunbar.

❧

Ambition

Once upon a time I planned to be
An artist of celebrity.
A song I thought to write one day,
And all the world would homage pay.
I longed to write a noted book,
But what I did was—learn to cook.
For life with simple tasks is filled,
And I have done not what I willed,
Yet when I see boys' hungry eyes
I'm glad I make good apple pies!

Elizabeth Thomas.

I Shall Not Pass Again This Way

The bread that bringeth strength I want
    to give,
The water pure that bids the thirsty live:
I want to help the fainting day by day:
I'm sure I shall not pass again this way.

I want to give the oil of joy for tears,
The faith to conquer crowding doubts
    and fears.
Beauty for ashes may I give alway:
I'm sure I shall not pass again this way.

I want to give good measure running o'er,
And into angry hearts I want to pour
The answer soft that turneth wrath away;
I'm sure I shall not pass again this way.

I want to give to others hope and faith,
I want to do all that the Master saith;
I want to live aright from day to day;
I'm sure I shall not pass again this way.

Ellen H. Underwood.

❧

From an old English parsonage
Down by the sea
There came in the twilight
A message to me;
Its quaint Saxon legend
Deeply engraven
Hath as it seems to me
Teaching from Heaven
And through the hours
The quiet words ring
Like a low inspiration
"DOE YE NEXTE THYNGE".

Minna Paul.

163

The Simple Things

I pray that I may do with joy the simple
  things
Of life, which somehow I must do from
  day to day;
Be it the baking of a loaf of bread
Or planting seed along the garden way.

Those ordinary little tasks which must
  be done,
I wish to do them with a singing heart,
That in the building of my life each day,
The work well done will be a perfect part.

Perhaps, I may not know how many will
  be fed,
Or how much joy my blooming flowers
  bring;
But this I know, the simple thing well
  done
Will lead me on to do some greater thing.

Hilda Ann Florin.

❧

No mystic voices from the heavens
  above
Now satisfy the souls which Christ
  confess
Their heavenly vision is in the works of
  love
A new age summons to new saintliness.

Before the uncloistered shrine of human
  needs
And all unconscious of the worth or
  price,
They lay their fragrant gifts of gracious
  deeds
Upon the altar of self sacrifice.

Francis G. Peabody.

For the New Year

Not what we have, but what we use;
Not what we see, but what we choose.
These are the things that mar or bless
The sum of human happiness.

The things nearby, not things afar,
Not what we seem, but what we are.
These are the things that make or break,
That give the heart its joy or ache.

Not what seems fair, but what is true;
Not what we dream, but what we do!
These are the things that shine like
  gems—
Like stars in heaven's diadems.

Clarence Urmy.

❧

To a child who had asked for something to keep, Anne Monroe quotes the
mother as answering, "We have nothing
to keep, dear, in all this wide world, only
things to use and love."

❧

Service

He has not served who gathers gold,
Nor has he served whose life is told
In selfish battles he has won,
Or deeds of skill that he has done;
But he has served who now and then
Has helped along his fellow-men.
The world needs many men today,
Red-blooded men along life's way,
With cheerful hearts and helping hands,
And with a faith that understands
The value of the simple deed
To serve another's hour of need.

His Proxies

Christ has no hands but our hands
To do His work today
He has no feet but our feet
To lead them to His way.

Christ has no tongues but our tongues
To tell men how He died
He has no help but our help
To bring them to His side.

We are the only Bibles
The careless world can read
We are the sinner's gospel
We are the scoffer's creed.

We are the Lord's last message
Given in deed and word
What if the lines are crooked?
What if the type be blurred?

What if our hands are busy
With other work than His?
What if our feet are walking
Where sin's allurement is?

What if our tongues are telling
No word of His dying love
How can we hope to lift men
From the mire to the things above?

Annie Johnson Flint.

❧❦

There is no end to the sky,
    And the stars are everywhere,
And time is eternity,
    And the here is over there;
For the common deeds of the common
        day
Are ringing bells in the far-away.

Henry Burton.

What He needs is better organs to reveal Himself through, richer, truer, holier lives to show His love through, more finely organized personalities for His grace to break through into the world.

He cannot do His work without us. He cannot preach without our lips, comfort without our help, heal without our hands, carry the truth without our feet, remove the shadow without our faith and effort. The invisible works through the visible, the unseen and eternal operates through little instruments like us!

Rufus M. Jones.

❧❦

Though my lamp be small, I am to give the flame. If I cannot give $100 but can give 10 cents a week, I rob the kingdom of my flame if I withhold the smaller gift. If I cannot teach in a church school or lead a discussion group, but can make friendly visits among the needy, and pleasant social calls in the parish, or help to make attractive the social gatherings of the church, I rob myself of joy and others of my influence, if I do not volunteer to do what is within my power. If I can not lead in public prayer, but can sit down with some baffled man or woman to point the way out of a business muddle or a social blunder, I fail myself, I fail others, and I fail God, if I do not give the flame. If I have little fitness for what is called "Church work" but can do something in the community to help others, I must remember that the flame burns just as brightly and with just as much warmth outside the pale of organized religion— and I must give the flame.

A Specialist Speaks

I have before me these precious opportunities for speaking this unto you. I can waste not. I can idle not. I will not take these hours from you for any less sublime task or privilege. I do not know enough of politics, sociology, art, literature, music or science to justify your coming to hear me speak on these topics. I know here but one thing, and if I am true to it, you will never weary of my use of your time and the expending of my limited strength. My theme has the breadth of God's love and the many-sidedness of His abundant goodness. It is perenially fresh and beautiful. I will not attempt to vie with your other sources of intellectual and spiritual vitality, in furnishing you delightful information or high entertainment. If they are valuable to you, it is because each to whom you give your attention is a specialist. So, also, am I. No one else has been traveling my path with Christ. No one else has met Him where I have met Him. No man can have another's experience. Others have more of genius, learning, eloquence, health, than I; no man has had my life and its history with Christ. Many have had greater vision porportionated to greater piety, but no one else's vision of Him do I know. I do know my own. I will preach only what I believe —the time is short. I will preach only what I know is supremely important in the thought of Jesus—the time is short. I will preach only what I have fallen down upon and found safe and able to bear me up —the time is short. I will preach only what I found true when lately I went up to the gate of Other-where—the time is short. I will preach these things with absoluteness of conviction that God will bless us, and I will look for the fruit of this ministry here, where the time is short, and there, also, where time shall vanish in the morning-glow of Eternity.

Frank W. Gunsaulus

❧

Sought by the greatest and the least as
    friend
He gave himself, unsparing, to the end;
He even kept death waiting at the door
Till he could do a friend one kindness
    more.

John H. Finley.

❧

The dear, long, quiet summer day
Draws to its close.
To the deep woods I steal away
To hear what the sweet thrush will say
In her repose.
Beside the brook the meadow-rue
Stands tall and white.
The water softly slips along,
A murmur to the thrush's song,
To greet the night.

Over and over, like a bell,
Her song rings clear;
The trees stand still in joy and prayer,
Only the angels stir the air,
High heaven bends near.
I bow my head and lift my heart
In Thy great peace.
Thy Angelus, my God, I heed.
By the still waters wilt Thou lead
Till days shall cease.

Alice Freeman Palmer.

166

Contentment

If I can lend a helping hand
To you, my friend, and understand
Your need, and give to you
A surety of friendship true,
   I'll be content.

If I can share with you a grief,
And help you see at most it's brief;
If I can hold your hand in mine
Through moments of a testing time,
   I'll be content.

If I can coax your weary eyes
To look above, to fairer skies;
If I can cause your ears to hear
The music of the heavenly sphere,
   I'll be content.

If I can guide you to the place
Of prayer, where by His matchless grace
Your soul will be restored and blessed,
Where God can do for you the rest—
   I'll be content.

           Roselyn C. Steere.

❦

Pass It On

Many years ago I heard the Rev. Mark Guy Pearse, one of England's most popular preachers, tell this gripping story:

Like many English boys, he was sent far from home to attend school. Vacation time had arrived and he was returning happily homeward. At a certain station he had to change trains, and in the transition lost his ticket. He was tearfully fumbling through his pockets for the third time when a man noticed his distress and inquired the cause.

Mark told him of his loss, and the man, looking round, saw on the boy's trunk the name, Mark Guy Pearse. "Can it be that you are the son of Mr. Mark Guy Pearse of ——?" The boy replied eagerly in the affirmative. "Well, this is wonderful," was the response. "Years ago your father did me a certain favor, and I remember that in rendering me the kindness he asked that when the chance came I should pass it on. So I shall gladly return the favor as you will, please, when opportunity offers."

He bought the boy a ticket and the homeward journey was joyfully completed.

Forty years passed by, and that boy, now a minister in London, was in the Paddington Station, waiting for a train. Presently he saw a boy evidently in trouble and at once went to the lad to learn what was the matter.

It seems that in this case the boy was going to spend a few weeks with relatives living in some distant place and had lost his ticket money. Immediately, of course, Mr. Pearse went back in memory to the similar circumstances of his boyhood days.

He told the lad of his experience as a youngster, stressing the point that this was his chance of passing on the kindness shown him forty years ago.

He bought a ticket and some candy for the boy, and then urged him to pass the favor on if ever occasion should arrive. As the train moved out of the station he saw the boy leaning out of the window, waving his cap and shouting, "All right, sir, I'll pass it on, I'll pass it on."

That is our business. That's what we're for.

           G. W. H.

Women Mending

All women at their mending wear a look
As legible as any open book;
And by the way in which they bend above
Each garment, shows their wisdom and
    their love.

A girl just mends her dress to make it do—
Impatiently—till she has something new.
A young wife darns an unaccustomed
    sock,
With proud, expectant eyes which seek
    the clock.

A mother sews a tiny button in place
On baby's gown, a glory on her face;
Or patches up a rent in son's best breeches
As if she'd reinforce the youth by stitches.

But grandma's fingers touch a boy's torn
    cap
As if it were his head upon her lap;
Her tremulous hands are light above the
    seam
Of grandpa's coat, as though she darned
    a dream—
More frail and beautiful—to make it last
Until his need, and hers, of dreams be
    past.

Old women know that women must
    repair
Life's worn habiliments, to keep life fair.
They know that mending is a sacred rite,
To be performed with prayer, while God
    gives light.
           Nelle Graves McGill.

My Debt

If I have strength, I owe the service of
    the strong;
If melody I have, I owe the world a song;
If I can stand when all about my post
    are falling,
If I can run with speed when needy hearts
    are calling,
And, if my torch can light the dark of
    any night—
Then, I must pay the debt I owe with
    living light.
If heaven's grace has dowered me with
    some rare gift,
If I can lift some load no other's strength
    can lift;
If I can heal some wound no other's
    hand can heal,
If some great truth the speaking skies
    reveal—
Then, I must go a broken, wounded
    thing,
If, to a wounded world my gifts no
    healing bring.
For any gift God gives to me, I cannot
    pay;
Gifts are most mine when I give them
    most away;
God's gifts are like His flowers, which
    show their right to stay
By giving all their bloom and fragrance
    away.
Riches are not gold, nor lands, estates,
    nor marts—
The only wealth there is, is found in
    human hearts.   *Charles Cooke Woods.*

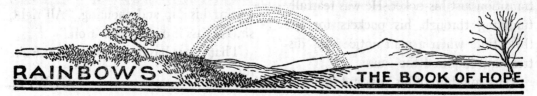

RAINBOWS   THE BOOK OF HOPE

Smiles HWS

The Simple Test
If a smile improves a man's face,
He is a good man;
If a smile disfigures his face,
He is a bad man.

William Lyon Phelps

Smiles

Never yet have we justly appraised the value of smiles among the world's assets. "Only A Smile" pleads one hymn of dubious melody. As if smiles were cheap. Sometimes to smile is a sterner test of character than to die.

Smiles through tears—was ever rainbow so transfiguring to a cloud? Smiles amid pain, smiles in spite of doubts and fears . . . . smiles of indulgence, smiles of pity, smiles of welcome for wayward feet—God give us a new rating for smiles.

The tradesman who smiles at me over the counter may cheat me a little and I shall not be too severe. The friend who smiles his love into my eyes helps me through the day. And the little child who looks Heaven at me with a radiant, trustful smile may own me.

Doubtless there are debts that can be paid with frowning brows and black displeasure. But there's a world-debt that never begins to be liquidated until we learn the divine craft of smiles.

George Clark Peck.

169

Mastery

Fate? I met her long ago
Met and measured will and strength
Whipped of her, I came to know
How to whip herself at length.

First, I fought her, brute to brute;
Every blow she smote me sore,
Dazed and mad with rage, and mute
Duly struck I back the more.

Striking blindly, striking hard
And forever striking wide—
With a broken arm for guard,
With a broken head beside.

So she mauled me as she would
So she bullied me the while;
Till I dropped my hands and stood—
Stood and whipped her with a smile!
                    Charles F. Lummis.

❧❧

Occupation, Housewife

After planning, marketing, cooking, after
Scouring the house from cellar to rafter,
After the dinner dishes are done
And the children disposed of, one by one,

After a day as domestic pearls,
We're supposed to turn into glamour
        girls,
Lovely and well worth a husband's
        wooing.
And it can't be done—and that's what
        we're doing!
                    May Richstone.

❧❧

Some women make a fool out of a man
and some can make a man out of a fool.

The Cheerful Caller

He dropped into my office with a grin
upon his face. He talked about the
weather and the college football race. He
asked about the family, and told the latest
joke. But he never mentioned anyone
who'd suddenly gone broke.

He talked of books and pictures, and
the play he'd been to see. A clever quip
his boy had made he passed along to me.
He praised the suit of clothes I wore; he
asked me what it cost. But he never said
a word about the money he had lost.

He was with me twenty minutes,
chuckling gaily, while he stayed, o'er the
memory of some silly blunder he had
made. He reminded me that tulips must
be planted in the fall; calamity and
tragedy he mentioned not at all.

I thought it rather curious, when he
had come and gone; he must have had
some tale of woe— but didn't pass it on.
For nowadays, it seems to me, that every
man I meet has something new in misery
and moaning to repeat.

So I write these lines to him who had
his share of woe, but still could talk of
other things, and let his troubles go. I
was happier with his visit. In a world
that's sick with doubt, 'twas good to meet
a man who wasn't spreading gloom about.

❧❧

Fortune

Fortune came and loudly knocked
    At my door with cheery hail,
But alas for Fortune's labors,
I was over at my neighbor's
    Pouring out a hard luck tale.

It's in Your Face

You don't have to tell how you live each
    day,
You don't have to say if you work or you
    play;
A tried, true barometer serves in the
    place—
However you live, it will show in your
    face.

The false, the deceit, that you bear in
    your heart
Will not stay inside where it first got the
    start;
For sinew and blood are thin veil of lace—
What you wear in your heart you wear
    in your face.

If you have gambled and won in the
    great game of life,
If you feel you have conquered the
    sorrow and strife,
If you've played the game fair and you
    stand on first base—
You don't have to say so, it shows on
    your face.

If your life is unselfish, and for others
    you live,
For not what you get, but how much
    you can give.
If you live in good will toward the whole
    human race,
You don't have to tell it—it shows in
    your face.

❧

They might not need me; but they might.
I'll let my head be just in sight;
A smile as small as mine might be
Precisely their necessity.
                Emily Dickinson.

Smiles

A smile costs nothing but creates much.
It happens in a flash and the memory of
it lasts forever. It cannot be bought,
begged, borrowed nor stolen, but it is
something that is no earthly good to anyone until it is given away. So if in your
hurry and rush you meet some one who
is too weary to give you a smile, leave one
of yours, for no one needs a smile quite
as much as the one who has none left
to give.

❧

A very unusual but, one may believe,
a very valid point is made by *Louise
Driscoll* who stresses in a poem that even
in talking to God one should say it with
a smile:—
The sorry prayers go up to God,
Day after weary day;
They whimper through the eternal blue,
And down the milky way.
And then a little, laughing prayer
Came running to the sky
Along the golden gutters, where
The sorry prayers go by.
I have no fear of anything
But in that holy place,
It found the very throne of God
And smiled up in His face.

❧

My first advice to young preachers
would be: Don't ask people how they
liked your sermon. They might tell you
the truth.

A student supply in my Seminary days
asked that question of a gruff old farmer
and the answer was, "I only heard a half
of it and only half liked the half I heard."

Only a Little Blossom

It was only a little blossom,
Just the faintest blush of bloom,
But it brought a glimpse of sunshine
To a dismal, darkened room.
It was only a glad "Good Morning,"
As he passed along the way,
But it spread the morning's glory
Over the livelong day.

Charlotte A. Perry.

The Glad Song

Sing a song, sing a song,
Ring the glad-bells all along;
Smile at him who frowns at you,
He will smile and then they're two.

Laugh a bit, laugh a bit,
Folks will soon be catching it,
Can't resist a happy face;
World will be a merry place.

Laugh a Bit and Sing a Song,
Where they are there's nothing wrong;
Joy will dance the whole world through,
But it must begin with you.

Joseph Morris.

Now don't forget, when things go wrong,
To try the magic of a song.
A cheerful heart, and smiling face
Pour sunshine in the darkest place.

Behind the Smile

I don't know how he is on creeds—I never heard him say; but he's got a smile that fits his face, and wears it every day. If things go wrong he won't complain—just tries to see the joke. He's always finding little ways of helping other folk.

He sees the good in every one, their faults he never mentions; he has a lot of confidence in people's good intentions. You soon forget what ails you, when you happen 'round this man; he can cure the melancholies quicker than the doctor can.

No matter if the sky is gray, you get his point of view, and the clouds begin to scatter, and the sun comes shining through. You'll know him when you meet him, and you'll find it worth your while to cultivate the friendship of the man behind the smile.

Sunshine

Just a song of sunshine!
  Let it flood the heart,
And of life's completeness
  Let it form a part.
Sing it though it cost you
  Hours of grief and pain,
You will reap a harvest
  Deep of golden grain,
Oh, the joy and comfort
  You through life may know,
With a song of sunshine
  Everywhere you go!

RAINBOWS · THE BOOK OF HOPE

*From a little spark may
burst a mighty flame.*
Dante.

Her Offering

A pair of pigeons Mary brought
  In humble offering;
Too deep her poverty, she thought,
  The wonted lamb to bring:
The lamb ordained to typify
One who should come to bleed and die.

Yet richer woman ne'er before
  The temple-pavement trod.
For in her gentle arms she bore
  Her Son, the Lamb of God.
The Lamb who takes our sins away
She offered in His courts that day.

             Mary Hoge Wardlaw.

Red Geraniums

I wonder why they always grow
In window-boxes green and prim.
They have a need of winds, to blow
Their scarlet skirts less neat and trim.
How can they flaunt their gypsy grace
In such a crowded, narrow space?

It must be rather hard for flowers
That are a blend of blood and flame,
To spend the warm, seductive hours
Being respectable and tame.
Born to dance wildly on a hill,
How dull must seem a window sill.

           Elizabeth Dillingham.

Values

When you are believing
  That the world is mad,
That both men and women
  Are most always bad,
If you pause a moment
  To give things their due,
You will find life lovely—
  Except for you.

        Edgar Daniel Kramer.

There were nuggets of gold in Moses that would never have been found had he remained in Pharaoh's palace. It took forty years of roughing it to bring them to the surface.

        E. P. Brown.

The two powers which, in my opinion, constitute a wise man are those of bearing and forbearing.

        Epictetus.

The gentleman is solid mahogany; the fashionable man is only veneer.

        Holland.

By these things examine thyself: By whose rules am I acting? In whose name? In whose strength? For whose glory? What faith, humility, self-denial, and love of God and to man have there been in all my actions?

        Mason.

Manners—the final and perfect flower of noble character.

        William Winter.

"I have never been hurt by anything I did not say."

        Calvin Coolidge.

"The highest mountain peak of human achievement is the hill called Golgotha."

A man can fail many times, but he isn't a failure until he begins to blame somebody else for it.

"Civilization had better find a way of doing away with war, or war will do away with civilization."

        Preston Bradley.

Made Stars

If there isn't a star within your sky,
  Pretend it's there!
Why, a make-believe one, swung wide
    and high,
  Is just as fair!
If you put it where you'll see it every
    night,
Just where the sky's particularly bright,
Your star is sure to guide your steps aright.

If there isn't any sunshine in your day,
  Why, put some in!
If you've never made your sun that way,
  Oh, do begin!
This sunshine-making's hard, but you
    won't mind:
Keep on, and when it's done you're apt
    to find
The home-made brand's the very nicest
    kind.

A propensity to hope and joy is real riches; one to fear and sorrow, real poverty.

Hume.

Virtue, if not in action, is a vice; and when we move not forward we go backward.

Loth.

Rest satisfied with doing well, and leave others to talk of you as they please.

Pythagoras.

Reading makes a full man, conversation a ready man, and writing an exact man.

Bacon.

The noblest revenge is to forgive.

Thomas Fuller.

Before you can get religion into any one else you have got to have a contagious case of it yourself.

Henry Sloane Coffin.

Is there anything so disenchanting as attainment? The want of a thing is perplexing enough, the possession of it is intolerable.

Sir John Vanbrugh.

God will probably ask more embarrassing questions in the field of finance on the day of judgement than in the field of theology.

Domestic peace can never be preserved in family jars.

Mrs. Partington.

A long face is the worst of bad manners.

Use life to get something that outlasts it.

Keep the path to the heart of your friend well weeded.

I asked John D. Rockefeller to what he most attributed his success, he replied "To others."

Forbes.

Some men have a den in their home, while others just growl all over the house.

Anon.

Hunt hard for the good points in the other fellow. Remember he has to do the same for you.

Anon.

The man whose house is on sand may talk boldly in fair weather, but how quickly he turns pale when thunder is heard!

E. P. Brown

Every noble life leaves the fiber of it interwoven forever in the work of thee world.

Ruskin.

Advice to Wives

A clever married woman knows when to be blind and when to be deaf. She will remember that the worst kind of seeing is to oversee and the worst kind of hearing is to overhear.

Be tenderly tactful toward an admittedly worried husband. A man is less likely to worry needlessly than a woman, and probably, if he shows manifest signs of anxiety, there is something worth being anxious about. At such a time the function of a wise wife is not to advise but to comfort. The odds are that he can get better advice elsewhere but nowhere else can he get comfort.

The superlatively tactful married woman will always remember when any difference of opinion arises that perhaps she may be wrong anyhow.

And that probably will be the only way by which she can induce her husband to concede that she is right.

As to personal tastes, which perhaps form the most serious incompatibility between the sexes, de gustibus non est disputandum.

Which being interpreted for the benefit of those who have forgotten Latin, means that there can be no disputing about tastes. It is a shrewd married team that can learn what subjects are not safely debatable.

A minor marital thunderstorm to clear the air may serve a purpose. In the wise policy of God man is born to trouble as the sparks fly upward. But be sure the flying sparks do not kindle into flame. For you cannot insure life's biggest things against fire.

Don't broadcast your differences. If there is a misunderstanding keep it a family secret. Not a breath of it even to your dearest friend. That is the surest way to put the case beyond remedy.

Don't get all worked up when some kindly friend tells you about your husband's former sweetheart. No wife ought to feel jealous of her husband's first love or loves. She has scored successfully over them all. And no husband ought to condemn himself if sometimes there comes through the golden haze of memory some once loved form and face.

But he could wisely remind himself that the poetry and romance might well vanish if he could see her now. The added thirty years and perhaps thirty pounds, would make him more than satisfied with things as they are.

Don't disturb your husband when he has retired to his den for a little while, unless something imperative demands. His disposition and soul need a little privacy.

G. W. H.

≫≪

Be good, get good, and do good. Do all the good you can; to all the people you can; in all the ways you can; as often as you can; and as long as you can.

Spurgeon.

The Mind

The mind which never held a seed
Will only grow a useless weed.
Who cultivates a fertile mind
Will have a crop of wealth to find;
And every seed grown tall and trim
Is but to view the soul of him.

I knew a man whose mind was keen.
He planted it, but in between
The furrows, where he had allowed,
He never hoed . . . he never ploughed;
And weeds grew up, and so assailed
The good of him until he failed.

A mind is nothing but a field
Which, if it ever is to yield,
Needs cultivation . . . careful, sure . . .
If seeds, and not the weeds, endure!

Christine Grant Curless.

❦

Dr. Fosdick said, "The most ruinous thing that ever comes on earth is a personality with charm who makes badness attractive." Then we nominate as the second most ruinous influence, the good person whose coldness makes goodness unattractive.

❦

Reminder

I have upon my finger
A little piece of string,
To help me with some items
That need remembering.

Sometimes I wish I had one
Tied in a magic knot,
To help me with the matters
That need to be forgot.

Clarence Edwin Flynn

There are certain test questions to ask concerning my participation in any "Doubtful Amusement." These are some:

Will it plunge me in a current that will carry me onward or backward?

Will it place me in the danger zone, close to the borders of unhallowed ground?

What effect would my participation have on others? Would it be best for my friends, my boy, my girl, to do the same?

What will be the effect of indulgement on my own finer nature, my mind's ideals, my heart's highest desires, my intimate fellowship with God?

❦

Some people seem to have little under perfect control except their generosity.

❦

Trouble

Better never trouble trouble until trouble troubles you, for you're sure to make your trouble double-trouble, if you do. And the trouble, like a bubble, you are troubling about, may be nothing but a cypher—with the rim rubbed out.

Better never cross your bridges till your bridge comes in view, for you're sure to lose your labor crossing bridges, if you do. And the bridges, or the ridges, you are worrying about, may be nothing but a cypher—with the rim rubbed out.

Better never spread a scandal till you know the story's true, for you're sure to make your neighbors needless trouble, if you do. And the matter of the chatter you are scattering about, may be nothing but a cypher—with the rim rubbed out.

David Keppel.

Earth's Common Things

Seek not afar for beauty Lo! it glows
In dew-wet grasses all about thy feet
In birds, in sunshine, childish faces sweet,
In stars and mountain summits topped
    with snows.
Go not abroad for happiness. For see,
It is a flower, that blossoms at thy door!
Bring love and justice home, and then
    no more
Thou'lt wonder in what dwelling joy
    may be.
Dream not of noble service elsewhere
    wrought
The simple duty that awaits thy hand
Is God's voice uttering a divine command
Life's common deeds build all that saints
    have thought.
In wonder-workings, or some bush-a-
    flame
Men look for God and fancy Him
    concealed;
But in earth's common things He stands
    revealed
While grass and flowers and stars spell
    out His name.

Minot J. Savage.

And he who gives a child a treat
Makes joy-bells ring in Heaven's street.
And he who gives a child a home
Builds palaces in Kingdom Come,
And she who gives a baby birth
Brings Saviour Christ again to earth.

John Masefield.

There's never a trouble that comes to stay
There's never a grievance but fades away;
Forget the heart-ache and bravely lend
A helping hand to some sadder friend.

The Circuit Rider

God tramps on through the scourging
    rains,
    God vaults into the saddle,
Rides alone past the dusty plains,
    God's back bends to the paddle—
Cedar branches and sunlight through!
    And on, still on, speeds the lone canoe!

God rides out on His ancient quest;
    Healing, saving, commanding.
Here in the savage, unknown West,
    Settlements, cabin, landing—
Well they know the steady beat,
    In the stillness of God's horses' feet.

God leads to grace the pioneers,
Who walk each hour with danger;
Knows these grim men for His peers;
    Gives His bread to the stranger—
Doing all that a neighbor can,
    God rides still, a weary man.

God rides out! And founds three states:
    Their scourger, their defender;
Guides their loves and tones their hates,
    Leads them into splendor!
God—in the Circuit Rider's breast—
    Once more, God built a world—Out
    West.

Mary Carolyn Davies.

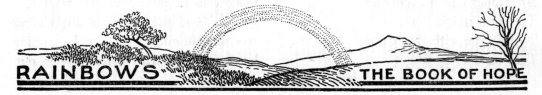

RAINBOWS   THE BOOK OF HOPE

He who cannot forgive others
Breaks the bridge over which
He must himself pass.

George Herbert

Open the door, let in the air;
The winds are sweet and the flowers are
    fair;
Joy is abroad in the world today,
If our door is wide, it may come this
    way—
        Open the door!

Open the door, let in the sun;
He hath a smile for every one;
He hath made of the raindrops gold and
    gems,
He may change our tears to diadems—
        Open the door!

Open the door of the soul; let in
Strong, pure thoughts which will banish
    sin;
They will grow and bloom with a grace
    divine,
And their fruit shall be sweeter than that
    of the vine—
        Open the door.

Open the door of the heart; let in
Sympathy sweet for stranger and kin;
It will make the halls of the heart so fair
That angels may enter unaware—
        Open the door!

179

St. Peter's Difficulty

One day Peter was greatly disturbed. He wanted to leave the Gate of Heaven and his duties there for a few minutes, so he called his brother Andrew to take his place . . .

Peter hastened away toward the throne, his business brooking no delay.

On the way he met Jesus, and after some hesitation could not help unburdening his heart to Him;

"A dreadful thing has happened, Master," he began, "and I want you to believe that I am not to blame. I have been given charge of the Gate and have never left it for one moment until now, and I pledge you my word I have never let a single person inside who has not a perfectly clean sheet. No one can be more grateful for all the privileges of Heaven than I am. You believe me, don't you?"

Jesus bowed His head with smiling eyes.

"I am sure, Peter, you have been an admirable guardian, but what is troubling you now?"

"The other day," began Peter, looking up at Him with sidelong intent eyes, "the other day I met a little blind girl whom I certainly never let into Heaven. Oh, Master, Master, someone is admitting them; I can do nothing and I shall be blamed for someone else's fault."

Jesus put his hand on Peter's shoulder: "We do not blame easily, do we, Peter? But who do you think is letting them in?"

"I cannot sleep or eat for thinking of it," replied Peter evasively; "please help me."

"How shall I help you?" asked Jesus.

"Come tonight at eleven o'clock when all is quiet and I will show you everything."

Jesus looked at him in some surprise, but answered simply: "I will be with you Peter."

That night Peter took Jesus and guided Him by the hand all along the rampart to the first great bastion; then he whispered to him to wait in the shadow and he would see. And lo! a few minutes later they were aware of a woman's figure close to the battlements. They both saw her unwind her girdle and let it down over the wall; in a few moments a little hunchback creature climbed up, took one or two halting steps and then cast himself down on his face before the woman and began kissing the hem of her garment.

At once Jesus drew Peter away, and as they went toward the gate, out of earshot, He said: "My Mother!"

"Yes, it is Mary," Peter began, "and what can I do? Those she lets in are all deformed like that wretched hunchback; she helps only the maimed and the halt and the blind, and some afflicted with bleeding, putrid sores—dreadful creatures; they would shame even an earthly city. But what am I to do, Master?"

"Peter, Peter!" said Jesus, and the luminous great eyes dwelt on him, "you and I had not even deformity to plead for us—"

Frank Harris.

Success

Before God's footstool to confess
A poor soul knelt and bowed his head;
"I failed" he cried, the Master said,
"Thou did'st thy best—that is success."

180

Before life's greatest crisis; before some unforeseen catastrophe makes the soul stagger and reel; before the last darkness falls, through which our failing eyes can no longer discern the hills and the woods, the skies and seas, let us realize that in ten minutes we may find that which some men spend all their lives in seeking—and oftentimes in vain, because they know not where to seek—the personal companionship of Jesus. He alone is sufficient for our need, and the only anchor of our soul.

In Him we find more than nature can ever give. There are Eyes that smile into our eyes. There are Hands stretched out to grasp our own. There is a Heart that understands.   *Leslie D. Weatherhead.*

❧❧

Sympathy

Is the way hard and thorny, oh, my
    brother?
Do tempests beat, and adverse wild winds
    blow?
And are you spent, and broken at each
    nightfall,
Yet with each morn you rise and onward
    go?
Brother, I know, I know!
I, too, have journeyed so.

Is your heart mad with longing, oh, my
    sister?
Are all great passions in your breast
    aglow?
Does the white wonder of your own soul
    blind you,
And are you torn with rapture and with
    woe?
Sister, I know, I know!
I, too, have suffered so.

Is the road filled with snare and
    quicksand, pilgrim?
Do pitfalls lie where roses seem to grow?
And have you sometimes stumbled in the
    darkness,
And are you bruised and scarred by many
    a blow?
Pilgrim, I know, I know!
I, too, have stumbled so.

Do you send out rebellious cry and
    question,
As mocking hours pass silently and slow,
Does your insistent "wherefore" bring
    no answer,
While stars wax pale with watching, and
    droop low?
I, too have questioned so,
But now I know, I know!
To toil, to strive, to err, to cry, to grow,
To love through all—this is the way to
    know.

          Ella Wheeler Wilcox.

❧❧

If I can feel sympathy—feel it within and without—then the dew falls and the desert begins to blossom. By sympathy I do not mean merely a fellowship in sorrow, but also, and no less truly, a fellowship in joy—a feeling for which we ought to have an English word. To be glad when your brother men are prosperous and happy, to rejoice in their success, to cheer for their victories; to be compassionate and pitiful when your brother men are distressed and miserable, to grieve over their failures, to help them in their troubles,—this is the fraternal spirit which blesses him who exercises it, and those toward whom it is exercised.

          Henry Van Dyke

A linnet who had lost her way
Sang on a blackened bough in Hell
Till all the ghosts remembered well
The trees, the wind, the golden day.
At last they knew that they had died
When they heard music in that land
And some one there stole forth a hand
To draw a brother to his side.

James Elroy Flecker.

If But One Hour

If but one hour were mine, of all your
days,
To come to you with all I owe of praise,
I would not choose from all, your shining
hour,
When joy at last seemed resting in your
power;
But I would take your darkest hour for
mine,
Praying that on your road some joy might
shine—
Because I took your hand in mine and
prayed.

This be my portion, this my final plea:
That others take your joys, but leave to
me
The weight to bear when you must walk
alone;
Whose load is mine, more than mine is
my own!
Oh, let me be still waters running deep,
In which you dip your cup, and therefrom
steep
The essence of a joy, grief but delayed.
If but one hour of all, then let it be
That lonely hour, when you've most need
of me!

Doris Virginia Couts.

Ah, friends, dear friends, as years go on
and heads get gray, how fast the
guests do go!
Touch hands, touch hands, with those
that stay.
Strong hands to weak, old hands to young,
around the Christmas board, touch
hands.
The false forget, the foe forgive, for every
guest will go and every fire burn low
and cabin empty stand.
Forget, forgive, for who may say that
Christmas day may ever come to
host or guest again.
Touch hands!

William H. Murray.

The superior man is the providence of
the inferior. He is eyes for the blind,
strength for the weak, and a shield for
the defenceless. He stands erect by bending above the fallen. He rises by lifting
others.

Robert G. Ingersoll.

Could we judge all deeds by motives,
see the good and bad within, often we
would love the sinner, even though we
loathe the sin.

Could we know the hidden sorrow,
could we guess the ceaseless pain, would
the grim external roughness seem I wonder just the same.

Would we help where now we hinder?
Would we pity where we blame?

Ah, we judge each other harshly seeing
not the grains of good; we should love
each other better if we only understood.

Sorrow

Sorrow brings people very close together. And sorrow not only creates the need of sympathy, but it makes the gracious ministry of sympathy possible. They who have never been touched by trouble have no power of sympathy. Only one who has been in the darkness of sorrow can enter into the darkness of another's sorrow.

We who have stood in need of comfort can comfort others as we have been comforted. Trouble thus puts new possibility and power into human life. You have a word to say which no untroubled soul can speak.

Sorrow is sometimes an excuse for selfishness. People go apart and separate themselves from the world's life, and think sad thoughts. And they wonder why they find no comfort. It is because they are going in the wrong direction; they are walking toward the darkness. The other way, is light. Sorrow must be made an opportunity for service. They who comfort others shall themselves be comforted. Unto those who minister to others shall the Father Himself minister. To such as these the old words shall have new and blessed meaning, and they will be able to say, as the psalmist said, "It is good for me that I have been in trouble." *George Hodges.*

❧❧

The Open Hand

See, dear, my hand is open—you are free!
I would not hold you by a single thread.
All love I give you, but with liberty,
For love held by restraint is cold and
　　dead.
Upon my palm a bird comes, wings
　　alight;
Love bids me clasp it closely to my breast;
But as it poises for its instant flight
My steady hand a haven makes, of rest.
So bird and man are mine, I leave them
　　free.
They fly into the world, but with a smile
I say, "Godspeed!" For surely back to me
Will come my man, my bird, to rest
　　awhile.
So, Love, I give you perfect liberty—
Look, dear, my hand is open! You are
　　free!

❧❧

To Eleanor

My very dear,
This poor hand lies so lightly in your own
As we sit here,
We two
Alone
I pray
That you may understand
Some day
Somewhere,
By a sweet miracle
The things that I would say,
And do not dare,
Or cannot.

My hand lies in your hand
And my mute heart is eloquent with tears,
And love that wells
Into my eyes:
And otherwise
No word:
My lips are inarticulate and dumb:
But a soft tightening of your fingers tells
That you have heard
The words that would not come.
Wilfred J. Funk.

183

O Captain! My Captain!

O Captain my Captain! our fearful trip
is done,
The ship has weather'd every rack, the
prize we sought is won,
The port is near, the bells I hear, the
people all exulting,
While follow eyes the steady keel, the
vessel grim and daring;
But O heart! heart! heart!
O the bleeding drops of red,
Where on the deck my Captain
lies,
Fallen cold and dead.

O Captain! my Captain! rise up and hear
the bells;
Rise up—for you the flag is flung—for you
the bugle trills,
For you bouquets and ribbon'd wreaths
—for you the shores a-crowding
For you they call, the swaying mass, their
eager faces turning:
Here Captain! dear father!
This arm beneath your head!
It is some dream that on the deck
You've fallen cold and dead.

My Captain does not answer, his lips are
pale and still,
My father does not feel my arm, he has
no pulse nor will,
The ship is anchor'd safe and sound, its
voyage closed and done,
From fearful trip the victor ship comes
in with object won;
Exult O shores, and ring O bells !
But I with mournful tread,
Walk the deck my Captain lies
Fallen cold and dead.

Walt Whitman.

Lincoln

The stuff God uses to make men
Is very rare indeed,
And God can use it only when
There is supremest need.
But when with wise and careful strokes
God moulds a man in shape,
The whole creation full of folks
Stands wandering and agape.

God saved and saved His precious stuff
While working out his plan,
Until at last he had enough
To make another man.
And then with sure and steady aim
The thunderbolt was hurled;
A great light out of darkness came—
And Lincoln filled the world.

James Larkin Pearson.

No poem more finely illustrates the truth that only when we climb do we march in brave company, than the following:—

As I went up by Heartbreak Road
Before the dawn of day,
The cold mist was all about,
And the wet world was gray;
It seemed that never another soul
Had walked that weary way.

But when I came to Heartbreak Hill,
Silver touched the sea;
I knew that many and many a soul
Was climbing close to me;
I knew I walked that weary way
In a great company.

Henry Gray Cone.

Stranger at the Door

When to your door I came the other day,
In ragged clothes and shaggy, unkempt
  hair,
I thought perchance you, too, would turn
  away—
And leave me standing, sorrowfully, there.
But no! you smiled and said to me,
  "Come in,
We have but little, yet delight to share."

And though I'm not entirely free from
  sin,
For you, from out my heart, I breathed a
  prayer.
You gave the best you had—no meagre
  crust,
You made me feel you cared, and I am
  glad.
So many give because they think they
  must—
But you so graciously shared all you had!
Ah, can it be that 'neath my ragged
  clothes,
You saw another, who so long ago,
Had but one seamless robe, and many
  woes—
Who died upon a cross—He loved you so?
                    Russell E. Kauffman.

A Strange Family

The father has not missed church in
twenty-three years. The mother has a
perfect record for eleven years. A son
has not missed for twelve years. A
daughter has been at the service every
Sunday for eight years.

What's the matter with this family?
Don't they ever have company to keep
them from church? Don't they ever feel
tired on Sunday morning? Don't they
ever have headaches, or colds, or parties,
or picnics, to keep them from church?
Don't they have a radio to get good sermons from other preachers? Don't they
ever think they can just as well read the
Bible at home? Don't they ever get mad
with their minister?

What is the matter with this family
anyway, that they go to church so regu-
larly and are so happy and cheerful?

❧

Calvary

Is the wonder all gone from the story so
  old
Of the heart that broke on the hill?
You once shed hot tears when that story
  was told
Can you weep over Calvary still?

Is it nothing to you that your Saviour
  should bleed
That they pierced His hands and His
  brow?
He was wounded and bruised and slain
  for your need
Can you weep over Calvary now?

Do you care that your Comrade in loneli-
  ness died
Because He cared greatly for thee
Does it pierce to your heart, that spear-
  thrust in His side
Can you weep over cruel Calvary?

To the Cross and its plea can you close
  heart and ears
It's message of mercy forget?
Nay, God grant you may say with eyes
  streaming tears
I can weep over Calvary yet.
                         G. W. H.

Twelve Good Men and True

Lord, God in Heaven, attend;
We are here to judge a man.
Be Thou in this tragic hour his friend,
None on a jury can.
Thou in the light, we in the dark,
When the scales of justice tilt,
How shall we find the outward mark
Of innocence or guilt?

Lord, God, we are gathered here
To analyze a crime.
What if we blunder through rage or fear,
Or lack of sufficient time?
How can we tell what label's best
To put to a prisoner's name?

How may we know in the selfsame test
We wouldn't have done the same?
Thou who art merciful and just,
We who are passion-swayed
How shall we judge a man
Like to our image made?

Helene Mullins.

If I Should Die To-night

If I should die tonight
My friends would look upon my quiet
face,
Before they laid it in its resting place,
And deem that death had left it almost
fair,
And laying snow-white flowers against my
hair,
Would smooth it down with tearful
tenderness,
And fold my hands with lingering caress,
Poor hands, so empty and so cold tonight!

If I should die tonight
My friends would call to mind with loving
thought
Some kindly deed the icy hand had
wrought;
Some gentle word the frozen lips had said;
Errands on which the willing feet had
sped.
The memory of my selfishness and pride,
My hasty words, would all be put aside,
And so I should be loved and mourned
tonight.

If I should die tonight,
Even hearts estranged would turn once
more to me,
Recalling other days remorsefully.
The eyes that chill me with averted glance
Would look upon me as of yore,
perchance
Would soften in the old familiar way;
For who would war with dumb
unconscious clay?
So I might rest, forgiven of all tonight.

O friends, I pray tonight
Keep not your kisses for my dead, cold
brow;
The way is lonely, let me feel them now.
Think gently of me; I am travel worn;
My faltering feet are pierced with many
a thorn.
Forgive, O hearts estranged, forgive I
plead!
When dreamless rest is mine, I shall not
need
The tenderness for which I long tonight.

Robert C. V. Meyers.

RAINBOWS — THE BOOK OF HOPE

TOMORROW
HWS

*I do not fear tomorrow. For I remember
yesterday and I love today.*

William Allen White

Unconquered

I have hoped, I have planned, I have
  striven,
  To the will I have added the deed;
The best that was in me I've given,
  I have prayed, but the gods would not
    heed.

I have dared and reached only disaster,
  I have battled and broken my lance;
I am bruised by a pitiless master
  That the weak and the timid call
    Chance.

I am old, I am bent, I am cheated
  Of all that Youth urged me to win;
But name me not with the defeated,
  To-morrow again, I begin.

Samuel E. Kiser.

Renascence

Yes, spring will come again! Beneath this
  snow
And ice, this frozen mass of death, I
  know
Are pregnant seeds, expectant blades of
  grass,
In readiness when numbered days shall
  pass
For their release—when sun's rays pene-
  trate
The earth and gently open freedom's gate.
And peace will come! Beneath this snow
  and ice
Of hate are fecund deeds of sacrifice.
They wait the cosmic touch of right and
  good
To liberate a nobler brotherhood.

John Calvin Slemp.

Life appears to me to be too short to be spent in nursing animosity or in registering wrongs. We are and must be, one and all, burdened with faults in this world; but the time will come, I trust, when we shall put them off in putting off our corruptible bodies; when debasement and sin will fall from us and only the spark will remain, the impalpable principle of life and thought, pure as when it left the Creator to inspire the creature; whence it came, it will return, perhaps to pass through gradations of glory.

It is a creed in which I delight, to which I cling. It makes Eternity a rest, a mighty home; not a terror and an abyss. Besides, with this creed revenge never worries my heart, degradation never too deeply disgusts me, injustice never crushes me too low; I live in calm looking to the end.

Charlotte Bronte'.

The One

I knew his face the moment that he
    passed
Triumphant in the thoughtless, cruel
    throng,—
Triumphant, though the quiet, tired eyes
Showed that his soul had suffered over-
    long.

And though across his brow faint lines
    of care
Were etched, somewhat of Youth still
    lingered there.

I gently touched his arm—he smiled at
    me—
He was the Man that Once I Meant to
    Be!

Where I had failed, he'd won from life,
    Success;
Where I had stumbled, with sure feet
    he stood;
Alike—yet—unalike—we faced the world,
And through the stress he found that life
    was good.

And I? The bitter wormwood in the glass,
The shadowed way along which failures
    pass!
Yet as I saw him thus, joy came to me—
He was the Man that Once I Meant to
    Be!

I knew him! And I knew he knew me for
The man He might have been. Then did
    his soul
Thank silently the gods that gave him
    strength
To win, while I so sorely missed the goal?
He turned, and quickly in his own firm
    hand
He took my own—the gulf of Failure
    spanned . . .
And that was all—strong, self-reliant free,
He was the Man that Once I Meant to
    Be!
We did not speak. But in his sapient eyes

I saw the spirit that had urged him on,
The courage that had held him through
    the fight
Had once been mine; I thought, "Can it
    be gone?"
He felt that unasked question—felt it so
His pale lips formed the one-word an-
    swer, "No!"

       *   *   *   *

Too late to win? No! Not too late for
    me—
He is the Man that Still I Mean to Be!

Everard Jack Appelton.

Prophecy

Somewhere beauty dwells, all undefiled
For I have seen a rose unfold
At dawn,
And wonder grow
In the eyes of a child.

Somewhere love shall live, all unafraid
For I have seen a woman clasp Death's
    hand
At child-birth
And pass into the shadows
Undismayed.

Somewhere life shall live, beyond the
    blue;
For I have seen the veil wear thin
And fall apart—
And the face of God shine through.

Nellie Burget Miller.

❦

The Closing Door

Tomorrow, ah, tomorrow,
The good we think to do,
The hearts we'll rob of sorrow,
The roses we shall strew.
And while we wait and contemplate
Our brood of golden plans,
The swift day dies, and darkened skies
Reprove our idle hands.

Tomorrow, ah, tomorrow!
Oh, friend, be wise, I pray.
This world, so full of sorrow,
Needs all your lips can say
Of comforts sweet and actions meet
To help it on its way.

Oh, speak before a fast-closed door
Shall mock you. Act today!

Thomas Curtis Clark.

I came to the desk with quivering lip
The day's work was done.
"Dear teacher I want a new page," I said
"I have spoiled this one."
He took the page so stained and blotted
And gave me a new one all unspotted
Then into my dim eyes smiled,
"Do better now, my child."
I went to the throne with quivering soul
The Day's work was done.
"Dear Father, I want a new page," I said
I have spoiled this one.
He took the page so stained and blotted
And gave me a new one all unspotted.
Then into my sad soul smiled,
"Do better now, my child."

Helen Field Fischer.

❦

Build upon resolve and not upon regret,
The structure of thy future. Do not grope
Among the shadows of old sins, but let
Thine own soul's light shine on the path
    of hope
And dissipate the darkness. Moist no tears
Upon the blotted record of lost years,
But turn the leaf, and smile, oh, smile to
    see
The fair white pages that remain to thee.

❦

And fierce though the fiends may fight
    And long though the angels hide,
I know that Truth and Right
    Have the universe on their side.
And that somewhere, beyond the stars
    Is a Love that is better than fate;
When the night unlocks her bars,
    I shall see Him, and I will wait.

Ships That Come Home

When my ship comes home! When my
  ship comes home!
  But shall I wait on shore
And dream of when my ship comes
  home—
  White sail and flashing oar?
I'm going to steer it home myself,
  Not wait on land without it;
For no one's ship comes drifting in
  With only dreams about it.

When my ship comes home! When my
  ship comes home!
  Myself I'll fill the hold—
I'll know that when my ship comes home
  With white sails flashing bold,
'Twill bring the things I wish. Our flag
  To ocean winds we'll fling it!
For each one's ship comes home at last
  If he helps Fate to bring it!

  Mary Carolyn Davies.

❧

Success lies not in achieving what you
aim at, but in aiming at what you ought
to achieve, and pressing forward, sure of
achievement here, or if not here, hereafter.

  R. F. Horton.

❧

There are two days about which I never
worry. Two carefree days, kept sacredly
free from fear and apprehension. One
of these days is yesterday. And the other
day I do not worry about is Tomorrow.

  Robert Jones Burdette.

Hope

'Tis better to hope, though clouds hang
  low,
  And keep the eyes uplifted,
For the sweet blue sky will soon peep
  through,
  When the ominous clouds are rifted.

There was never a night without a day
  Or an evening without a morning,
And the darkest hour, as the proverb goes,
  Is the hour before the dawning.

❧

When?

If fortune, with a smiling face,
  Strews roses on your way;
When shall we stoop to pick them up?
  Today, my friend, today!

But should she frown with face of care,
  And talk of coming sorrow;
When shall we grieve, if grieve we must?
Tomorrow, friend, tomorrow.

  Anon.

❧

Only a little while now and we shall
be again together and with us those other
noble and well-beloved souls gone before.

I am sure I shall meet you and them;
that you and I shall talk of a thousand
things and of that unforgettable day and
of all that followed it, and that we shall
clearly see that all were parts of an infinite plan which was wholly wise and
good.

  Richard Maurice Burke.

Now, while the sounds of martial wrath
assail,
While the red banner floats upon the gale;
While dark destruction, with his legion
bands,
Waves the bright sabre o'er devoted
lands;
While War's dread comet flashes through
the air,
And fainting nations tremble at the glare;
To thee Futurity from scenes like these,
Pale fancy turns, for heaven-imparted
ease;
Turns to behold, in thy unclouded skies
The orb of peace in bright perspective
rise;
And pour around, with joy-diffusing ray,
Life, light and glory, in a flood of day.

Mrs. Hemans.

The Old Year's Pack

When the New Year in at the front door
peeps,
And out at the back door the Old Year
creeps
I hope he will carry away on his back
A load as big as a peddler's pack;
And we'll stow away in his baggage then
Some things that we never shall want
again.

We will put in the puckery little pout
That drives all the merry dimples out,
And the creasy scowls that up and down
Fold nice little foreheads right into a
frown;
And the little quarrels that spoil the plays,
And the little grumbles on rainy days,
And the bent-up pins, and the teasing
jokes
That never seem funny to other folks;

And we'll throw in the bag some cross
little "don'ts,"
And most of the "can'ts," and all of the
"wont's,"
If we get all these in the Old Year's pack,
And shut it so tight that they can't come
back,
When the old year's done, I think we'll
see
A Happy New Year for you and me.

For another day is dawning as the winged
darkness flies,
And the silver stars keep sentry till another sun shall rise,
For the daylight is eternal and the sunshine never dies,
It is always marching on . . .
For an empty tomb is waiting, and **the**
east is silver gray
As the angels of the morning trumpet in
another day!

Thick Is the Darkness

Thick is the darkness—
  Sunward, O, sunward!
Rough is the highway—
  Onward, still onward!

Dawn harbors surely
  East of the shadows.
Facing us somewhere
  Spread the sweet meadows.

Upward and forward!
  Time will restore us:
Light is above us,
  Rest is before us.

William Ernest Henley.

191

Is It Raining Little Flower?

Is it raining, little flower?
  Be glad of rain.
Too much sun would wither thee,
  'Twill shine again.
The sky is very black, 'tis true,
  But just behind it shines
    The blue.

Art thou weary, tender heart?
  Be glad of pain;
In sorrow the sweetest things will grow
  As flowers in the rain.
God watches and thou wilt have sun.
  When clouds their perfect work
    Have done.

                      Anon.

Sunset

I saw the sun set golden on a hill
With crimson streamers of the dying day,
Mid molten copper clouds, with many a
  ray,
And glowing shaft of dazzling light, and
  still
The sunlight faded not, but seemed to fill
The sky with splendor as if it would stay
Forever beautiful, nor pass away,
Except in glory and with dauntless will.
I thought of souls who bravely journeyed
  on
Beneath dull skies, beset by pain and
  strife,
Without the light of gladsome sun to
  send
Them strength until, when every hope
  seemed gone,
The clouds had melted into radiance, and
  life
Appeared serene and splendid at the end.

             John D. M. Brown.

This is the time of sadness and farewell,
The time of welcome and of new delight;
The old year drifts upon the wind tonight
Into that limbo where the dead years
  dwell.
From some strange, distant bourne no
  tongue can tell,
O'er moonlit ways and paved with shin-
  ing white,
The new, swift-footed year—a vision
  bright—
Comes at the clamor of the old year's
  knell!
Time turns his glass! The sands full
  slowly run,
Freighted, in each dropped grain, with
  memory—
The failures wrought, the few successes
  won!
I cry, "O Time, what brings the new for
  men?"
The brave-tongued bells peal answer back
  to me,
"A chance to fail; a chance to try again!"

            Charles C. Jones.

The Look Ahead

I am done with the years that were;
I am quits;
I am done with the dead and old;
They are mines worked out;
I delved in their pits;
I have saved their grain of gold.

Now I turn to the future for wine and
  bread;
I have bidden the past adieu.
I laugh and lift hand to the years ahead;
Come on! I am ready for you.

            Edwin Markham.

To-Morrow

By Lope De Vega

Lord, what am I, that, with unceasing
    care,
Thou didst seek after me, that thou didst
    wait,
Wet with unhealthy dews, before my
    gate,
And pass the gloomy nights of winter
    there?

Oh, strange delusion, that I did not greet
Thy blest approach! and oh, to Heaven
    how lost,
If my ingratitude's unkindly frost
Has chilled the bleeding wounds upon
    thy feet!

How oft my guardian angel gently cried,
"Soul, from thy casement look, and thou
    shalt see
How he persists to knock and wait for
    thee!"
And, oh, how often to that voice of sor-
    row,

"To-morrow we will open," I replied,
And when the morrow came I answered
    still, "To-morrow."

Translated by H. W. Longfellow.

❧

Compensation

I never knew a night so black
Light failed to follow in its track;
I never knew a storm so gray
It failed to have its clearing day;
I never knew such bleak despair
That there was not a rift somewhere;
I never knew an hour so drear
Love could not fill it full of cheer.

Edwin H. Stuart.

Faith and common sense are two twin
sisters and neither is of use without the
other.

A great leader used to give the command "Trust in God and keep your pow-
der dry." And John Wesley once said he
was saved by supplication and sulphur.

Hundreds were drowned in the Titanic
disaster because of their faith that the
great liner with her separate airtight com-
partments was unsinkable. Hence they
refused to heed the counsels of common
sense and take to the lifeboats.

Faith and reason must travel together.
You must watch as well as pray.

❧

There will be other Springs
That o'er this land
Shall spread their golden light,
Their perfumed airs,
That we have loved together.

Yes, other Springs,
When guns have ceased to roar,
And darkened skies no longer rain de-
    struction:
When on this earth once more
Sweet peace shall give
Her silent benediction;
And feet, long absent from our silent
    streets,
Shall be turning—wearily, gladly turning
Homeward to us who wait,
Keeping love's bright flame burning.

There will be other Springs,
When God shall give to us again
Joy all pain transcending.

Ethel Parton Rainey.

Alpine Journey

Twice I have climbed to those high shoulders of the Central Alps where the road which you follow brings you to the very edge of the Rhone glacier and to the sources of those rivers which seek the Mediterranean. Once I came there at the end of a long day's tramp, when the clouds which had been slowly gathering for twenty-four hours finally settled down upon the mountains.

It was at best a broken and shadowed world of hopes and prophecies; all things were lost and darkened by the clouds. Again I came by the same road at the end of a day when a cloudless dawn had moved through light to a sunset unobscured by a single breath of mist, and there, all which had been before lost in clouds and deepening shadows stood in such glory as he must have seen who saw the gold and ivory walls of the New Jerusalem. Every snow clad mountain was an altar and the very shining of their summits a white and moving glory.

Our hope of the kingdom is like that. It is overlaid by clouds and much obscured by fear and folly. We see, here and there, but brokenly, the lesser summits; the far prophetic slopes are lost in darkness. But the clouds will clear away —and where we now see but broken contours we shall see the shining table-lands of God; where now we see but broken hopes our children's children shall discover divine fulfillment.   *Atkins.*

Journeys' End

When the long day's tramp is over, when
the journey's done,
I shall dip down from some hill-top at
the going down o' the sun,
And turn in at the open door, and lay
down staff and load,
And wash me clean of the heat o' the day
and white dust o' the road.

Cecily Fox Smith.

❦

The Last Sonnet

The earthly limitations that are mine
Have taught me that I cannot reach one
star,
For which long years ago I did repine,
And worshipped there in ecstasy afar.

Sometimes at eventide and morning, too,
In the soft twilight and at dawning day
When hopes were young and every dream
seemed new
I thought that always life would be that
way.

But now I know the fragrant rose must
die,
That from a heart a tender love will fade,
While often in an unexpected way
The things at which I laughed leave me
afraid.

But tho' despair adds discord to my song
The vision of far better things inspires
me on.   *Charles Bancroft.*

RAINBOWS   THE BOOK OF HOPE

VICTORY

I saw the powers of darkness
Take their flight;
I saw the morning break.

With every rising of the sun
Think of your life as just begun.

The Past has cancelled and buried deep
All yesterdays. There let them sleep.

Concern yourself with but Today
Grasp it and teach it to obey

Your will and plan. Since time began
Today has been the friend of man.

You and Today! A soul sublime
And the great heritage of time.

With God Himself to bind the twain,
Go forth, brave heart! Attain! Attain!

Ella Wheeler Wilcox.

Oh, may we follow undismayed
    Where'er our God shall call!
And may His spirit's present aid
    Uphold us lest we fall!
Till in the end of days we stand
    As victors in a deathless land.

John Henry Newman.

Sportsmanship

I chuckled as he faltered when we neared
    the goal,
And as I passed I heard him gasp, "Well
    run."
They gave to me the victor's silver bowl;
To him, the King of Heaven said, "Well
    done."

George W. Humphreys.

Upper Road

The "Upper Road" over life's journey is traveled by those who have the qualities and virtues to overcome difficulties, surmount obstacles and stick to ideals.

It is up hill and down. You will pass through foul and fair weather—you will encounter steep grades, rocky slopes and narrow passages, and there are many evidences of struggle by the wayside.

You will see the by-paths here and there which lead off to the "Lower Road"—but the main highway is plainly marked at every fork and junction so that he who runs may read—and if you follow the sign of Progress that marks the way you will reach your goal and experience the keen joy of victory.

❧

The Landing of the Pilgrim Fathers

The breaking waves dashed high
  On a stern and rock bound coast,
And the woods, against a stormy sky,
  Their giant branches tost:

And the heavy night hung dark
  The hills and waters o'er,
When a band of exiles moored their bark
  On the wild New England shore.

Not as the conqueror comes,
  They, the true hearted, came
Not with the roll of the stirring drums,
  And the trumpet that sings of fame;

Not as the fleeing come
  In silence and in fear,—
They shook the depth of the desert
    gloom,
  With their hymns of lofty cheer.

Amidst the storm they sang,
  And the stars heard and the sea!
And the sounding aisles of the dim woods
    rang
  To the anthem of the free.

The ocean-eagle soared
  From his nest by the white wave's foam,
And the rocking pines of the forest
    roared—
  This was their welcome home!

There were men with hoary hair,
  Amidst that pilgrim-band—
Why had they come to wither there
  Away from their childhood's land?

What sought they thus afar?
  Bright jewels of the mine?
The wealth of seas, the spoils of war?—
  They sought a faith's pure shrine!

Ay, call it holy ground,
  The soil where first they trod!
They have left unstained what there they
    found—
  Freedom to worship God!
                    Mrs. Hemans.

❧

The words of the late *Sylvester Horne* have meaning for the Protestant church today:

We are watchers of a Beacon, whose light must never die.

We are guardians of an Altar, that shows God ever nigh.

We are children of Thy freeman, who sleeps beneath the sod.

For the might of Thine arm, we bless Thee, our God, our fathers' God.

For life as it now is, in the individual of the race, is but an unfinished symphony, a design sketched but not completed, a prophecy pathetically unfulfilled. Can death defeat God? I will not believe it. The dead, small and great, are with Him. He will finish His work.

Gains Glenn Atkins.

❧❧

Setbacks

Let me speak of setbacks in our moral life. Probably there is not one of us who has not now, or has not had at some time in the past, some hard moral battle to fight. When you are struggling against all the demons of your lower self to do right and keep straight, and the demons get the upper hand, and you do wrong and have reason to be ashamed of yourself, will you accept that defeat as absolute? Will you say to yourself that, having failed once, you must therefore keep on failing, so that there is no further use in trying to do better? Then at and from that point you will be a moral failure. But if you will but look at yourself from God's viewpoint—taking the long view of your spiritual development—you will achieve a patience with your own shortcomings born not of surrender to them, but of resolved and confident determination that, in due season, they shall yet be utterly overcome. With such a bearing toward your temptations, you will be likely to win the final victory long before this lifetime is over; and, in any event, another life is to follow, in which you will achieve the moral goals for which you strenuously strive in the life that now is.   *Russell Henry Stafford.*

Victory

I call no fight a losing fight
If, fighting, I have gained some straight
     new strength;
If, fighting, I turned ever toward the
     light,
All unallied with forces of the night;
If, beaten, quivering, I could say at length:
"I did no deed that needs to be unnamed;
I fought—and lost—and I am unashamed."

Miriam Teichner.

❧❧

When the outlook for Britain was still dark, Winston Churchill closed one of his great speeches by quoting these lines of Arthur Hugh Clough:

"Say not, 'The struggle naught availeth,
     The labor and the wounds are vain;
The enemy faints not, nor faileth,
     And as things have been they remain.'

"If hopes were dupes, fears may be liars;
     It may be through yon smoke concealed
Your comrades chase even now the fliers,
     And but for you possess the field.

"For while the tired waves vainly break-
     ing
Seem here no painful inch to gain,
Far back, through creeks and inlets mak-
     ing,
Comes silent, flooding in, the main.

"And not by eastern windows only
     When daylight comes, comes in the
     light;
In front the sun climbs slow, how slowly!
     But westward look! the land is bright."

The Game

I can't expect luck to be coming my way in all of the games that I happen to play. So, if now and then I must forfeit a trick, though badly I need it, I oughtn't to kick, for that is just part of the game.

And whoever played in a game that was fun, that called for small effort, that it might be won? My victory can never —no, never—be sweet unless I have snatched it away from defeat. The fight's the best part of the game!

And who is it wants to be always in luck, relying on Fortune instead of on Pluck? And who is it wants to go smiling through life, unable to say he has weathered the strife—unable to prove he was game?

And though I may win, or be last in the race, may I never cringe at the troubles I face. And when I have finished, may honest men write: "In winning or losing, he fought a good fight, from the start to the end of the game!"

Charles S. Kinnison

※

I do not dare to pray
For winds to waft me on my way,
But leave it to a higher Will
To stay or speed me, trusting still
That all is well, and sure that He . . .
Will land me——every peril past——
Within the harbor of Heaven at last.

Then whatsoever wind doth blow,
My heart is glad to have it so;
And blow it east, or blow it west,
The wind that blows, that wind is best.

Caroline A. Mason.

Oh, I have slipped the surly bonds of earth,
And danced the skies on laughter-silvered wings;
Sunward I've climbed and joined the tumbling mirth
Of sun-split clouds—and done a hundred things
You have not dreamed of—wheeled and soared and swung
High in the sunlit silence. Hov'ring there.
I've chased the shouting wind along and flung
My eager craft through footless halls of air.
Up, up the long delirious, burning blue
I've topped the wind-swept heights with easy grace,
Where never lark, or even eagle, flew;
And, while with silent, lifting mind I've trod
The high untrespassed sanctity of space,
Put out my hand and touched the face of God.

John Gillespie Magee, Jr.

※

This is not absolutely the best world God could have made. But it is the best world for the purpose He had in making it . . . God willed to make a moral universe and the only condition upon which morality is possible is freedom.

Virtue is possible only in a world where man may be vicious. Sacrifices possible only in an order in which man may be selfish. Bravery is possible only in a universe in which a man may be a coward. Love is possible only when it is possible not to love. It is the possibility of saying 'No' which gives so much charm to the heart when it says 'Yes.'

Hence God made a world in which man and woman would rise to moral heights, not by that blind driving power which makes the sun rise each morning, but rather by the exercise of that freedom in which one may fight the good fight and enjoy the spoils of victory, for no one shall be crowned unless he has struggled.

Fulton J. Sheen.

※

A Late Lark Twitters From the Quiet Sky

A late lark twitters from the quiet skies;
And from the west,
Where the sun, his day's work ended,
Lingers as in content,
There falls on the old, grey city
An influence luminous and serene,
A shining peace.

The smoke ascends
In a rosy-and-golden haze. The spires
Shine, and are changed. In the valley
Shadows rise. The lark sings on. The sun
Closing his benediction,
Sinks, and the darkening air
Thrills with a sense of the triumphing
    night—
Night with her train of stars
And her gift of sleep.

So be my passing!
My task accomplished, and the long day
    done,
Some late lark singing,
Let me be gathered to the quiet west,
The sundown splendid and serene,
Death.

William Ernest Henley.

Saturday Evening and Sunday Morning

Saturday night *Robert Burns* has haloed forever in his immortal poem.

The picture of the humble cottage, the peasant family, the reunion with those who have worked away from home through the week, the fireside glow, the open Book, the simple prayer—all quite unforgettable.

Similarly around Sunday morning *Hamilton Wright Mabie* sheds a tender glory.

He says, we need "the vast quiet of Sunday morning, the repose of universal rest and of immemorial worship.

"The calm of those fresh and fragrant hours is no figment of the imagination . . . it is a symbol of the peace of God which passes understanding."

※

"This rest is glorious!" said John Ericsson on his death-bed. "Gladly I lived, and gladly I die," was the sentiment of the confident spirit whose epitaph Mr. Stevenson undertook to provide.

That is the right feeling. We are not half glad enough to be alive, not nearly as pleased as we should be at the prospect of dying. We should . . . form our opinions of death less by its concomitants immediately on this side of the grave, and much more by the splendid company of the brave, the kind, the wise, and the true, who know what we can only guess about its benefits.

Edward Sanford Martin.

Requiem

Under the wide and starry sky
Dig the grave and let me lie,
Glad did I live and gladly die,
And I laid me down with a will.

This be the verse you grave for me:
Here he lies where he longed to be;
Home is the sailor, home from the sea,
And the hunter home from the hill.

Robert Louis Stevenson.

❧❧

The Duke of Wellington is reported to have said, "The British are not braver than the French—they are only brave for five minutes longer."

❧❧

My Triumph

The autumn time has come;
On woods that dream of bloom,
And over purpling vines,
The low sun fainter shines.

The aster-flower is failing,
The hazel's gold is paling;
Yet overhead more near
The eternal stars appear!

And present gratitude
Insures the future's good,
And for the things I see
I trust the things to be;

That in the paths untrod,
And the long days of God,
My feet shall still be led,
My heart be comforted.

O living friends who love me!
O dear ones gone above me!

Careless of other fame,
I leave to you my name.

Sweeter than any sung
My songs that found no tongue;
Nobler than any fact
My wish that failed of act.

Others shall sing the song,
Others shall right the wrong,—
Finish what I begin,
And all I fail of win.

What matter, I or they?
Mine or another's day,
So the right word be said
And life the sweeter made?

Hail to the coming singers!
Hail to the brave light-bringers!
Forward I reach and share
All that they sing and dare.

The airs of heaven blow o'er me;
A glory shines before me
Of what mankind shall be,—
Pure, generous, brave, and free.

Ring bells in unreared steeples,
The joy of unborn peoples!
Sound, trumpets far off blown,
Your triumph is my own!

Parcel and part of all,
I keep the festival,
Fore-reach the good to be,
And share the victory.

I feel the earth move sunward,
I join the great march onward,
And take, by faith, while living,
My freehold of thanksgiving.

John Greenleaf Whittier.

"They have triumphed who have died;
They have passed the porches wide
Leading from the House of Night
To the splendid lawns of light.
They have gone on that far road
Leading to their new abode,
And from curtained casements we
Watch their going wistfully.

"They have won, for they have read
The bright secrets of the dead;
And they gain the deep unknown,
Hearing Life's strange undertone.
In the race across the days
They are victors; theirs the praise,
Theirs the glory and the pride—
They have triumphed, having died."

Charles Hanson Towne.

Victory

(Found on the body of an Australian
soldier in first World War)

Ye that have faith to look with fearless
eyes
Beyond the tragedy of a world at strife,
And know that out of death and night
shall rise
The dawn of ampler life:
Rejoice, whatever anguish rend the heart,
That God has given you the priceless
dower
To live in these great times and have
your part
In freedom's crowning hour,
That ye may tell your sons who see the
light
High in the heavens—their heritage to
take—
"I saw the powers of darkness take their
flight;
I saw the morning break."

Crowns of roses fade—crowns of thorns
endure. Calvaries and crucifictions take
deepest hold of humanity—the triumphs
of might are transient—they pass and are
forgotten—the sufferings of right are grav-
en deepest on the chronicle of nations.

Abram J. Ryan.

General William Booth
Enters Heaven

(Drums)

Booth led boldly with his big bass drum—
(Are you washed in the blood of the
Lamb?)
The saints smiled gravely, and they said,
"He's come,"
(Are you washed in the blood of the
Lamb?)
Walking lepers followed, rank on rank,
Lurching bravoes from the ditches dank,
Drabs from the alley ways and drug-fiends
pale—
Minds still passion-ridden, soul-power's
frail!
Vermin-eaten saints with mouldy breath
Unwashed legions from the ways of
death—
(Are you washed in the blood of the
Lamb?)

(Banjos)

Every slum has sent its half-a-score
The round world over—Booth had
groaned for more.
Every banner that the wide world flies
Bloomed with glory and transcendent
dyes.
Big-voiced lassies made their banjos bang,
Tranced, fanatical, they shrieked and
sang,

(Are you washed in the blood of the
Lamb?)

Hallelujah! It was queer to see
Bull-necked convicts with that land make
free!
Loons with trumpets that blowed a blare,
blare, blare—
On, on, upward through the golden air!
(Are you washed in the blood of the
Lamb?)

(Bass drums slower and softer)

Booth died blind, and still by faith he
trod,
Eyes still dazzled by the ways of God.
Booth led boldly and he looked the chief:
Eagle countenance in sharp relief,
Beard a-flyin', air of high command
Unabated in the Holy Land.
Jesus came out from the Court-House
door,
Stretched his hand above the passing
poor.

(Flutes)

Booth saw not, but led his queer ones
there
Round and round the mighty Court-
House square,
Yet in an instant all that blear review
Marched on spotless, clad in raiment new.
The lame were straightened, withered
limbs uncurled
And blind eyes opened on a new sweet
world.

(Bass drums louder and faster)

Drabs and vixens in a flash made whole!
Gone was the weasel-head, the snout, the
jowl;
Sages and sibyls now, and athletes clean,
Rulers of empires, and of forests green!
(Are you washed in the blood of the
Lamb?)

(Grand chorus of all instruments—Tambourines in the foreground)

The hosts were sandalled and the wings
were fire!—
(Are you washed in the blood of the
Lamb?)
And their noise played havoc with the
angel choir.
(Are you washed in the blood of the
Lamb?)
O, shout Salvation! It was good to see
Kings and princes by the Lamb set free.
The banjos rattled and the tambourines
Jing-jing-jingled in the hands of queens!

(Reverently sung; no instruments)

And when Booth halted by the curb for
prayer
He saw his Master through the flag-filled
air.
Christ came gently with a robe and crown
For Booth the soldier, while the throng
knelt down.
He saw King Jesus, they were face to face,
And he knelt a-weeping in that holy place!
(Are you washed in the blood of the
Lamb?)   *Vachel Lindsay.*

RAINBOWS   THE BOOK OF HOPE

WORK

Make Dust

My son, remember you have to work. Whether you handle pick or wheelbarrow or a set of books, digging ditches or editing a newspaper, ringing an auction bell or writing funny things, you must work.

Don't be afraid of killing yourself by overworking on the sunny side of thirty. Men die sometimes but it is because they quit at nine P. M. and don't go home until two A. M. It's the intervals that kill, my son.

The work gives you appetite for your meals; it lends solidity to your slumber; it gives you a perfect appreciation of a holiday. There are young men who do not work but the country is not proud of them. It does not even know their names; it only speaks of them as old So-and-So's boys.

Nobody likes them; the great busy world doesn't know they are here. So find out what you want to be and do. Take off your coat and make dust in the world. The busier you are, the less harm you are apt to get into, the sweeter will be your sleep, the brighter your holidays and the better satisfied the whole world will be with you.

Robert Jones Burdette.

Success

Success is not represented by a bag of gold at the end of the rainbow—it is not a sudden streak of luck on a long chance —it is not necessarily enjoyed in a palace surrounded by luxuries and servants.

Success is a state of mind which comes to you or me through any degree of progress and achievement.

Drops of sweat from honest effort are always more gracious than idle tears from weak wishing.

Happiness is in doing—success is in the step forward, however steep the grade.

❧

Success never comes spontaneously; it is the result of quality put into work all down the line, quality put into work one loves. Most notable editors were printers' devils and loved the smell of printer's ink. Most notable mothers worshipped their dollies as little girls, and had infinite patience in dressing and undressing them, putting them to sleep, and taking them for an airing. That railway president you hold as a model before your little son was an oiler only yesterday, and as good an oiler as he is a president. That head of a great school you so admire first taught in remote country districts.

❧

Those can conquer who think they can.

Emerson.

Work

The world is made up of two great classes of people—those who want success and wish for it and those who want success and work for it.

Work is the net price all must pay to travel the highway of progress.

❧

In his autobiography *Lord Tweedsmuir* declares: "I would be content with any job, however thankless, in any quarter, however remote, if I had a chance of making a corner of the desert bloom like the rose and a solitary place glad."

❧

After all, if you work all day in God's sunshine, when evening comes you are pleasantly tired and ready for rest and not much inclined to find fault with your lot.

Elizabeth and her German Garden.

❧

Do your work—not just your work and no more, but a little more for the lavishing's sake; that little more which is worth all the rest. And if you suffer as you must, and if you doubt as you must, do your work.

Put your heart into it and the sky will clear. Then out of your very doubt and suffering will be born the supreme joy of life.

Dean Briggs.

On the Cloud of Witnesses

Oh, do not wrong the generations past
  By scorn, or bitter prating of dead
    hands;
It is not chance that their achievements
    last,
  Nor whim of fortune that their build-
    ing stands.
It is for us they strove; we are the heirs
  Of all their agony and sweat and tears;
And, willing or ungrateful, each one
    shares
  In the vast legacy of toilsome years.
They would not bind us; theirs no selfish
    aim
  To chain the future to their halting-
    place.
They mourn our failures, glory in our
    fame,
  Thrill with our struggle in this mortal
    race.
A Cloud of Witnesses, O doubtful Soul,
  Applauds your straining footsteps to-
    ward the goal.
           George Meason Whicher.

❧

The idle man does not know what it
is to enjoy rest. Hard work, moreover,
not only tends to give us rest for the
body but what is even more important,
peace to the mind.
           Lord Avebury.

❧

"Not slothful in business," so that the
world will learn that Christ's men are the
first in that realm as in all others.

"Fervent in Spirit, serving the Lord."
So that business will not push bigger
things from their place.

Doing nothing is the most tiresome
thing in the world, because you can't
quit and rest.
           Anon.

❧

Banish the future; live only for the
hour and its allotted work. Think not of
the amount to be accomplished, the difficulties to be overcome, but set earnestly
at the little task at your elbow, letting
that be sufficient for the day; for surely
our plain duty is not to see what lies dimly
at a distance, but to do what lies clearly
at hand.
           Osler.

❧

We give the closing lines of *Angela
Morgan's* battle hymn of labor:

Work!
Thank God for the swing of it,
For the clamoring, hammering ring of it,
Passion and labor daily hurled
On the mighty anvils of the world.
Oh, what is so fierce as the flame of it?
And what is so huge as the aim of it?
Thundering on through dearth and
    doubt,
Calling the plan of the Maker out.
Work, the Titan, the friend,
Shaping the earth to a glorious end,
Draining the swamps and blasting the
    hills,
Doing whatever the Spirit wills—
Rending a continent apart,
To answer the dream of the Master heart.
Thank God for a world where none may
    shirk—
Thank God for the splendor of work!

When Earth's Last Picture Is Painted

When Earth's last picture is painted and
  the tubes are twisted and dried,
When the oldest colors have faded, and
  the youngest critic has died,
We shall rest, and, faith, we shall need
  it—lie down for an aeon or two,
Till the Master of All Good Workmen
  shall set us to work anew.

And those that were good will be happy:
  they shall sit in a golden chair;
They shall splash at a ten-league canvas
  with brushes of camel's hair.
They shall find real saints to draw from
  —Magdalene, Peter, and Paul;
They shall work for an age at a sitting
  and never be tired at all!

And only the Master shall praise us, and
  only the Master shall blame;
And no one shall work for money, and
  no one shall work for fame,
But each for the joy of the working, and
  each, in his separate star,
Shall draw the Thing as he sees It for the
  God of Things as they are!

                    Rudyard Kipling.

❧

No man needs sympathy because he
has to work . . . Far and away the best
prize that life offers is the chance to
work hard at work worth doing.

  Theodore Roosevelt,
    in a Labor Day Address, 1903.

❧

Strength of mind is exercise, not rest.
                              Pope.

So this is the beautiful philosophy of
life, that the more we have to do, the
more we are rested, and the less we have
to do the more tired we are. Nothing
rests a man so much as plenty to do.

              William Alfred Quayle

❧

We have barely begun to live, begun
to work, begun to discover the continents
we craved for, when the sun goes westering down into the sea.

Without a sunrise elsewhere, it is hopeless. To me life is inexplicable and mean-
ingless—unfair, unequal, unbalanced and
unjust—unless we are to carry on elsewhere the task which here with such toil
we have begun.

So God stoops down to us in infinite
mercy and says "Child, all your life on
earth is but a beginning; and I shall do
better for you than at your beginnings.
When sorrow and sighing shall have fled
away." In that hope we can be strong and
steadfast; we can begin again after a hundred failures; we can ask for no other
triumph here than the triumph of never
giving in.

                    G. H. Morrison.

❧

"Our business in life is not to get ahead
of other people, but to get ahead of ourselves. To break our own record, to out-
strip our yesterdays by todays, to bear our
trials more beautifully than we ever
dreamed we could, to whip the temper inside and out as we never whipped him
before, to give as we have never given, to
do our work with more force and a finer
finish than ever—this is the true idea—to
get ahead of ourselves."

The first fault is the child of simplicity;
but every other, the offspring of guilt.

Goldsmith.

❧

The Gospel of Labor

But I think the king of that country
    comes out from his tireless host
And walks in the world of the weary, as
    if he loved it the most:
For here in the dusty confusion, with
    eyes that are heavy and dim
He meets again the laboring men who are
    looking and longing for Him.

He cancels the curse of Eden, and brings
    them a blessing instead,
Blessed are they that labor for Jesus par-
    takes of their bread,
He puts His hand to their burdens, He
    enters their homes at night:
Who does his best shall have as his guest
    the Master of life and light.

And courage will come with His presence,
    and patience return at His touch,
And manifold sins be forgiven to those
    who love Him much;
And the cries of envy and anger will
    change to the songs of cheer,
For the toiling age will forget its rage
    when the Prince of Peace draws near.

This is the gospel of labor, ring it, ye
    bells of the kirk,—
The Lord of Love comes down from
    above to live with the men who work,
This is the rose that He planted, here in
    the thorn cursed soil—
Heaven is blessed with perfect rest, but
    the blessing of earth is toil.

Henry Van Dyke.

Bruce Barton said, "In Bethlehem
two thousand years ago, there stood a
little inn. And behold it was so full of
Business that the greatest event in history
knocked at its doors and could not come
in."

❧

We may know something of the re-
morse of lost opportunities, which can
never come to us though we seek with
tears. Death closes doors not only for the
dead, but for some of the living. In Carlyle's reminiscences of his wife Jane
Welsh Carlyle there are some sad passages, where he recalls scenes of the past.
One cannot read them without almost
hearing the sob in the words from the
old man's breast, as he brings back in
memory the occasions when his wife had
been his unwearied helper, and he longs
for the chance to tell her what he felt.
Many a man has known that moment,
it may be when the first sod fell clattering
upon the lowered coffin. Or he recalls
tired eyes that are closed, and thinks of
patient lips that no longer can speak their
comforting word, and remembers loving
hands that lie still. At such time we know
too poignantly that there are some things
that are irreparable. It may be that we
would fain show some of the love we felt
but never expressed, lavish tenderness on
the dear head, or sob repentance to the
gentle soul. Too late! The door is shut.

Hugh Black.

❧

As far as the east is from the west, so
far may Resolutions be from Resolution.

The people of the civilized world will deal with all tyrants. Their very existence brings their downfall, as Ebenezer Elliott sets forth in blazing lines in his "Battle Song:"

Madmen, they trample into snakes
 The wormy clod!
Like fire beneath their feet awakes
 The sword of God!

Behind, before, above, below,
 They rouse the brave,
Where'er they go they make a foe
 Or find a grave."

The only effective proof of God is an entirely good man. The one thing which will recall this wild and disorderly time of ours in which, beneath the surface, the heart is craving for its lost peace, is the vision of happy communities of people who are satisfied with God and with the way of Jesus Christ, people of quiet manners and healthy minds.

John A. Hutton.

"I cannot do much," said a little star,
"To make the dark world bright;
My silver beams cannot travel far
Through the folding gloom of night,
But I'm a true part of God's great plan,
And I'll cheerfully do the best I can."

The story is told of *Josephine Butler.* She came home late one night and her only child, a little girl, excitedly rushed out of her bedroom upstairs to greet her mother, who stood at the foot of the stairs. In her eagerness she fell over the baluster at her mother's feet and was taken up dead! What did that mother do with that hardship? Well, there are many things she might have done. That grief might have closed for her all the windows of life. It might have pulled down all the shades, and life for her might have become forever a darkened room. She might have become cynical and embittered.

But she chose another way. She went out to mother thousands of little orphan girls, who otherwise would have known nothing of a mother's love. And she wrote:

"Because of little pallid lips which once
 My name did call,
No childish voice in vain appeal upon
 My ears doth fall.
I count it all my joy their joys to share,
 And sorrows small.

Because of little death-cold feet, for earth's
 Rough roads unmeet,
I'd journey leagues to save from sin and harm
 Such little feet;
And count the lowliest service done for them
 So sacred sweet." *Harold C. Phillips.*

RAINBOWS   THE BOOK OF HOPE

AUTHOR INDEX

212